T0207150

Wireshark for Network Forensics

An Essential Guide for IT and Cloud Professionals

Nagendra Kumar Nainar
Ashish Panda

Apress®

Wireshark for Network Forensics: An Essential Guide for IT and Cloud Professionals

Nagendra Kumar Nainar
North Carolina, NC, USA

Ashish Panda
Bangalore, Karnataka, India

ISBN-13 (pbk): 978-1-4842-9000-2
https://doi.org/10.1007/978-1-4842-9001-9

ISBN-13 (electronic): 978-1-4842-9001-9

Managing Director, Apress Media LLC: Welmoed Spahr
Acquisitions Editor: Aditee Mirashi
Development Editor: James Markham
Coordinating Editor: Aditee Mirashi

Cover image designed by eStudioCalamar

Distributed to the book trade worldwide by Springer Science+Business Media New York, 1 New York Plaza, Suite 4600, New York, NY 10004-1562, USA. Phone 1-800-SPRINGER, fax (201) 348-4505, e-mail orders-ny@springer-sbm.com, or visit www.springeronline.com. Apress Media, LLC is a California LLC and the sole member (owner) is Springer Science + Business Media Finance Inc (SSBM Finance Inc). SSBM Finance Inc is a **Delaware** corporation.

For information on translations, please e-mail booktranslations@springernature.com; for reprint, paperback, or audio rights, please e-mail bookpermissions@springernature.com.

Apress titles may be purchased in bulk for academic, corporate, or promotional use. eBook versions and licenses are also available for most titles. For more information, reference our Print and eBook Bulk Sales web page at http://www.apress.com/bulk-sales.

Any source code or other supplementary material referenced by the author in this book is available to readers on GitHub via the book's product page, located at www.apress.com/. For more detailed information, please visit http://www.apress.com/source-code.

Printed on acid-free paper

Nagendra Kumar Nainar: *I would like to dedicate this book to my late Chitappah Asokan who never failed to inspire me during my young age.*

Ashish Panda: *I would like to dedicate this book to my parents for making possible everything that I have in life and to my wife and daughter for all the encouragement and sacrifices.*

Naren: *I would like to dedicate my contribution to my father Manikandan and mother Kavithamani who dedicated their time to support and encourage me in making this contribution possible. I would also like to dedicate this to my loving sister Dhanya.*

Table of Contents

About the Authors xi

About the Contributor xiii

About the Technical Reviewer xv

Acknowledgments xvii

Introduction xix

Chapter 1: Wireshark Primer 1

Introduction 1

Get Me Started! 3

    macOS 3

    Linux 4

    Windows Install 5

    The First Capture 6

    Understanding a Packet 7

    Data Representation 13

Big Picture: I/O Graphs 14

Big Picture: TCP Stream Graphs 15

    Time Sequence (Stevens) 15

    Time Sequence (tcptrace) 15

    Throughput 16

    Round Trip Time 17

    Window Scaling 18

Bigger Picture: Following a Packet Stream 19

    Biggest Picture: Flow Graphs 20

    CloudShark: The Floating Shark 21

Summary 27

Chapter 2: Packet Capture and Analysis **29**

Sourcing Traffic for Capture 30

    Setting Up Port Mirroring.. 30

    Remote Port Mirroring 31

    Other Mirroring Options 34

    Capture Point Placement 35

OS-Native Traffic Capture Tools.. 36

    UNIX, Linux, BSD, and macOS 36

    Windows.. 39

Wireshark-Based Traffic Capture 41

    CLI-Based Capture with Dumpcap or Tshark.. 41

    GUI-Based Capture with Wireshark 43

Capture Modes and Configurations... 45

    Promiscuous Mode 45

Remote Packet Capture with Extcap... 47

    Remote Capture with Sshdump.. 47

    Mobile Device Traffic Capture 49

    Android Devices.. 49

    Using Third-Party Android App and Sshdump... 52

Capture Filtering 54

    Capture Filter Deep Dive... 56

    High Volume Packet Analysis.. 60

    Advanced Filters and Deep Packet Filter 61

Summary.. 63

References for This Chapter... 64

Chapter 3: Capturing Secured Application Traffic for Analysis **65**

Evolution of Application Security 66

Capturing and Analyzing HTTPS.. 69

    Basics of HTTPS 69

    Capturing and Filtering HTTPS Traffic.. 72

Analyzing HTTPS Traffic 73

HTTPS Filters for Analysis 82

Capturing and Analyzing QUIC Traffic 85

Basics of QUIC 85

Capturing and Filtering QUIC Traffic 89

Analyzing QUIC Traffic 90

Decrypting QUIC/TLS Traffic 98

QUIC Filters for Analysis 98

Capturing and Analyzing Secure DNS 99

Basics of DNS 99

Secure DNS 102

Summary 105

References for This Chapter 105

Chapter 4: Capturing Wireless Traffic for Analysis **107**

Basics of Radio Waves and Spectrum 107

Basics of Wireless LAN Technology 110

Setting Up 802.11 Radio Tap 117

Wireless Capture Using Native Wireshark Tool 118

Wireless Capture Using AirPort Utility 119

Wireless Capture Using Diagnostic Tool 120

Wireless Operational Aspects – Packet Capture and Analysis 121

802.11 Frame Types and Format 122

Wireless Network Discovery 125

Wireless LAN Endpoint Onboarding 127

Wireless LAN Data Exchange 136

Wireless LAN Statistics Using Wireshark 140

Summary 141

References for This Chapter 142

Chapter 5: Multimedia Packet Capture and Analysis **143**

Multimedia Applications and Protocols.. 143

Multimedia on the Web.. 144

Multimedia Streaming 144

Real-Time Multimedia 146

How Can Wireshark Help 150

Multimedia File Extraction from HTTP Capture 151

Streaming RTP Video Captures 152

Real-Time Media Captures and Analysis.. 153

Decrypting Signaling (SIP over TLS) 153

Decrypting Secure RTP.. 158

Telephony and Video Analysis... 163

Summary.. 171

References for This Chapter... 172

Chapter 6: Cloud and Cloud-Native Traffic Capture **173**

Evolution of Virtualization and Cloud.. 173

Basics of Virtualization 174

Hypervisor – Definition and Types 177

Virtualization – Virtual Machines and Containers... 178

Traffic Capture in AWS Environment 181

VPC Traffic Mirroring.. 182

Traffic Capture in GCP Environment.. 187

Traffic Capture in Docker Environment 193

Traffic Capture in Kubernetes Environment 195

Summary.. 201

References for This Chapter... 201

Chapter 7: Bluetooth Packet Capture and Analysis **203**

Introduction to Bluetooth 204

Communication Models.. 204

Radio and Data Transfer 205

Bluetooth Protocol Stack 207

Controller Operations.. 208

HCI 209

Host Layer Operation 209

Application Profile–Specific Protocols... 210

Tools for Bluetooth Capture.. 212

Linux 212

Windows 213

macOS... 214

Bluetooth Packet Filtering and Troubleshooting 215

Controller-to-Host Communication.. 215

Pairing and Bonding 216

Paired Device Discovery and Data Transfer.. 218

Summary.. 220

References for This Chapter... 220

Chapter 8: Network Analysis and Forensics.. 221

Network Attack Classification 221

Packet Poisoning and Spoofing Attacks.. 222

Network Scan and Discovery Attacks.. 225

Brute-Force Attacks... 229

DoS (Denial-of-Service) Attacks 230

Malware Attacks 232

Wireshark Tweaks for Forensics 234

Autoresolving Geolocation.. 234

Changing the Column Display.. 235

Frequently Used Wireshark Tricks in Forensics 235

Wireshark Forensic Analysis Approach 236

Wireshark DDoS Analysis 236

Wireshark Malware Analysis 241

Summary.. 244

References for This Chapter... 244

Chapter 9: Understanding and Implementing Wireshark Dissectors.................... 245

Protocol Dissectors 250

    Post and Chain Dissectors 253

Creating Your Own Wireshark Dissectors... 253

    Wireshark Generic Dissector (WSGD) 253

    Lua Dissectors 254

    C Dissectors... 257

Creating Your Own Packet... 258

Summary.. 261

References for This Chapter... 262

Index.. 263

About the Authors

Nagendra Kumar Nainar (CCIE#20987, CCDE#20190014) is a Principal Engineer with Cisco Customer Experience CX Organization, focusing on enterprise and service provider customers. He is the coinventor of more than 150 patent applications in different technologies including virtualization/container technologies. He is the coauthor of multiple Internet RFCs, various Internet drafts, and IEEE papers. Nagendra Kumar also coauthored multiple technical books with other publishers such as Cisco Press and Packt. He is a guest lecturer in North Carolina State University and a speaker in different network forums.

Ashish Panda (CCIE#33270) is a Senior Technical Leader with Cisco Systems Customer Experience CX Organization primarily focused on handling complex service provider network design and troubleshooting escalations. He has 19+ years of rich experience in network design, operation, and troubleshooting with various large enterprises and service provider networks (ISP, satellite, MPLS, 5G, and cloud) worldwide. He is a speaker at various Cisco internal and external events and is very active in the network industry standard bodies.

About the Contributor

Naren Manikandan is a sophomore at Research Triangle High School, a voracious technology learner who is potentially working toward positively impacting the technology industry. His passion about technology inspired his mentor to involve him as a contributing author for this book. He is part of the First Robotics Competition (FRC) team leading the development of computer vision for robots that participates in international robotics competitions. Naren actively indulges in intraschool and interschool discussions and other industry technical meetups.

About the Technical Reviewer

 **Brahma Nath Pandey** is currently working as Vice President at Blackrock, one of the world's leading financial institutions. He has extensive experience working in telecom, automobile, IOT, and finance domains. At Blackrock, he is leading a team of talented engineers in designing and implementing several critical data engineering projects. In his past organizations, he has designed and deployed Java-based distributed cloud-native autoscalable solution to the cloud. He got acquainted with Wireshark while working for InfoVista, using it to analyze SNMP packets being sent to and from an application.

Apart from his day job, he is a curious tech and science enthusiast whom you can find trying out new things. He has a keen interest in space and green technologies, and he loves playing chess.

Acknowledgments

Nagendra Kumar Nainar: First, I would like to thank my wife Lavanya and daughter Ananyaa for their patience and support not just during the time of this book authoring but always.

I would also like to thank my coauthor, mentee, and good friend Ashish Panda who shared the load with me writing the chapters. I would like to thank my other (high school) mentee Naren Manikandan for his enthusiasm and energy shown to engage and contribute to finish this book on time.

I would like to thank my good friend Arun Arunachalam for helping with details around dissector development. A very special thanks to Aditee Mirashi, Shonmirin PA, and other Apress publication crew for helping us get this book published on time.

Ashish Panda: I would like to thank my mentor and coauthor Nagendra who always encouraged and inspired me to take the road less traveled, including taking this project of authoring the book. Thanks also to Naren for all the contributions. His energy and enthusiasm at such a young age amaze me.

A big thanks to my wife Pallabi and daughter Akanksha for being my strength and support always. This wouldn't have been possible without their patience and sacrifices.

I would like to thank all my friends who were by my side and supported me even during odd hours while writing this book. Also, I would like to thank the whole Apress team, especially Aditee and Shonmirin, who made sure that the book gets published on time.

Naren Manikandan: I would like to thank my history teacher Mr. Jefferson Guilford for inspiring me to think outside the box even in simple matters. I would also like to thank Nagendra Kumar Nainar for giving me this opportunity to exhibit my passion to the world.

Introduction

Traffic capture and analysis is an integral part of the overall IT operation, and accordingly Wireshark is an essential skillset required for any IT operation team. This community developed and managed open source tool powers the operation team with the ability to dissect the traffic across the layers for security analysis and troubleshooting purposes. This book will help the readers gain essential knowledge about the Wireshark tool and how to use the same for capturing and analyzing various types of traffic.

The book starts by sprucing up the knowledge of the readers about the Wireshark architecture and its basic installation and use. Further, the book explains the use of this tool to capture the traffic in different unique scenarios. This explains helps the readers to capture the traffic from mobile devices, Bluetooth captures along with cloud and cloud-native environment. The book also explains the use of different cypher techniques to capture the keys and decode encrypted traffic for deep analysis. Overall, this book will help the readers to gain strong knowledge about the tool and its usage in different, latest technology scenarios.

CHAPTER 1

Wireshark Primer

This chapter introduces you to Wireshark and covers basics of the tool, packet capture, and display and filtering techniques. Some of the topics covered in this chapter will be discussed in detail in subsequent chapters. The following is a summary of the concepts you will learn in this chapter:

- Introduction to Wireshark architecture

- Wireshark package installation and usage

- Basic analysis and filtering

- Wireshark cloud services

- Version and feature parity

- Data stream and graphs

Introduction

Wireshark is an open source network packet analyzer used to capture packets in real time flowing through the network. Wireshark is also used to analyze packets captured by other applications or Wireshark in an offline manner. It provides a simple command line (CLI) or graphical user interface (GUI) to analyze and sniff network traffic over an interface like Ethernet, Wi-Fi, Bluetooth, token ring, frame relay, and many more. Wireshark presents a flexible way to filter the desired data to be captured through capture filters and, while analyzing, limit packets being shown in a capture through display filters. Wireshark has many other robust packet flow analysis and decode tools integrated, which makes it an indispensable weapon in the armory of networking and security professionals. Also at the same time, it's used in educational institutes for teaching networking protocols.

© Nagendra Kumar Nainar and Ashish Panda 2023
N. K. Nainar and A. Panda, *Wireshark for Network Forensics*, https://doi.org/10.1007/978-1-4842-9001-9_1

The idea of an open source packet analysis tool occurred to Gerald Combs after wanting to troubleshoot and understand his network, creating Ethereal (original Wireshark) in 1997. Wireshark is an open source software released under the GNU General Public License (GPL). This means the source code is available freely under the GPL, and we don't need to worry about license keys or fees to use on any number of computers. In addition, Wireshark has got good community support. From its release in July of 1998 to now, Wireshark had several contributors continually improving the program by adding new features and protocol support to Wireshark, either by integrating to the source code or as dissector (parser) plugins.

The following is a summary of some of the important features available on Wireshark:

- Available on all popular OSs like Windows, Linux, UNIX, and MacOSx.

- Live packet capture from network interfaces and save data.

- *Analyze capture data* by other applications like tcpdump, Windump, tshark, and many others capable of storing captures in pcap and pcapng format.

- *Import* and analyze packet data in hex dumps.

- *Export* captured packets in various file formats.

- Display, filter, colorize, or search packets with *very detailed protocol information*.

- Create various *statistics* and graphs based on packet flow information.

- Decode encrypted data and analyze when all relevant data is available.

- …and *a lot more!*

Get Me Started!

Wireshark development and tests frequently occur in Linux, Microsoft Windows, and macOS. The quickest GUI way to explore and install Wireshark is by visiting the official website at `www.wireshark.org/download.html` and choosing the right download specific for your operating system.

macOS

The official macOS Wireshark package bundle (.dmg) can be downloaded from the Wireshark download page, and contents can be copied to the */Applications* folder.

Note   In order to capture packets on macOS, the "ChmodBPF" package is required. It can be installed by opening the "Install ChmodBPF.pkg" file in the Wireshark .dmg during installation or post-installation from the Wireshark application by navigating to the "*About Wireshark*" section, selecting the "*Folders*" tab, and double-clicking "*macOS Extras.*"

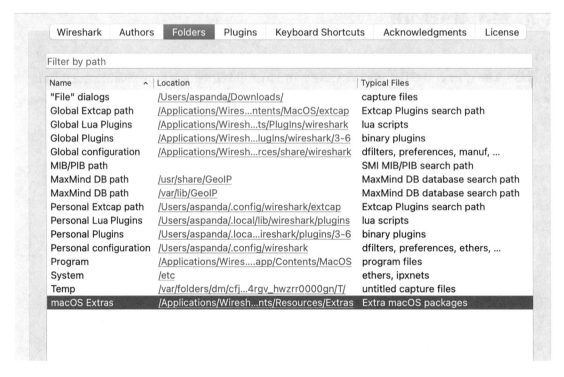

Figure 1-1. *ChmodBPF package path*

The ChmodBPF and system path packages are included along with the Wireshark installer package.

The geeky CLI way that uses Homebrew to install Wireshark on macOS is

```
brew install Wireshark
```

Linux

Command-line installation varies based on Linux distributions. We have covered examples for Red Hat and Debian types, but other variants will follow the standard install approach.

Red Hat and Alike

For the distribution that supports yum, the following command can be used to install Wireshark along with the Qt GUI package:

```
yum install wireshark wireshark-qt
```

Ubuntu and Debian Derivatives

On Debian, you can follow the apt way, and it should take care of the dependencies:

```
sudo apt-get install wireshark
```

Allowing Non-root User to Capture Packets

Note   By default, Wireshark doesn't allow non-root users to do packet captures.

The following steps will help to allow non-root users to capture packets on Linux:

a. Try reconfiguring Wireshark by running

```
sudo dpkg-reconfigure wireshark-common
```

In response to the question, "Should non-superusers be able to capture packets," select "<Yes>".

b. Create a Wireshark user and group:

```
sudo adduser wireshark
```

c. Add the non-root user to the "wireshark" group by executing

```
sudo usermod -a -G wireshark <non-root user>
```

d. Log out the non-root user and log back in again.

Windows Install

The Wireshark installer can be downloaded from www.wireshark.org/download and executed. During the installation, several optional components and the location of the installed package can be selected. For most users, default settings will work and are recommended.

On 32-bit Windows, the default install path is "%ProgramFiles%\Wireshark", and on 64-bit Windows, the default install path is "%ProgramFiles64%\Wireshark", and this % ... % maps to "C:\Program Files\Wireshark" on most systems.

Wireshark on Windows needs **npcap** for capturing packets. The latest npcap installer is part of the Wireshark installer. If **npcap** is not installed, live network traffic packet capture won't be allowed, but Wireshark will still be able to open and analyze saved capture files. By default, the latest version of npcap is installed, but if a different version is required or reinstallation of npcap is needed, it can be done by triggering the install and checking the *Install Npcap* box as appropriate.

The First Capture

Chapter 2 covers the packet capture approach, dependencies, capture filter, etc. in detail. In this section, we are covering basics to get you started with Wireshark.

Once the Wireshark application is launched, the main interface is shown including sections for basic capture controls, capture filters, and display filters. Select the desired interface from the list by clicking and hit the start capture button to start the capture. To select multiple interfaces, press the Ctrl key (Command on MacOSx) and select the needed interfaces.

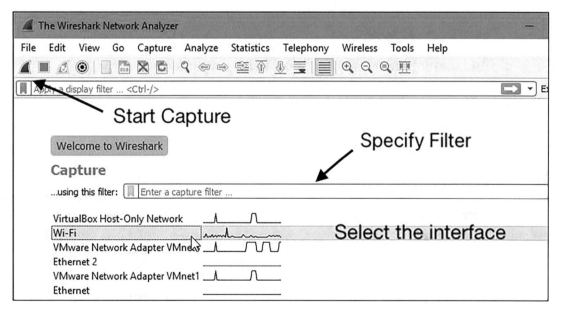

Figure 1-2. *Wireshark launch page*

When capture is in progress, by default it shows live the packets being captured in various colors for different packet types. To stop, click the red square "Stop Capturing" button right next to the "Start Capturing" button. At first glance, you'll notice the data split into various columns.

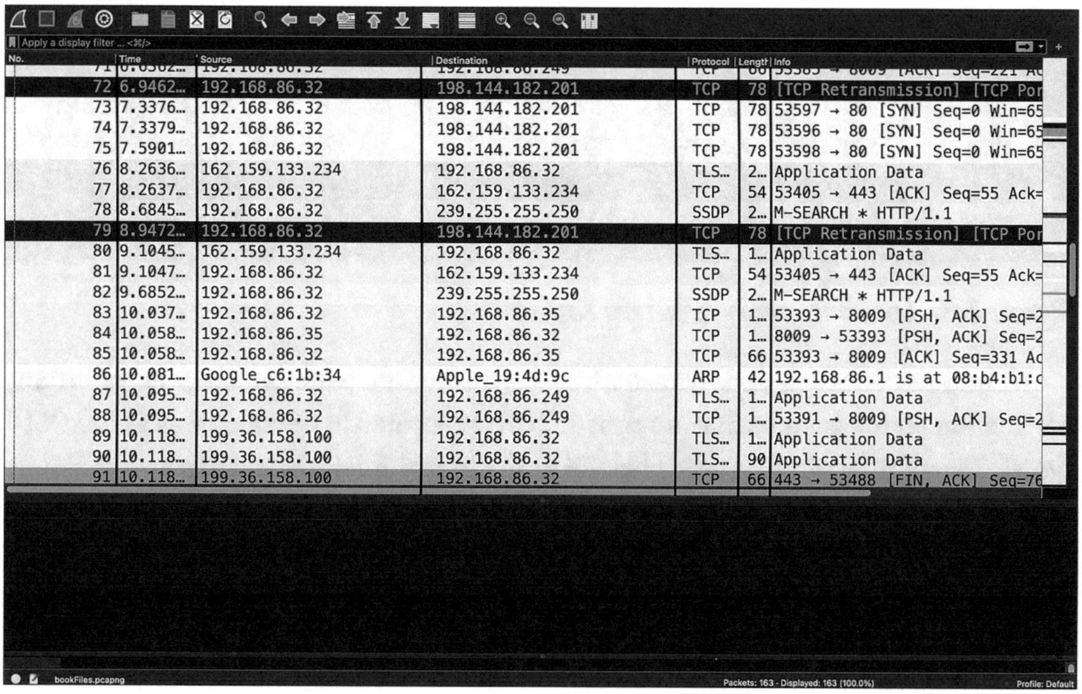

Figure 1-3. *Wireshark live capture*

Understanding a Packet

It's time to investigate a capture at the individual level. This is an example of one of the TCP packets captured.

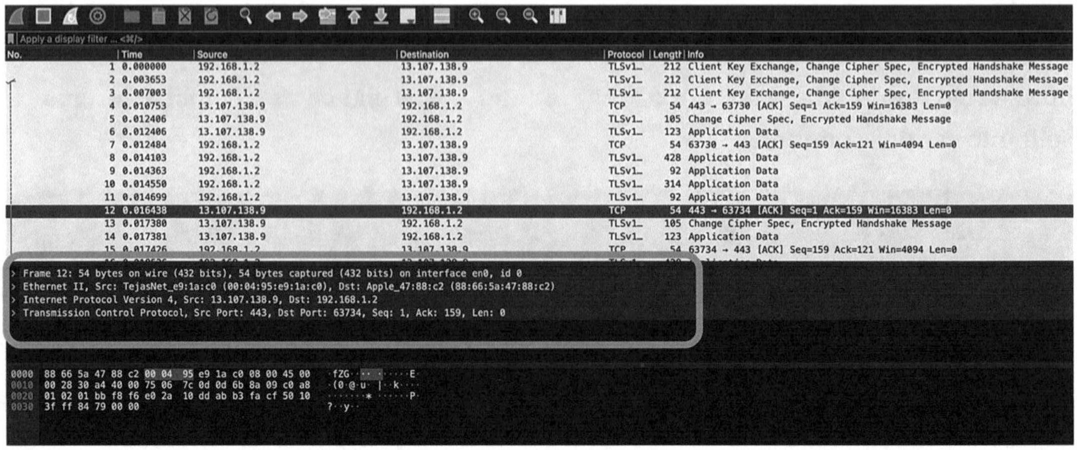

Figure 1-4. *Understanding a packet capture*

When a packet is selected, Wireshark opens the bottom panel which gives important information on the features that are conveniently presented in the same way as the OSI model. The number of layers seen changes as the protocol selected changes.

In the preceding example, from the top down we can see the frame layer, the Ethernet (data link) layer, the IP (network) layer, and the TCP (transport) layer.

If there are more layers or headers in the packet, it is sequentially decoded in the Wireshark packet view. For a packet with multiple encapsulated protocols to be decoded properly, there must be a dissector available that decodes the corresponding protocol layer.

Every packet decode starts with the Frame dissector. It dissects the details of the captured metadata itself (e.g., timestamps). The Frame dissector passes the data to the lowest-level data dissector in the data link layer, for example, the Ethernet dissector gets triggered for the Ethernet header. The packet is then passed to the next dissector in the network layer, for example, the IPv4/v6 dissector gets triggered and so on. Each stage of dissectors decodes and displays the details of the packet.

Dissectors can be written as a self-registering plugin (a shared library or DLL) or built into Wireshark source code. The biggest benefit of going with the plugin approach is that rebuilding a plugin is much faster. If the dissector is built into the source code, then Wireshark needs to be completely recompiled and rebuilt. Hence, it makes more sense to write a dissector as a plugin. More details on dissectors are available in Chapter 9.

Capture Filters

We will discuss in detail capture filters in Chapter 2. Only basics have been included here for completeness on the getting started discussion.

Capture filters are used to decrease the size of captures by filtering out only relevant packets matching the condition before they are added to the capture file. Clicking the Capture Options button shows a screen containing a list of interfaces.

To set a filter, either an interface can be double-clicked, or a custom filter can be entered in the text box. The following list shows examples of some simple capture filters:

host 192.168.2.1: Packets to and from host 192.168.2.1

src host 192.168.2.1: Packets from host 192.168.2.1

dst host 192.168.2.1: Packets to host 192.168.2.1

net 192.168.2.0/24: Packets to and from all host part of network 192.168.2.0/24

port 8080: Packets to or from TCP or UDP port 8080

Figure 1-5. *Capture filter*

Display Filters

This is one of the main advantages of using Wireshark: its clean, simple style to display filtered packets. Wireshark display filters help filter out the matching packets and limit the number of packets displayed on a live capture or while analyzing a file with captured packets. Display filters are different from capture filters, and the syntax is slightly different and simpler than capture filters.

To apply a display filter, simply add the filter text in the display filter box and hit the enter key or apply button. When the display filter is removed from the filter box, all packets are shown.

A display filter can filter matching on a protocol type or a specific field(s) in the protocol. Also, the filter can use logical comparison operators and parentheses to create complex expressions.

The following is a list of some simple frequently used display filters:

`arp or icmp`: Packets of type ARP or ICMP

`ip.addr == 192.168.2.1`: Packets to and from ipv4 host 192.168.2.1

`ip.src != 192.168.2.1`: Packets *not* from ipv4 host 192.168.2.1

`ip.dst == 192.168.2.1`: Packets to ipv4 host 192.168.2.1

`ip.addr == 192.168.2.0/24`: Packets to and from all host part of network 192.168.2.0/24

`tcp.port eq 443 or udp.port == 443`: Packets to or from TCP or UDP port 443

Wireshark allows automatic display filter creation based on a packet or protocol fields in the packet. Simply right-click the desired packet of interest or protocol fields inside the packet and apply it as a filter. This method uses the device's IP address, but the conversation filter below it can use its protocol.

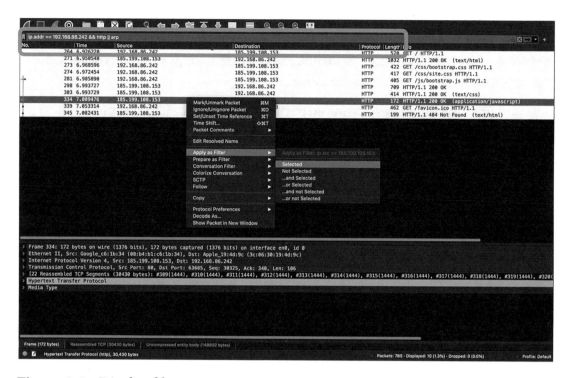

Figure 1-6. *Display filter*

Also, Wireshark allows adding a custom display filter button for frequently used or complex filters. This can be added by clicking the + button beside the display filter box which launches another text box.

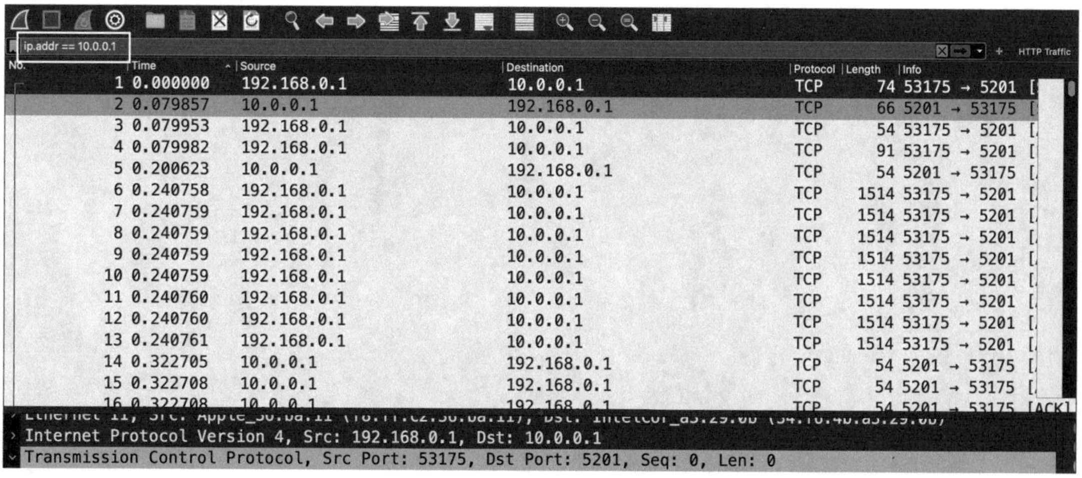

Figure 1-7. *Custom display filter button*

Pcap vs. Pcapng

Wireshark also gives capabilities to save captures to a file, supporting both pcap and pcapng formats. The latter is a newer format that supports

- **Multiple interfaces**: Captured packets from multiple interfaces (e.g., wlan0 and eth0) can all be stored in a single file.

- **Tagged metadata**: Wireshark tags metadata about what machine captured the data, including the OS type and sniffer application.

- **Precise timestamps**: Time is now expressed as 64-bit time units, number, in seconds relative to January 1, 1970, UTC, instead of the former microseconds.

- **Individual comments**: "Annotations" can be saved to individual frames of a capture.

The Capture Options tab gives a few additional settings useful to personalize user experience.

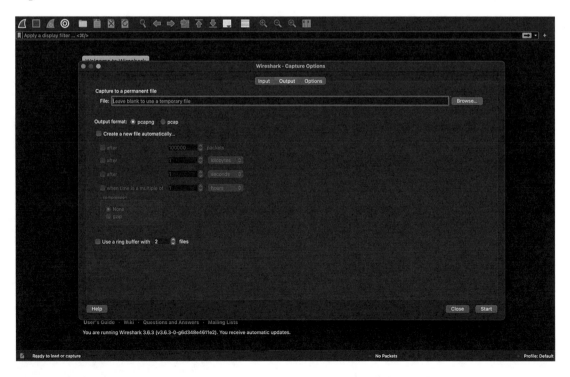

Figure 1-8. *Capture options*

Data Representation

While capturing, there are packets continuously popping up with different symbols and colors, and it can be overwhelming to make sense of it. One of the neat features is a mini map to the left of each packet. Although they may not be very informative, these symbols are helpful from tracing TCP conversations to tracking HTTP responses. Few example representations are shwon in the below table.

Table 1-1. *Data Representation*

┌	First packet in a conversation.
|	Part of the selected conversation.
┊	*Not* part of the selected conversation.
└	Last packet in a conversation.
⊤►	Request.
⊩	Response.
↓	The selected packet acknowledges this packet.
⇓	The selected packet is a duplicate acknowledgment of this packet.
↓	The selected packet is related to this packet in some other way, e.g., as part of reassembly.

Big Picture: I/O Graphs

To see a broader view, I/O graphs can be used to track the packet flow rate and pattern activity using graphs. It is always easier to visualize a flow pattern graphically than the packet list view. An I/O graph can be used for live packet captures or completed captures through capture files. This helps in troubleshooting application issues and TCP/UDP transport layer issues.

To launch a default I/O graph, click **Statistics ➤ I/O Graphs**. The x axis represents the time interval (this can be altered through the interval drop-down), and the y axis represents packets per chosen interval for the flow type. The Y Axis unit type can be changed by double-clicking the flow type and choosing the desired options (bytes or bits or count, etc.). Additional graphs can be added by clicking the + button and defining a display filter for the flow type. In our example, we have added a custom graph for the dns response time.

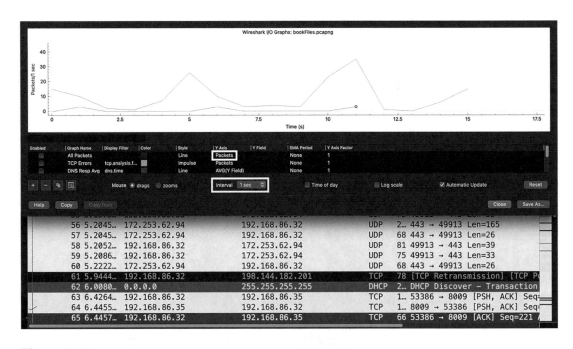

Figure 1-9.

Big Picture: TCP Stream Graphs

TCP stream graphs show a pictorial map of the packets within the TCP flow in a capture. The visual representation depicts how each packet in the flow is related to each other. There are multiple flavors of the stream graph, and using them can help with the deep-dive troubleshooting of a TCP flow.

Time Sequence (Stevens)

This graph shows visually the graph of TCP sequence numbers over time, similar to the graph in Richard Stevens' *TCP/IP Illustrated* series of books.

In the following example capture, pauses in a transfer can be noticed by zooming into one section of the graph where there is no packet gain over a duration of time. Then clicking this portion takes the packet screen directly to that packet.

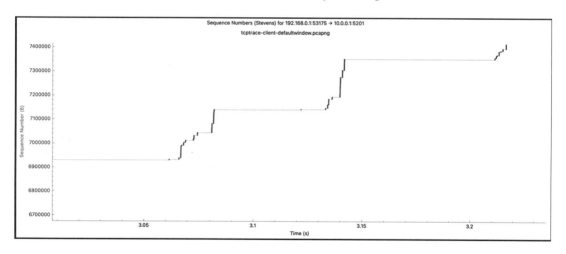

Figure 1-10. *TCP stream graphs – time sequence (Stevens)*

Time Sequence (tcptrace)

This graph shows TCP metrics details similar to the ones seen through the tcptrace utility, including acknowledgments, selective acknowledgments, forward segments, reverse window sizes, and zero windows.

The blue lines show the bytes of each packet sent by one device, and the green lines above represent the receive window size. If at any point, the vertical blue line reaches the green one, the maximum bytes allowed at that time is reached and the sender cannot live up to its name.

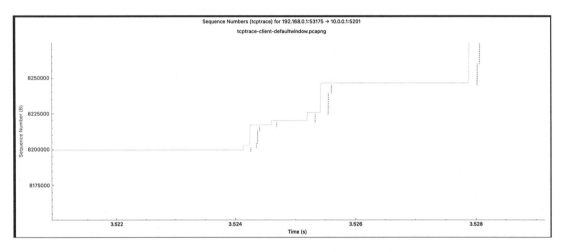

Figure 1-11. *TCP stream graphs: time sequence (tcptrace)*

Throughput

This graph shows the average throughput and goodput for a TCP flow.

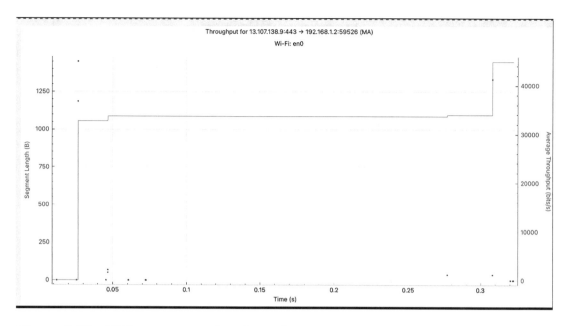

Figure 1-12. *TCP stream graphs: throughput*

Round Trip Time

This graph shows the round trip time against the time or sequence number. RTT considered here is the acknowledgment timestamp corresponding to a particular packet segment.

17

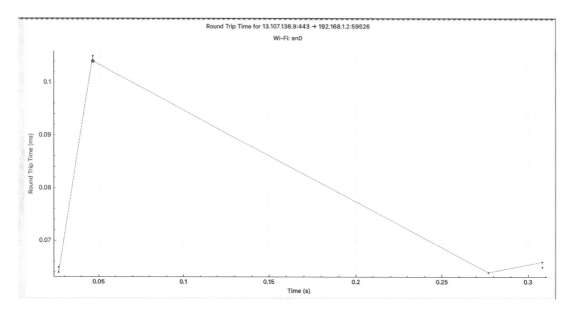

Figure 1-13. *TCP stream graphs: round trip time*

Window Scaling

This graph shows the TCP window size and outstanding bytes.

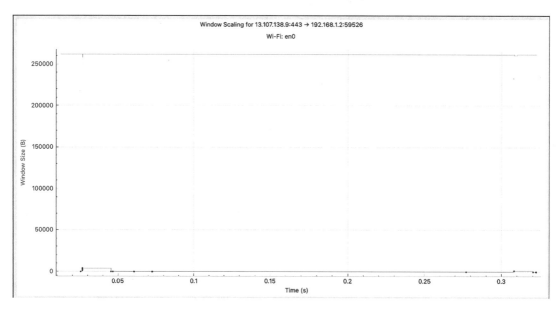

Figure 1-14. *TCP stream graphs: window scaling*

Bigger Picture: Following a Packet Stream

Display filters or graphs won't make the cut when we need a complete application view of the packet communication. Perhaps you are trying to understand how the application data looks like when we merge the individual packets of a TCP or UDP data stream. This is where following a data stream helps. It gives the overall application-level visibility of the combined payload of a packet stream. The supported protocols are TCP, UDP, DCCP, TLS, HTTP, HTTP/2, QUIC, and SIP.

To filter out, right-click the packet of interest, click Follow, and choose the right protocol type.

The following TCP conversation shows the entire conversation with colors, client packets in red and server packets in blue. If the stream has encrypted data, additional steps will be needed to show the decoded data.

Figure 1-15. *Following a packet stream*

Clicking the "Show Data as" drop-down menu and selecting YAML encoding can format the data contained within the flow in an easily readable way.

peers:
  - peer: 0
    host: 192.168.86.32
    port: 49818
  - peer: 1
    host: 192.168.86.35
    port: 8009
packets:
  - packet: 19
    peer: 0
    index: 0
    timestamp: 1651093814.711767000
    data: !!binary |
      FwMDAGlz3zdFsTDjPry41zp8LKmURXClzf4TdJxi/x5QOdZ6DZdEP/CKwl5cNNgILrX1ED26DKaJ
      ze+PZI+On9Zu5RUl6oMXa0VHaziVR6ZmyAvjmad9BcLWZCDZtop6HR75GHAx/4S8+B08yZc=
  - packet: 22
    peer: 1
    index: 0
    timestamp: 1651093814.801125000
    data: !!binary |
      FwMDAGm5M6V2h04JpE/VMkMkzn8e+hT330hOm3YYUsNTUBz8ubwha6PkAPk0R48lnPOSiq7YHZkM
      A69C/T+1uVZD4Cu+RyhfhuG+wkb0eR+Nx5BGdQTCKsgswa7Us6Kn0PPCUar8yV3tuLL6Enc=
  - packet: 105
    peer: 0
    index: 1
    timestamp: 1651093819.802924000
    data: !!binary |
      FwMDAGmBoqfhIMcO0PKAObcorQBonsphtSmpWJyjKEeDuXs1QRPX8FZ6sUa24edNjK7L/8uRRa2S
      yxuayILt6dPgl6Winhx9AiC+IzRw6MibV52k5tdtUQyr566PP5ZrXFXyy74Db91ebWjjamw=
  - packet: 107
    peer: 1
    index: 1
    timestamp: 1651093819.812316000
    data: !!binary |
      FwMDAGmB0qQ16G80c6jIh6kqcwr1MhFxU3alEh5GNzyyAY4jZR9ZTxs7U8a7GzRskLR3vPKN6Fb
      krmMuDNTIkg9ctaJSKQw2oj1004AoGI4zzcBicPNOwaqr8eLOhj0pI0uHyfzxRoLLorNlqo=
  - packet: 3295
    peer: 0
    index: 2
    timestamp: 1651093824.814519000
    data: !!binary |
      FwMDAGnm5368aOZdsdm5jaKxwMRI0gniWUlQGtmQOc6hCqsPn2Gcvz3kDbERvrtNqB5k+UC/M3XM
      0JCNAGdZxZpOJ8+INJao9LCpLBfg/DmJ/SITgix1WEAdDR99BpsFUkTa3xA1kOJuKtMvrb0=
  - packet: 3297

3 client pkts, 3 server pkts, 6 turns.

Entire conversation (660 bytes)   Show data as   YAML   Stream   3

Find: Find Next

Help   Filter Out This Stream   Print   Save as...   Back   Close

Figure 1-16. *Following a packet stream: YAML*

Biggest Picture: Flow Graphs

The previous representation of the TCP flow graph was specific to one protocol or flow, but what if there is a visual way to see the entire capture with all its hosts and conversations? Flow graphs!

It shows a consolidated visual representation of multiple host endpoints and the communication between them. The graph shows the flow direction, ports, flags, sequence number, and many more with nice comments explaining the state of the communication. You can scroll through the graph showing packet relative time and inspect all packets or filter connections by ICMP Flows, ICMPv6 Flows, UIM Flows, and TCP Flows. Also, instead of showing for all packets, you can limit the graph to a subset by applying a display filter.

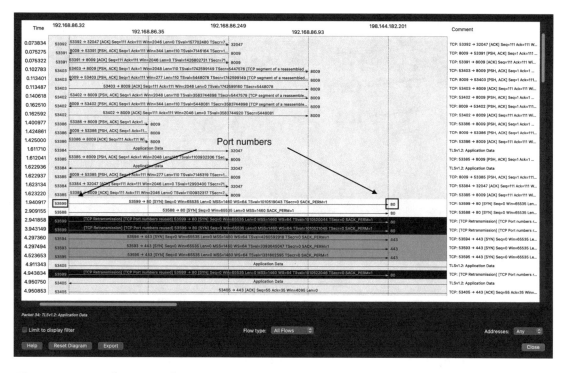

Figure 1-17. *Flow graph*

CloudShark: The Floating Shark

What if we don't have Wireshark or any other packet analysis utility locally installed and still we need to analyze a capture file or we want to analyze a capture file in the cloud, what do we do?

The networking company QA Café introduced a paid web-based cloud software named CloudShark. It was built around Wireshark's cousin TShark, a packet-capturing console utility, and it mimics the style, but not functionality like Wireshark, as it cannot capture packets, but analyze them.

Get Me Started!

There is a sign-in and sign-up option at this web page: `www.cloudshark.org/login`. This is a paid service, but they offer a free 30-day trial.

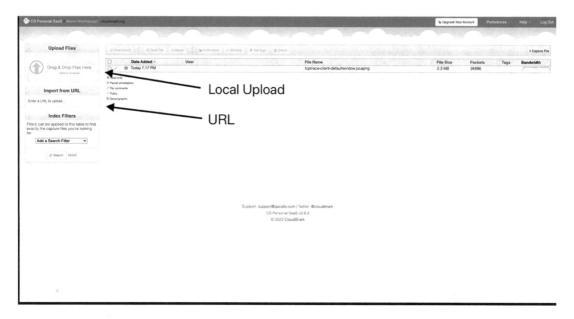

Figure 1-18. *CloudShark login*

Once logged in, a homepage is shown with a side panel of upload options and a main file panel. The local upload can put pcap or pcapng files to the cloud. If the capture file is available on some FTP or HTTP server, a URL import can be done with HTTP and FTP:

- http://username:password@server/path/file.pcap

Import server user credentials are hidden from any viewers of the file and are only stored in the CloudShark database. If the username or password contains special characters, follow these encoding rules. The search button at the bottom left of the page allows searching for previous uploaded files.

Feature Parity with Wireshark

The main packet panel, the variable bottom panel, and even the display filter text box are all kept the same as Wireshark.

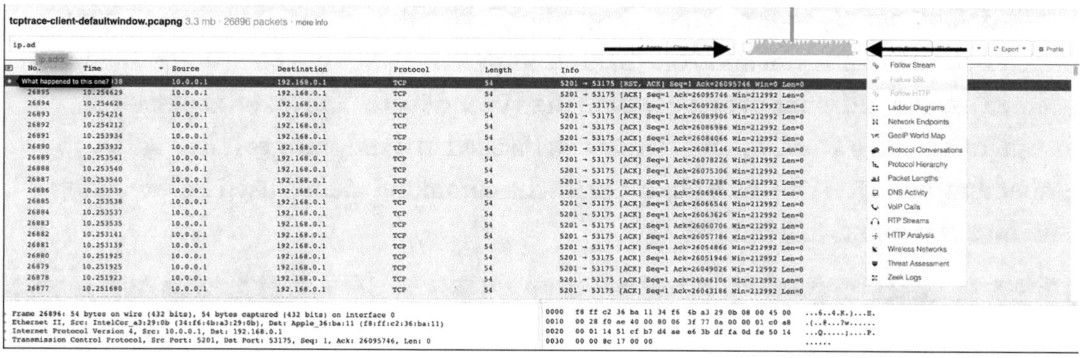

Figure 1-19. *CloudShark packet analysis*

The CloudShark interface displays a mini graph that can specify within which duration the application should display. This helps when the capture is big, and we can alter the timeline to focus on packets or the timeline of our interest.

The analysis tool and graph options shown in the menu are very similar to the ones in Wireshark with a few extra security features. Even annotations can be created for each individual packet, making it easier for collaborators to quickly find issues.

To share the capture file, select the export button and either download the current file with all its revisions or create a new one only including the filtered data (Create New Session).

CloudShark API

CloudShark offers a programmable way of interacting with the capture files through an API that allows users to gain packet data, upload/download documents, and expand their network infrastructure. Each registered user will have an API token that behaves like a typical username and password. You can find your default API token by clicking the **Preferences ➤ API token** option.

Its default permissions can be changed by clicking the token name and applying preferences. The authentication checkbox is important, since not checking it allows users to use the API without being logged in to CloudShark. The token is passed in as a parameter in a search query, which can be used in a script to get information, to embedding it in an HTML web page. Curl is the command mainly used for executing calls on a command-line interface.

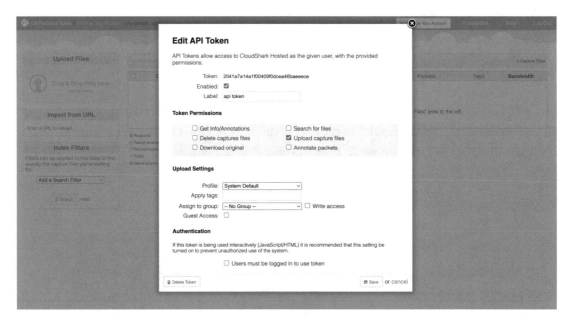

Figure 1-20. *Editing CloudShark API options*

CloudShark API Interaction with Curl

In this example, we have used CURL to test the API. However, other methods can be used to explore the API. Curl comes default on macOS (use `www.confusedbycode.com/curl/` for Windows), and it is used to send data between a client and a URL endpoint or server, thus its name, client URL. With CURL form encoding is automatically done with the -F flag, so either a URL or a direct path can be used.

Here are examples of both uploading and downloading via this method:

- **Upload capture file**
  - URL and HTTP authentication when the capture file is located on a remote HTTP server

```
curl -F url=http://path/to/capture/file https://www.cloudshark.org/api/v1/<api-key>/upload
```

- Upload local file (POST)

```
curl -F file=@filename.cap https://www.cloudshark.org/api/v1/<api-key>/upload
```

- Upload local file (PUT)

```
curl --upload-file filename.cap https://www.cloudshark.org/api/v1/<api-key>/upload
```

- More details are available on the upload API in the Cloudshark website.
- **Download** (-s flag silences the call) **capture file**
- Save to a file with a file ID as cid to a local file "example.cap"

```
curl -s https://www.cloudshark.org/api/v1/<api-key>/download/<cid> > example.cap
```
Query   Output

More details about API can be found in the Cloudshark website.

Auto Upload to CloudShark (Raspberry Pi, Linux, MacOSx)

Even capture files from a Raspberry Pi, Linux, or MacOSx or a remote machine can be uploaded onto CloudShark using a shell script. The script uses dumpcap, a network capturing tool part of TShark.

- If TShark is not installed (test by executing the tshark command), it can be installed by the following commands on a terminal window:

  Raspbian

  ```
  sudo apt-get update
  sudo apt-cache search tshark
  sudo apt-get install tshark
  ```

  Ubuntu

  ```
  sudo apt-get update
  sudo apt-get install tshark
  ```

  MacOSx

  Follow the usual Wireshark install. TShark comes along with it.

The cloudshark_capture.sh script is available at the GitHub repository: `https://github.com/cloudshark/cloudshark-capture`.

- Either directly download the zip file onto your local machine or use the wget command to download

```
wget https://github.com/cloudshark/cloudshark-capture/archive/
refs/heads/master.zip
unzip master.zip
cd cloudshark-capture-master/
```

- Edit the cloudshark_capture.sh script and enter the API token. Changing the prompt variable to n will disable further optional confirmations after capture.

```
nano cloudshark_capture.sh
```

```
chmod +x cloudshark_capture.sh
```

- Run the shell script.

```
./cloudshark_capture.sh -c <number of packets>
```

Example output

```
% ./cloudshark_capture.sh -c 10
Capturing on 'Wi-Fi: en0'
File: /tmp/traffic-2022-06-28-055557.pcapng
Packets captured: 10
Packets received/dropped on interface 'Wi-Fi: en0': 10/19 (pcap:0/
dumpcap:0/flushed:19/ps_ifdrop:0) (34.5%)
Send to CloudShark via https://www.cloudshark.org (y|n=default) y
Additional Tags? (optional)
```

```
Capture Name? (optional) tshark_auto1
A new CloudShark session has been created at:
https://www.cloudshark.org/captures/5a2a617d87b7,
If you get errors related to dumpcap or python, their
corresponding executable path can be corrected in the script
manually.
```

Summary

In this chapter, we got introduced to Wireshark.

- Went through the installation and basic deployment of this software on various operating systems.

    - Explored the user interfaces and CLI of Wireshark and learned about basics of display and capture filters

    - Learned about various packet flow analysis tools like I/O graphs, TCP stream graphs, flow graphs, etc.

Finally, we looked at a cloud packet analyzer tool, CloudShark. Although this might not have the same multitude of features Wireshark does, it is much easier to collaborate and share. It can even integrate with Wireshark and TShark, so you have the best of both sides.

All in all, you have learned the foundation of Wireshark and the features it provides which will help you shark more efficiently and happily.

CHAPTER 2

Packet Capture and Analysis

In today's world, the underlying network protocols and the applications running on the network can be complex. Many times, issues involving applications and networks require visibility at the packet communication level to understand the problem and solve it.

One of the important applications of Wireshark is to capture packets and analyze them. Wireshark is a simple application to set up a capture. However, you should be aware of what packets you are trying to capture, the source and location of the packet flow, the volume of the flow, etc.

Wireshark is very flexible in terms of capturing packets of interest and ignoring other packets. This helps isolate your packets of interest when there is a lot of background traffic.

Packet capture and analysis through Wireshark can be done on all popular operating systems including mobile devices. But the approach may vary a bit.

This is an important chapter that focuses on deep diving into packet capture methods, but some basic details are also included for the sake of completeness. At the end of this chapter, you will learn about

- Capture point placement and how to source packets for capture

- Wireshark and OS-native packet capture tools

- Various capture modes

- Packet capture on mobile devices

- Specific packet capture with simple and complex capture filters for high volume data analysis

© Nagendra Kumar Nainar and Ashish Panda 2023
N. K. Nainar and A. Panda, *Wireshark for Network Forensics*, https://doi.org/10.1007/978-1-4842-9001-9_2

Sourcing Traffic for Capture

Wireshark or similar applications running on a device listen to the packets traversing through a network interface and can capture the same. For the captures to work, the packets should be seen on the network interface first.

The packets seen on a network interface can be of two types:

- Packets generated by the device or packets destined to the device

- Redirected or mirrored packets that are meant for other devices in the network but sent to a central device for capturing

In the subsequent sections, we will learn more about capturing mirrored packets and the basics of capture point placement.

Setting Up Port Mirroring

Port mirroring is a feature of network devices like routers, switches, and firewalls which helps replicate and redirect packets. Port mirroring can be called a port monitor or Switched Port Analyzer (SPAN) by various networking vendors.

Port mirroring continuously monitors the mirrored source ports, creates a copy of packets seen on the source port, and sends it to the mirror destination port. Both transmit and receive packets on mirrored source ports can be sent to the destination port for capture. The device running Wireshark or any other packet capture application is connected to the mirror destination port.

As shown in Figure 2-1, the requirement is to capture packets traversing between S1 and the firewall. So ports 1 and 2 connecting to these devices are defined as mirror sources, and all these mirrored packets are sent to mirror destination port 3 which connects to the capture point.

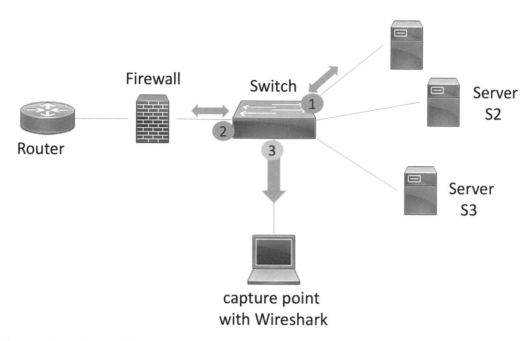

Figure 2-1. *Port mirroring*

The actual configuration of setting up port mirroring on the network device is vendor specific. It is out of the scope of this book.

Remote Port Mirroring

In the previous scenario, the packet source devices which need the packets captured are connected to the same switch where our capture device is connected.

However, this may not be the scenario always when your network is big and spans across a number of devices and geographies. The switch or router where your capture device is connected may be separated by one or many devices. Sometimes, it may not be convenient to send someone to the remote packet source device to connect the capture device locally.

In such scenarios, the mirrored packets on the source device can be sent to the remote device by either of the following methods depending on the network type:

   1.   Over a layer 2 trunk if it's an L2 switching domain. This is known
        as Remote SPAN or remote monitoring depending on the network
        equipment vendor type.

2. It can be encapsulated with an appropriate Generic Routing Encapsulation (GRE) header and tunneled across the IP network to the destination device. This is known as Encapsulated Remote SPAN (ERSPAN) or "mirroring to GRE" depending on the network equipment vendor type.

The mirror destination device decapsulates the captured packets if encapsulated and redirects them to the network port where the capture device is connected.

Figure 2-2 illustrates both the remote port mirroring capabilities.

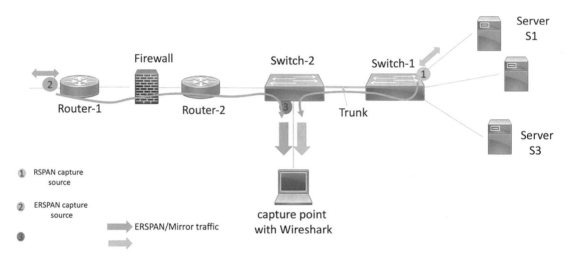

Figure 2-2. *Remote port mirroring*

Switch-1 mirrors the packets going in and out of port 1 and redirects to the remote switch, Switch-2, over a layer 2 trunk link between the switches.

Similarly, Router-1 mirrors the packets going in and out of port 2 and redirects to the remote switch, Switch-2, over a layer 3 IP network by encapsulating the captured packet in an ERSPAN and GRE header.

Figure 2-3 shows details of the encapsulation headers and how the actual packet was encapsulated and sent to the destination device with IP address 1.1.1.1.

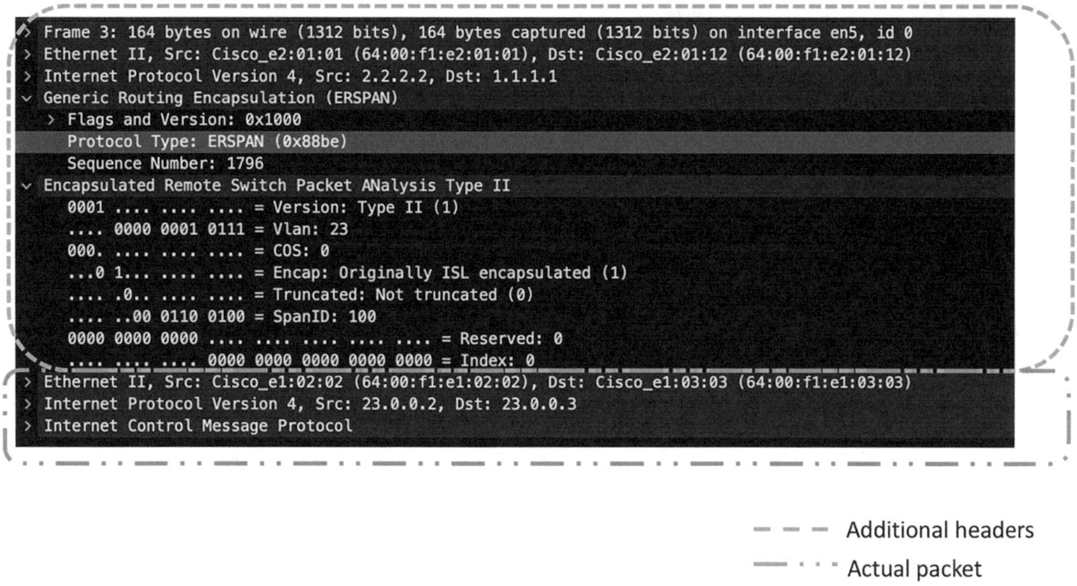

```
> Frame 3: 164 bytes on wire (1312 bits), 164 bytes captured (1312 bits) on interface en5, id 0
> Ethernet II, Src: Cisco_e2:01:01 (64:00:f1:e2:01:01), Dst: Cisco_e2:01:12 (64:00:f1:e2:01:12)
> Internet Protocol Version 4, Src: 2.2.2.2, Dst: 1.1.1.1
∨ Generic Routing Encapsulation (ERSPAN)
   > Flags and Version: 0x1000
     Protocol Type: ERSPAN (0x88be)
     Sequence Number: 1796
∨ Encapsulated Remote Switch Packet ANalysis Type II
     0001 .... .... .... = Version: Type II (1)
     .... 0000 0001 0111 = Vlan: 23
     000. .... .... .... = COS: 0
     ...0 1... .... .... = Encap: Originally ISL encapsulated (1)
     .... .0.. .... .... = Truncated: Not truncated (0)
     .... ..00 0110 0100 = SpanID: 100
     0000 0000 0000 .... .... .... .... .... = Reserved: 0
     .... .... .... 0000 0000 0000 0000 0000 = Index: 0
> Ethernet II, Src: Cisco_e1:02:02 (64:00:f1:e1:02:02), Dst: Cisco_e1:03:03 (64:00:f1:e1:03:03)
> Internet Protocol Version 4, Src: 23.0.0.2, Dst: 23.0.0.3
> Internet Control Message Protocol
```

– – – Additional headers
— · · · Actual packet

Figure 2-3. *ERSPAN header*

The actual vendor-specific configuration of the mirroring is out of the scope of this book.

Important Note   Remote mirroring (RSPAN), encapsulated remote mirroring (ERSPAN), etc. are vendor dependent and may not be supported on all your network devices. When you choose this option, do make sure to check vendor documentation.

While doing remote mirroring, all your mirrored traffic is carried over the network between source and network devices. This may overwhelm the underlying network if the sufficient capacity doesn't exist. For example, if you are mirroring ten 1 Gbps ports and sending to the remote device, more than the 10 Gbps traffic may hit the underlying link. Make sure the transport link is of higher capacity than 10 Gbps and sufficient headroom is available to accommodate this. Otherwise, this will affect all other traffic flowing through.

Other Mirroring Options

The main purpose of port mirroring is to redirect capture traffic from the source switch or router to the destination port where the capture device is connected. However, the end hosts or network devices do not always connect to a switch or a router. There can be a direct link between the devices, and we need to capture the packets or errors on the link, etc. In this case, a low-cost solution of TAP or hub may help.

TAP

A network TAP or Test Access Point is a passive three-port device which can be inserted like a bump on the wire between two network equipment. All the packets between the devices are sent to the third port where the capture device can be connected. TAP uses splitters internally to replicate the data toward the capture destination port, while actual communication remains uninterrupted.

Advantages of TAP

- There is no limit on the size of a packet which can be replicated.

- Capturing errored frames due to link issues, etc. is easy. These are normally dropped by switches during normal port mirroring.

- Simple and cost-effective. No complex configurations are needed.

Note   The link between the devices is interrupted while introducing the TAP. Hence, this operation should be carried out during a maintenance window.

Hub

A hub is a half-duplex device where packets sent or received on one port of the hub is also visible to other ports of the hub. As it's a half-duplex communication, it may affect the actual data communication between the source devices.

Hubs are not commonly used when port speed is above 100 Mbps. This is a cost-effective solution for mirroring traffic but should be your last choice if other options don't work.

Capture Point Placement

In the previous sections, we learned how we can source traffic from other network devices redirected toward the capture point. The general rule of thumb is to place the capture device or sniffer as close to the suspected network device as possible.

However, as the network size grows, it becomes a challenge to have capture devices at each location. To reduce efforts, we have to decide on what are the optimum points where we can do the packet capture. The approach varies based on different scenarios.

The following are some of the suggested guidelines which will help you decide:

- Collect information related to the network problem at hand in detail.

  - Find the nature of drop or degradation and source and destination endpoints involved.

  - Find out the path of the packet taken by the affected flow and the suspected devices and interfaces involved in the packet drop or degradation.

  - Understand the direction of the issue on the suspected path or devices.

- If the problem description is clear and we have a limited set of suspected devices and interfaces or segments, then

  - Capture as close to the suspected locations as possible. If the desired device supports packet capture capability, leverage it for packet capture. E.g. many hosts and servers natively support packet capture utilities like tshark, Wireshark etc. Most of the network equipment like routers, switches, and firewalls also support on-the-box packet capture capabilities which can be leveraged.

  - If on-box capture is not available or we need to capture the packets traversing on the wire, we can use a port mirroring technique or TAP to redirect packets to a capture device.

  - If local SPAN is possible, it's recommended. But if field engineer presence is a challenge, due to logistic reasons, then Remote SPAN or Encapsulated Remote SPAN can be done to mirror the packets toward a centralized capture device.

- If the problem description is unclear and multiple devices or multiple paths are involved, then we will end up having captures from multiple suspected locations.

OS-Native Traffic Capture Tools

There are many external packet capture applications available for any operating system. However, many times a user may run into authorization issues that don't allow the application to be installed or the application itself may not run properly. At that point, the native packet capture utilities which are available by default come in handy.

Some of the available native utilities are discussed in detail in subsequent sections.

UNIX, Linux, BSD, and macOS

All UNIX-like platforms have **tcpdump** natively available as a standard package. **tcpdump** offers a command-line interface which can print the contents of network packets to standard output or a file.

In many cases, it's more useful and easy to capture packets using tcpdump rather than Wireshark. For example, you might want to do a packet capture remotely and either don't have your OS GUI access or Wireshark is not installed on the remote device. In such scenarios, you can run **tcpdump** and capture the packets to a file for viewing through Wireshark on a local machine. Detailed ways of doing remote capture are discussed in the section "Remote Packet Capture with Extcap" of this chapter.

Usage:

Capture interface en0 and show on terminal

```
% sudo tcpdump -i en0
tcpdump: verbose output suppressed, use -v or -vv for full protocol decode
listening on en0, link-type EN10MB (Ethernet), capture size 262144 bytes
19:46:22.978547 IP somedomain.com.https > 192.168.1.3.54372: UDP,
length 109
19:46:22.978918 IP 192.168.1.3.54372 > somedomain.com.https: UDP,
length 109
19:46:23.167737 IP somedomain.com.https > 192.168.1.3.54372: UDP,
length 125
```

Save captures to a file

$ **tcpdump -i <interface> -w <file> -C <file size MB> -c <packet count>**

The correct *interface* and the name of a *file* to save into will have to be specified in the preceding command. The interface name can be found from the "*ifconfig*" or "*ip addr*" command. In addition, in case you are not mentioning capture size or capture count, the capture can be terminated with ^C when enough packets are captured.

Example: Capture to a file on macOS

```
% sudo tcpdump -i en0 -w test_capture.pcap -C 1 -c 100
Password:
tcpdump: listening on en0, link-type EN10MB (Ethernet), capture size
262144 bytes
100 packets captured
107 packets received by filter
0 packets dropped by kernel
%
```

Example: Capture displayed on the terminal

```
% sudo tcpdump -vvv
tcpdump: data link type PKTAP
tcpdump: listening on pktap, link-type PKTAP (Apple DLT_PKTAP), capture
size 262144 bytes
11:50:12.671775 AF IPv4 (2), length 1043: (tos 0x60, ttl 64, id 0, offset
0, flags [DF], proto TCP (6), length 1039)
    192.168.200.1.56526 > somedomain.com.sip: Flags [P.], cksum 0x17bd
    (correct), seq 2639251502:2639252489, ack 1230333462, win 2048, options
    [nop,nop,TS val 4273941536 ecr 3103280548], length 987
11:50:12.672009 88:66:5a:47:88:c2 (oui Unknown) > 00:04:95:e9:1a:c0 (oui
Unknown), ethertype IPv4 (0x0800), length 1143: (tos 0x60, ttl 64, id
19633, offset 0, flags [none], proto UDP (17), length 1129)
    192.168.1.3.60828 > somedomain.com.https: [udp sum ok] UDP, length 1101
11:50:12.678223 00:04:95:e9:1a:c0 (oui Unknown) > 88:66:5a:47:88:c2 (oui
Unknown), ethertype IPv4 (0x0800), length 503: (tos 0x60, ttl 244, id
54512, offset 0, flags [none], proto UDP (17), length 489)
    somedomain.com.https > 192.168.1.3.60828: [udp sum ok] UDP, length 461
```

- When you want to see a detailed packet, decode with the verbose
  option (-vvv) with an Ethernet header (-e).

Example: Capture displayed on the terminal with verbose and Ethernet header info

```
% sudo tcpdump -vvv -e
tcpdump: data link type PKTAP
tcpdump: listening on pktap, link-type PKTAP (Apple DLT_PKTAP), capture
size 262144 bytes
11:50:12.671775 AF IPv4 (2), length 1043: (tos 0x60, ttl 64, id 0, offset
0, flags [DF], proto TCP (6), length 1039)
    192.168.200.1.56526 > somedomain.com.sip: Flags [P.], cksum 0x17bd
    (correct), seq 2639251502:2639252489, ack 1230333462, win 2048, options
    [nop,nop,TS val 4273941536 ecr 3103280548], length 987
11:50:12.672009 88:66:5a:47:88:c2 (oui Unknown) > 00:04:95:e9:1a:c0 (oui
Unknown), ethertype IPv4 (0x0800), length 1143: (tos 0x60, ttl 64, id
19633, offset 0, flags [none], proto UDP (17), length 1129)
    192.168.1.3.60828 > somedomain.com.https: [udp sum ok] UDP, length 1101
11:50:12.678223 00:04:95:e9:1a:c0 (oui Unknown) > 88:66:5a:47:88:c2 (oui
Unknown), ethertype IPv4 (0x0800), length 503: (tos 0x60, ttl 244, id
54512, offset 0, flags [none], proto UDP (17), length 489)
    somedomain.com.https > 192.168.1.3.60828: [udp sum ok] UDP, length 461
```

Additional expressions can be provided to filter out only the desired packets:

- The following could capture two-way packets for SSH:

  ```
  sudo tcpdump -n port 22 and host 25.67.35.68 -w capture_ssh.pcap
  ```

- And/or statements can be used to have a desired filter:

  ```
  tcpdump -w <filename> -i <if name> -C <file size MB> src port 22
  and host 25.67.35.68 or host 1.1.1.1
  ```

Other tcpdump capture options can be found at the tcpdump man page: www.
tcpdump.org/manpages/tcpdump.1-4.99.1.html. We will discuss more on the filters in
the "Capture Filtering" section of this chapter.

Windows

Windows has a built-in packet capture component called "ndiscap." This is implemented as an ETW (Event Tracing for Windows) trace provider. This ETW technology allows applications to produce trace messages or events. ndiscap should be preferred compared to other popular packet capture methods (WinPcap, included with older versions of Wireshark) due to performance problems. A capture can be collected as follows.

Note   Administrator privilege may be required for the captures.

Example 2-1. Find available interface name or GUID

```
C:\Users\User1\Downloads>netsh trace show interfaces

Wireless LAN adapter Local Area Connection* 1:
    Description:     Microsoft Wi-Fi Direct Virtual Adapter
    Interface GUID:  {0DA7302A-AFF6-4E42-A373-86A9A19276F6}
    Interface Index: 3
    Interface Luid:  0x47008001000000

Wireless LAN adapter Local Area Connection* 2:
    Description:     Microsoft Wi-Fi Direct Virtual Adapter #2
    Interface GUID:  {1ADCE923-0FBF-47E4-8FC6-2730E25F37B4}
    Interface Index: 4
    Interface Luid:  0x47008002000000

Wireless LAN adapter Wi-Fi:
    Description:     Intel(R) Wi-Fi 6 AX201 160MHz
    Interface GUID:  {A6F04A17-3118-449A-82B2-80DC35CBCD26}
    Interface Index: 17
    Interface Luid:  0x47008000000000
```

Example 2-2. Start the capture with interface GUID or interface name

```
C:\Users\User1\Downloads>netsh trace start capture=yes captureinterface="{A
6F04A17-3118-449A-82B2-80DC35CBCD26}" tracefile="C:\Users\User1\Downloads\
capture_1.etl"

Trace configuration:
-------------------------------------------------------------------
Status:               Running
Trace File:           C:\Users\User1\Downloads\capture_1.etl
Append:               Off
Circular:             On
Max Size:             512 MB
Report:               Off
```

Example 2-3. Stop the capture

```
C:\Users\User1\Downloads>
C:\Users\User1\Downloads>netsh trace stop
Merging traces ... done
Generating data collection ... done
The trace file and additional troubleshooting information have been
compiled as "C:\Users\User1\Downloads\capture_1.cab".
File location = C:\Users\User1\Downloads\capture_1.etl
Tracing session was successfully stopped.
```

ndiscap packet capture generates a file in *etl* format, which cannot be opened by Wireshark. *etl* files can be opened by ETW-centric tools like Microsoft Message Analyzer, but that may not help here. There is an open source tool available by Microsoft known as **etl2pcapng.exe** that can convert the *etl* file to a pcapng file which can be opened with Wireshark. The etl2pcapng can be downloaded from the GitHub link: https://github. com/microsoft/etl2pcapng/.

Note   Administrator privilege may be required for this.

Example 2-4. Convert the .etl file to .pcapng for Wireshark viewing

```
C:\Users\User1\Downloads>etl2pcapng.exe capture_1.etl capture_1.pcapng
IF: medium=wifi                 ID=0     IfIndex=17
Converted 86 frames

C:\Users\User1\Downloads>
```

Wireshark-Based Traffic Capture

Compared to the native capture utilities, Wireshark is more flexible and advanced. Wireshark is available on all popular operating systems, and wherever available, it is recommended to be the first choice for packet capture and analysis.

Wireshark is a GUI-based application, but it comes with command-line options with dumpcap or tshark which almost fulfills the same requirements.

CLI-Based Capture with Dumpcap or Tshark

Dumpcap comes as part of the Wireshark suite of packages in all OS installations. But tshark may need to be installed manually if required. You may need to search the path in case it's not directly accessible from the environmental executable PATH.

```
% sudo find /Applications/ -name "*tshark*"
/Applications//Wireshark.app/Contents/MacOS/tshark
<SNIP>
% sudo find /Applications/ -name "*dumpcap*"
/Applications//Wireshark.app/Contents/MacOS/dumpcap
```

Dumpcap and tshark behave the same way, use the same pcap library and have similar flags, and capture filters as tcpdump discussed in the earlier section. In fact, tshark uses dumpcap as its capturing engine. There are some minor differences between dumpcap and tshark.

The choice of which CLI-based tool to use can be decided by referring to Table 2-1. In normal applications, any of the two should work.

Table 2-1. *Difference Between Dumpcap and Tshark*

Difference	Dumpcap	Tshark
Default availability	Part of the Wireshark suite	Optional package in some OS
Capture display	Can't display on the terminal. Dumps to a file	By default, displays on the terminal and dumps to a file
Extcap interface detection (for remote capture)	Can't detect	Works well with extcap interfaces
Performance	Performs better than tshark in heavy load	Compared to dumpcap, some packets can be missed in heavy load
Additional flags	-N: Number of packet buffers -C: Number of byte buffers -t: Separate capture thread per interface	These flags not available

```
% ./tshark -i en0
Capturing on 'Wi-Fi: en0'
 ** (tshark:72470) 16:26:57.784999 [Main MESSAGE] -- Capture started.
 ** (tshark:72470) 16:26:57.785643 [Main MESSAGE] -- File: "/var/folders/
    dm/cfjmqx7x1ddc674rgv_hwzrr0000gn/T/wireshark_Wi-Fi4WIVL1.pcapng"
    1    0.000000   192.168.1.3   → 192.168.200.1DTLSv1.2 1415 Application Data
    2    0.000050   192.168.1.3   → 192.168.200.1DTLSv1.2 407 Application Data
    3    0.061736 192.168.200.1→ 192.168.1.3   DTLSv1.2 199 Application Data
    4    0.062055   192.168.1.3   → 192.168.200.1DTLSv1.2 151 Appli

% ./dumpcap -i en0
Capturing on 'Wi-Fi: en0'
File: /var/folders/dm/cfjmqx7x1ddc674rgv_hwzrr0000gn/T/wireshark_Wi-
Fi10PPL1.pcapng
Packets captured: 195
Packets received/dropped on interface 'Wi-Fi: en0': 195/0 (pcap:0/
dumpcap:0/flushed:0/ps_ifdrop:0) (100.0%)
%
```

GUI-Based Capture with Wireshark

In Chapter 1, you have got a good understanding of Wireshark installation, basics of the user interface, etc. In this chapter, we will focus on how to get a simple packet capture started.

When you launch Wireshark, it shows a list of recently opened capture files (in the following image, it's empty and not shown) and also a list of available interfaces.

The traffic rate graph is also shown against each interface. This helps identify quickly which interfaces are active and have traffic flowing.

To start a capture

1. Select the desired interface.

2. [Optional] Specify a capture filter if want to limit capture to packets of interest. If not specified, all packets are captured.

3. Hit the start button.

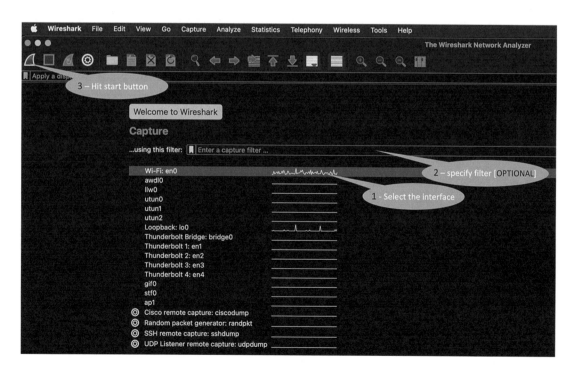

Figure 2-4. *Starting a packet capture*

Capturing Traffic from Multiple Interfaces

Sometimes, we need to correlate data from multiple interfaces. In such cases, we can choose multiple interfaces by pressing the CONTROL key (Windows, Linux) or COMMAND key (macOS) and select desired interfaces by clicking the mouse.

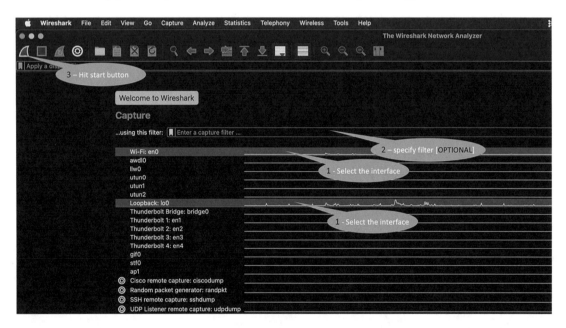

Figure 2-5. *Capturing on multiple interfaces*

Stopping Capture

Once the desired data is captured, it can be stopped by hitting the stop button. The capture file can be saved by selecting the save option.

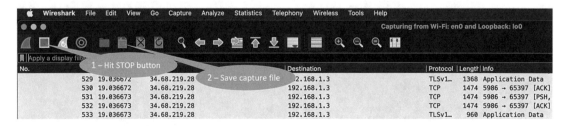

Figure 2-6. *Stopping capture and saving*

Capture Modes and Configurations

Promiscuous Mode

Promiscuous mode is related to how a network adapter processes a packet received on its interface. By default, if the destination MAC is not the adapter MAC, the adapter may drop the unicast Ethernet frame. This means the received packet may be destined to a different adapter or device, and the local adapter shouldn't process.

Promiscuous mode if activated on the adapter allows a network adapter to process all frames whether it's meant for this adapter or not.

In some virtual machines, the adapter settings may need to be tweaked to allow promiscuous mode, but normally we don't have to change anything for hardware adapters.

Once the network adapter passes the frames not meant for itself for further processing by applications like Wireshark, capture behavior can be controlled at the application level too.

Wireshark by default captures in promiscuous mode. This is very important for capturing packets coming to the capture device redirected by switch port mirroring (SPAN) other device network interfaces. For successful capture of such frames, the network adapter should be operating in promiscuous mode, and Wireshark should have activated promiscuous mode.

This setting can be changed at the **Capture ➤ Options** window by checking or unchecking the enable promiscuous mode as shown in Figure 2-7.

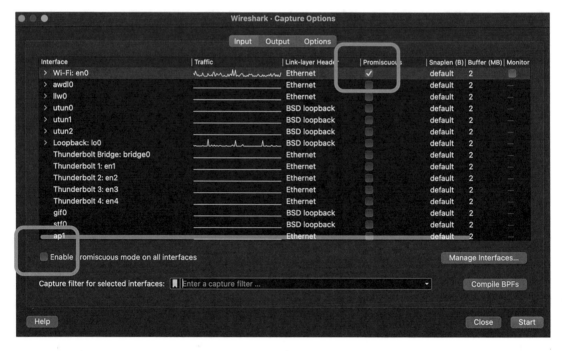

Figure 2-7. *Configuring promiscuous mode*

Pitfalls

Vlan Tag Is Not Seen in Captured Frames

On Windows platforms, some of the network adapters strip off the dot1q vlan tag/ header before passing the frame to Wireshark for processing. This may be seen if promiscuous mode is not enabled. To fix this, appropriate registry settings can be done as recommended by the vendor. We have the reference link for Intel adapters in the "References for This Chapter" section.

Monitor Mode

The monitor mode is related to Wi-Fi adapters, which allow packet capture at the 802.11 radio level and not at the Ethernet level.

The Wi-Fi adapter has to support the monitor mode, and not all adapters and OSs may have support for the same. Details on monitor mode are discussed in the "wireless capture in Chapter 4."

Remote Packet Capture with Extcap

In previous sections, we have seen how to use Wireshark to do a live capture of traffic traversing through the network interface locally. If the packet doesn't hit the local interface, capture can't be done.

This concept can be further evolved for remote device capture through extcap. The extcap interface plugin makes available remote device interfaces as virtual capture interfaces on local machines. These virtual capture interfaces can be used directly in Wireshark to trigger packet captures.

There are several extcap utilities that are bundled with Wireshark. You may have access to more or fewer depending on your platform operating system:

- androiddump

- ciscodump

- randpktdump

- sshdump

- udpdump

In the Wireshark GUI, extcap interfaces are normally presented as interfaces with a picture of a gear. In the interface capture list, they will be at the bottom, so you may need to scroll down. In tshark, you can list which ones are available with tshark -D. Note that dumpcap -D will not show extcap interfaces.

We can discuss more on this with an example of sshdump.

Remote Capture with Sshdump

Sshdump is an extcap tool that makes available locally an interface of a device accessible through SSH. This allows running a capture tool remotely and tunneling the captured packets over an SSH connection to the local device running the sshdump extcap plugin.

Requirements

- Some packet capture executables (like tcpdump, wireshark, etc.) must have been installed on the remote device.

- SSH connection is allowed to the remote device.

- The SSH user is allowed to run the capture utility.

The following is the way to trigger sshdump from the Wireshark GUI.

Step 1: From the Wireshark home page, click the gear icon corresponding to the "*SSH remote capture: sshdump*" interface.

Step 2: Fill the server IP/hostname, SSH port, and authentication details.

Step 3: Fill the optional interface (name will be specific to the device), sudo, or capture command details and start.

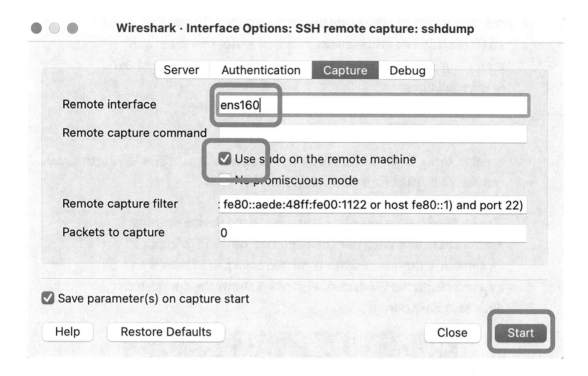

Mobile Device Traffic Capture

Wireshark supports packet capture on mobile devices. However, it can have a lot of other tool dependencies. In the following section, we have discussed some of the approaches like Wireshark native ways and third-party apps.

Android Devices

Using Native Androiddump Utility

Like **sshdump**, **androiddump** is an extcap plugin that makes available a remote-connected Android device interface on the local device for packet captures. The following are some of the requirements:

1. You must have installed an Android SDK. Android SDK for various platforms is available at the following:

   `https://developer.android.com/sdk/index.html#Other`

2. Add the SDK to the PATH environment variable. The environment PATH specified should contain a directory with tools like "adb" and "android" required for the capture. They come as part of the SDK installation.

   The following is an example in macOS to update the environment PATH:

   ```
   export PATH="${HOME}/Library/Android/sdk/tools:${HOME}/Library/
   Android/sdk/platform-tools:${PATH}"
   ```

3. The Android device must be connected to the device running Android SDK and Wireshark through USB or Wi-Fi pairing. Without this, the androiddump-related extcap interfaces won't be available on the Wireshark. Figure 2-8 shows the connected devices in the Android Studio.

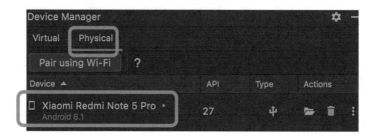

Figure 2-8. *Android Studio device manager connections*

4. For network interface packet capture, the Android device must be rooted, and the tcpdump binary should be installed. Binaries can be found at this location: `www.androidtcpdump.com/android-tcpdump/downloads`.

5. Some Android devices require on-screen authentication, and hence you must have required (root) permission to the Android device.

The following are the supported Android interfaces:

1. Logcat Main (binary [<=Jelly Bean] or text)

2. Logcat System (binary [<=Jelly Bean] or text)

3. Logcat Events (binary [<=Jelly Bean] or text)

4. Logcat Radio (binary [<=Jelly Bean] or text)

5. Logcat Crash (text; from Lollipop)

6. Bluetooth Hcidump [<=Jelly Bean]

7. Bluetooth Bluedroid External Parser [Kitkat]

8. Bluetooth BtsnoopNet [>=Lollipop]

9. Wi-Fi tcpdump [need tcpdump on phone]

Once the preceding requirements are satisfied, the respective androiddump extcap interfaces will be visible on Wireshark on the capture device running Wireshark and Android Studio (Android SDK).

Choose the desired androiddump extcap interface and start the capture with default settings. In the following example, as shown in Figure 2-9, we have used a logcat radio interface.

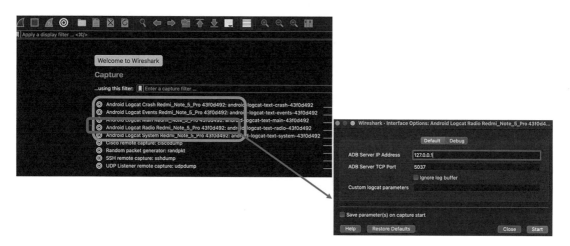

Figure 2-9. *Androiddump interfaces*

This starts the capture, and it can be seen in real time on the Wireshark GUI interface.

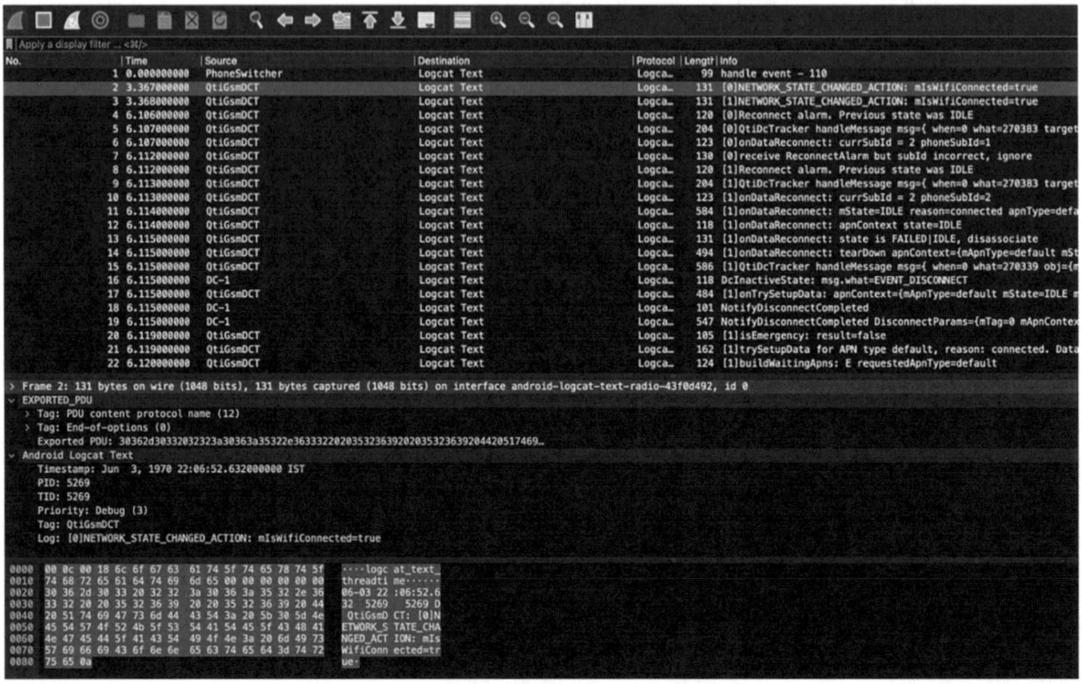

Figure 2-10. *Androiddump capture*

Using Third-Party Android App and Sshdump

There are multiple free and paid Android-based applications available which allow packets to and from the Android-based mobile device to capture packets on the required interface and locally save them to a pcapng file or send remotely to a Wireshark capture device through the sshdump extcap utility.

In this section, we are discussing one such free application called "PCAP Remote," which captures the packets on a required interface and streams packets to an SSH server interface on the Android device. We can utilize the sshdump extcap utility available on Wireshark running on a remote capture device to open a connection with the Android device SSH server and receive packets in real time.

Step 1: On the Android device

Install the Android app and start capture mode as the SSH server.

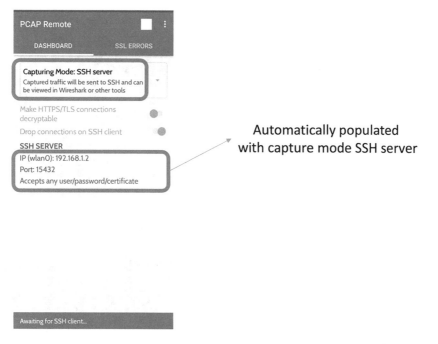

Figure 2-11. *PCAP Remote Android app settings*

Step 2: From the remote device running Wireshark

Start capture on the sshdump extcap interface and use details seen in step 1. Here, the username and password have to be specified. This can be any random text but can't be left empty.

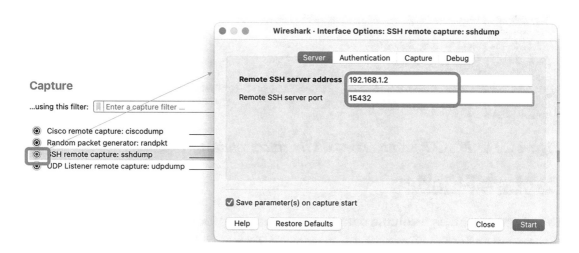

Figure 2-12. *PCAP Remote Wireshark settings – 1*

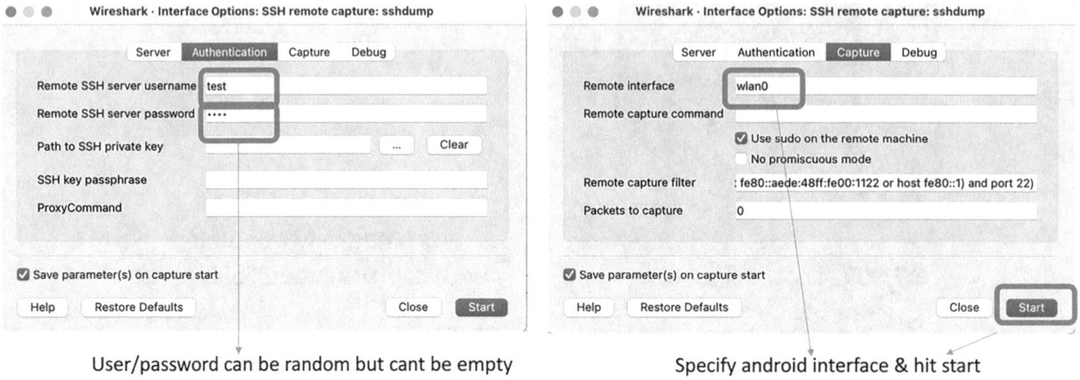

User/password can be random but cant be empty   Specify android interface & hit start

Figure 2-13. *PCAP Remote Wireshark settings – 2*

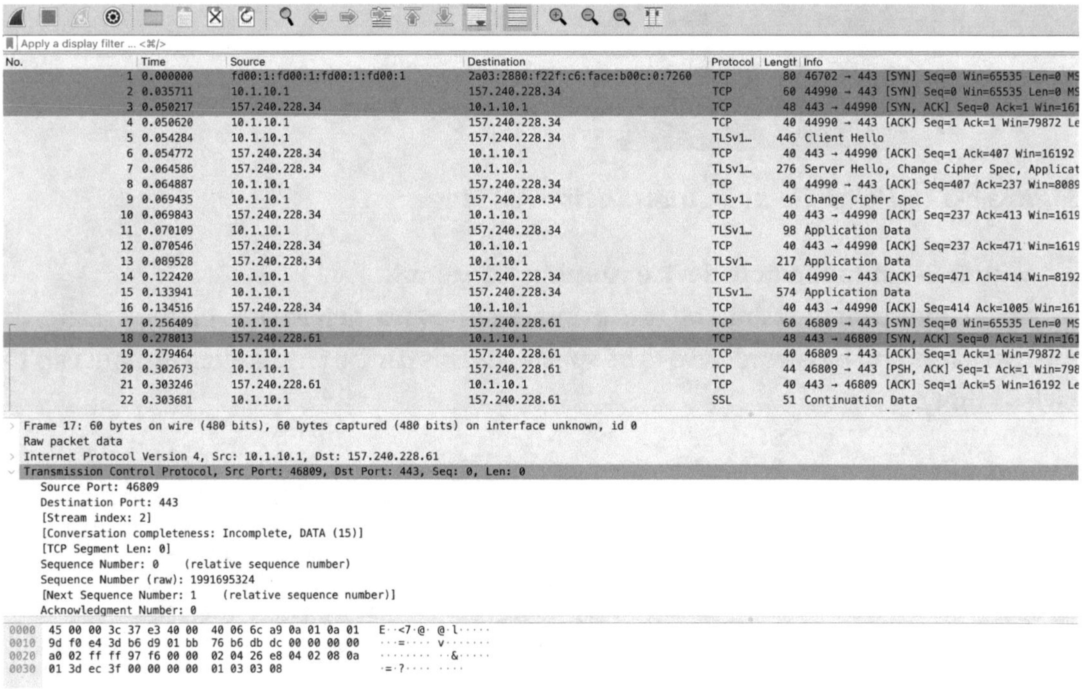

Figure 2-14. *PCAP Remote Android Wireshark sshdump capture*

Capture Filtering

On a network with high volume data, if we capture every frame that is being discovered, the capture buffer can be exhausted very quickly. Capture filters are used to decrease the size of captures by filtering out only relevant packets matching the condition before they are added to the capture file.

Prior to packet capture, the filter can be specified at the Wireshark "Capture Options" dialogue box in the "Capture Filter" field as shown in Figure 2-15.

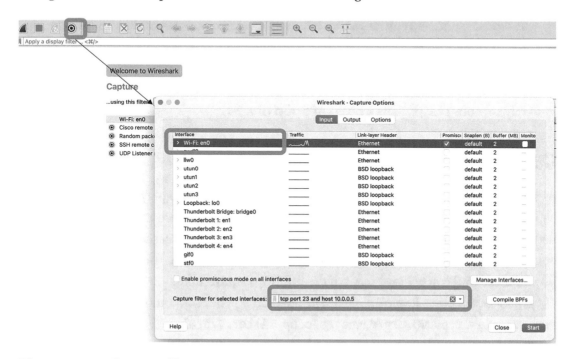

Figure 2-15. *Capture filter*

A capture filter consists of primitive expressions like protocol type, protocol parameters, etc. connected by logical expressions like "and," "or," "not," etc.

The following is an example of a capture filter that captures **telnet** traffic to and from a particular endpoint 192.168.1.1:

```
tcp port 23 and host 192.168.1.1
```

Detailed supported capture filter expressions can be found on the tcpdump man page: `www.tcpdump.org/manpages/pcap-filter.7.html`. Some examples of common capture filters are the following:

```
dst host 192.168.1.1
```

Only capture packets with IPv4 destination as 192.168.1.1

```
ip proto <Protocol>
```

Only capture IPv4 packets with protocol value matching *<Protocol>*

```
ip6 proto <Protocol>
```

Only capture IPv6 packets with protocol value matching *<Protocol>*

<Protocol> specified earlier can be a numeric value or corresponding name like **arp**, **tcp**, **udp**, **icmp6**, **nd**, etc.

```
tcp src port 1234
```

Only capture TCP packets with source port of *1234*.

Capture Filter Deep Dive

At first glance, capture filters might seem like the ugly twin of display filters. However, capture filters are not the same as display filters and have a different syntax. If you are used to working with display filters, the syntax can feel less expressive. It may seem as if you are not able to filter for most protocols or expert information, but capture filters are powerful too and can achieve most of the filtering requirements.

Wireshark capture filters follow the libpcap filter syntax documented at the tcpdump man page: `www.tcpdump.org/manpages/pcap-filter.7.html`.

The filter expressions in turn get converted to the BPF (Berkeley Packet Filter) syntax in the backend. The BPF architecture executes the BPF filter code on the network packets to find a match. This helps in the real-time computation of the network packets for the kernel to decide if it can drop or truncate incoming packets as early as possible. This eliminates user space application involvement for further analysis. BPF can compile the filter expressions to a code that the Linux kernel understands and can act on.

All the libcap-based capture applications like Wireshark, tshark, dumpcap, and tcpdump use the same uniform BPF syntax for capture filters. When you specify the capture filter, the text strings are converted to a set of BPF instructions and compiled automatically by the BPF compiler.

Understanding BPF: What Goes Behind the Capture Filters

If you want to understand the corresponding BPF instructions or want to troubleshoot why sometimes the capture filter string did not work the way expected, it can be easily found as follows:

CLI way

```
% sudo dumpcap -d -f "tcp"
Capturing on 'Wi-Fi: en0'
(000) ldh      [12]
(001) jeq      #0x86dd           jt 2    jf 7
(002) ldb      [20]
(003) jeq      #0x6             jt 10   jf 4
(004) jeq      #0x2c            jt 5    jf 11
(005) ldb      [54]
(006) jeq      #0x6             jt 10   jf 11
(007) jeq      #0x800           jt 8    jf 11
(008) ldb      [23]
(009) jeq      #0x6             jt 10   jf 11
(010) ret      #524288
(011) ret      #0
```

GUI way

After specifying the capture filter in the dialogue box, hit the Compile BPFs button. This generates the compiled BPF code.

In Table 2-2, we have an explanation of the BPF instructions corresponding to the preceding filter. Details about the BPF syntax can be found here: `https://man7.org/linux/man-pages/man8/bpfc.8.html`.

Table 2-2. *BPF Instructions Explained*

BPF Instruction		Meaning
(000) ldh	[12]	Load 2 bytes from byte 12. This corresponds to the Ethertype value
(001) jeq	#0x86dd jt 2 jf 7	If loaded value, i.e., Ethertype, is 0x86dd (ipv6 packet) is TRUE, go to #2, or if FALSE, go to #7
(002) ldb	[20]	Load 1 byte from byte 20 (IPv6 Next Header)
(003) jeq	#0x6 jt 10 jf 4	IPv6 Next Header: If TCP, then **MATCH**, go to #10, else #4
(004) jeq	#0x2c jt 5 jf 11	If IPv6 packet has extension header
(005) ldb	[54]	Load 1 byte from byte 54 (IPv6 Extension Header)
(006) jeq	#0x6 jt 10 jf 11	IPv6 Extension Header: If TCP, then **MATCH**, go to #10, else #11
(007) jeq	#0x800 jt 8 jf 11	If loaded value, i.e., Ethertype, is 0x800 (ipv4 packet) is TRUE, go to #8, or if FALSE, go to #11
(008) ldb	[23]	Load 1 byte from byte 23 (IPv4 protocol value)
(009) jeq	#0x6 jt 10 jf 11	IPv4 protocol value: If TCP, then **MATCH**, go to #10, else #11
(010) ret	#524288	MATCH. Capture the packet
(011) ret	#0	No match. Do not capture

Using the preceding filter, we captured the IPv4 TCP packet shown in Figure 2-16. If we look closely at the preceding BPF instruction set, lines #7, #8, #9, and #10 result in the packet match in Figure 2-16.

BPF #8,9   Protocol 06 = TCP   BPF #7   Ethertype 0800

```
0000    00 04 95 e9 1a c0 88 66 5a 47 88 c2 08 00 45 00
0010    00 40 00 00 40 00 40 06 47 57 c0 a8 01 04 28 63
0020    09 52 ff 0f 01 bb a2 87 a9 de 00 00 00 00 b0 02
0030    ff ff 32 5b 00 00 02 04 05 b4 01 03 03 06 01 01
0040    08 0a 02 13 c1 fb 00 00 00 00 04 02 00 00
```

Figure 2-16. BPF example

High Volume Packet Analysis

Let's take a use case where we need to find a DHCP packet flowing randomly at a very low rate across a service provider core router on multiple 100 Gbps interface. The background data rate can be very high close to the line rate of 100 Gbps where the packet of interest can be flowing at less than one packet per second.

This is like searching a needle in the haystack, and if we don't use any capture filtering, the capture file will exhaust the disk space very quickly, and postcapture analysis will also be very difficult. The following are some of the approaches that will help in the capture.

When the Packet Characteristics Are Known

If we know that our packet is not going to be encapsulated with any other header and it is always deterministic, then we can deploy a capture filter that completely matches the packet. In this case, as it's a DHCP packet, we can use the filter in Figure 2-17 which can capture the DHCP packet.

Figure 2-17. Capture filter for DHCP packets

When the Packet Encapsulations Is Unknown

Sometimes, we are not clear about what additional headers can be added on the packet. Say there may be a vlan tag on the DHCP packet if it's going across an Ethernet trunk. In case it's carried across an MPLS layer 2/3 VPN, there can be additional MPLS headers and tags also. There can be scenarios also where the packet may not be given required treatment and missing some of the expected headers. We can use packet size/range-based filter to minimize the overall capture. We may have to do multiple trial runs to fine-tune the range.

The filter in Figure 2-18 considers that the packet is tagged with one or multiple MPLS headers and within 250–400 bytes in size.

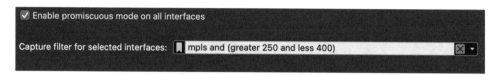

Figure 2-18. *Capture filter for MPLS packets 250–400 bytes*

When we don't know if there can be an MPLS tag or any other packet header, but we are sure about the size range, the filter in Figure 2-19 can help.

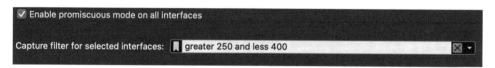

Figure 2-19. *Capture filter for all packets 250–400 bytes*

Advanced Filters and Deep Packet Filter

Filters based on byte offset

Byte offset notation–based filters can be a bit confusing initially, yet are the most powerful. Once you understand the logic, you can design a filter to capture *any* kind of packet even though standard protocol expressions are not available for the same.

The syntax is

Protocol [*X* : *Y*]

Protocol = Can be an expression like `ip,icmp,icmpv6,tcp,udp`

X = Offset in bytes from the start of the specified **protocol** header

Y = Number of bytes to check

The filter tries to match Y bytes located X bytes from the start of the specified **protocol** header.

Note   The default value of X = 0, which means the protocol header starts with zero bytes. The default value of Y = 1, which means if you do not mention anything, 1 byte will be checked.

This is simple yet so powerful as any packet can be filtered just by specifying the value of the number of bytes to match and the offset or location of the bytes from the start of the protocol header.

Consider the following Ethernet IPv4 packet:

> IP header bytes: Colored in Blue
>
> TCP header bytes: Colored in Red

```
0000    00 04 95 e9 1a c0 88 66 5a 47 88 c2 08 00 45 00
0010    00 34 00 00 40 00 40 06 26 79 c0 a8 01 05 8e fa
0020    c3 a3 cb c7 01 bb bf 28 32 3f 81 f7 f7 0c 80 11
0030    08 00 fa b0 00 00 01 01 08 0a 60 77 44 a9 1e e1
0040    63 cf
```

Example:

To match the preceding packet based on the TTL value of 64 (0x40), the following filter will work. Here, we are matching 1 byte (default value considered) which is at the offset of 8 bytes from the IP header:

`ip[8] = 64`

To match the preceding packet based on the TCP destination port value of 443 (0x01 bb), the following filter will work. Here, we are matching 2 bytes which are at the offset of 8 bytes from the IP header:

`tcp[2:2] = 443`

In the preceding example, we used the "=" operator. But other logical operators (>, <, >=, <=, =, !=) can be used to form a filter.

Masking with byte offset filters

62

In many scenarios instead of the whole byte, it is useful to isolate nibbles or a few bits for matching. Bit masking helps in extracting the desired bits.

For example, the first byte of the IP header consists of the version number (4 bits) and IPv4 header length (last 4 bits):

```
0100  = Version: 4
0101 = Header Length: 20 bytes (5)
```

If we want to check the IPv4 header length, then we can mask the version number field by doing a binary AND operation of the first byte with 0x0f:

```
ip[0] & 0x0f
```

For IPv4 packets without an option field, the header length is always 20 bytes. The header length is expressed in terms of the number of 4 byte fields present in the IP header (5 x 4 = 20 bytes). So, in case we want to match all IPv4 packets without the option field, then we can use the bit masking operator earlier to mask the version field, and the value of the first byte should always be 5 in this case (0000 0101) post masking:

```
ip[0] & 0x0f = 5
```

Using the preceding approach, complex filters can be designed to match packets based on specific TCP flags, IP flags, or for that matter any field inside any packet.

Summary

This chapter is all about capturing the packet.

We learned about

- How to source packets for capturing using various port mirroring methods

- How to use the OS-native capture utilities available by default

- How to leverage Wireshark and related utilities for better packet capture experience

- How to remotely capture packets using various SPAN and extcap methods

- How to capture packets on mobile devices

- How to use capture filters for efficient packet captures

References for This Chapter

BPF: https://man7.org/linux/man-pages/man8/bpfc.8.html

tcpdump: www.tcpdump.org/manpages/pcap-filter.7.html

androiddump: www.androidtcpdump.com/android-tcpdump/downloads

Intel preserving VLAN tag: www.intel.com/content/www/us/en/support/articles/000005498/network-and-i-o/ethernet-products.html

CHAPTER 3

Capturing Secured Application Traffic for Analysis

Following the famous adage that goes "***Necessity is the mother of any invention***," securing end-to-end traffic is an evolution happening for the past couple of decades in an attempt to secure the user and data privacy from malicious hackers.

Cyber-attack is ever evolving right from 1986 when the very first computer virus known to the industry, named "Brain," was introduced infecting the boot sectors of computers. While the industry and the technology enthusiasts frantically worked on digitally transforming the society through radical technology inventions, a fair share of efforts are being spent by the malicious hackers to compromise the user and the data privacy and security. These malicious hackers may be a novice trying to prove their prowess by identifying any application or transit node vulnerabilities and exploiting the same to corrupt the data for fun or can be cyber criminals performing such attacks for monetary benefits such as identity theft or ransomware. Such attacks can be performed on both data in rest and data in motion.

In order to defend such cyber-attacks and protect the user privacy, various security measures such as data encryption, secured channels or tunnels, secure name resolution, etc. have been introduced. While such security enhancements definitely help improve the data privacy by making it hard for the hackers to capture or decode the captured data, these also introduce operational challenge for the network and application administrators with a genuine intention to analyze the captures for performance or other corporate policy compliances. For example, a corporate security compliance team would like to sniff all the traffic from the employees leaving the domain to ensure that the data

© Nagendra Kumar Nainar and Ashish Panda 2023
N. K. Nainar and A. Panda, *Wireshark for Network Forensics*, https://doi.org/10.1007/978-1-4842-9001-9_3

downloaded or the websites visited by the employees are not violating any country or corporate regulation policies.

In this chapter, we will look into the various end application security concepts and further look into how to use the Wireshark tool for capturing and analyzing the encrypted traffic exchanged from the secured application client to the server.

Note   While the administrators may need to perform analysis on encrypted data where the data can be in rest or in transit, the Wireshark tool has a major role in analyzing the data in transit. Accordingly, this chapter will focus on analyzing the encrypted data captured while in transit.

Evolution of Application Security

As part of the digital transformation, applications have become an integral part of not just the business vertical but also in other verticals such as education, lifestyle essentials, and entertainment. The one thing that is common among all these applications spanning across various verticals is the confidential user-centric data generated. Any compromise in this information-rich data may result in compromising the user privacy and making them vulnerable for various social and monetary attacks.

The revolutionary start of the Dotcom bubble in the early 1990s resulted in the surge of numerous Internet-based businesses that leverage web technologies for the business application development. During the early days of the Dotcom bubble, almost all the web traffic ubiquitously used and adopted the Hypertext Transfer Protocol (HTTP) as the application layer protocol for exchanging data between the client and the server. But HTTP was originally designed to be extremely simple in an attempt to accelerate the adoption of the protocol for the World Wide Web (WWW). In fact, the initial version of HTTP is known as the one-line protocol as the request sent from the client to the server is normally a single-line request, and the response from the server is usually the HTML file itself. An example is shown as follows:

```
GET www.somedomainexample.com/index.html
```

As more and more critical business applications began to proliferate, the sensitivity of the data exchanged and the simplicity of the HTTP protocol used to exchange the data intrigued the malicious hackers to find vulnerabilities and compromise the data and the user privacy. To address this issue and to strengthen the overall data privacy, Hypertext Transfer Protocol Secure (HTTPS) was introduced that encrypts the application data exchanged over the HTTP protocol with authentication and security protocols such as Secure Socket Layer (SSL) or Transport Layer Security (TLS). Most of the current browsers support HTTPS, and many modern sites mandate the use of HTTPS to access the site or the data.

Note   Most of the current web browsers support HTTPS, and in fact, many sites mandate the need to use HTTPS to access the website or the data. While TLS1.2 is the current version in most of the browsers, TLS1.3 was introduced and standardized by RFC8446.

While traditionally HTTP traffic used TCP as the transport layer protocol, the recent development started replacing TCP with UDP and use QUIC as the encryption layer instead of TLS. The use of HTTP over TCP/TLS is collectively referred to as HTTP2, while the use of HTTP over QUIC is referred to as HTTP3.

While HTTPS protected the web traffic, there are a plethora of other types of traffic that are not natively exchanged over HTTPS. While one option is to redesign the applications to use HTTPS instead of any native or non-web protocols, it is too complex and not a brownfield deployable solution. Instead, the industry experts created a suite of encryption protocols that operated at the network layer. A point-to-point IPSec tunnel is created between different endpoints to encrypt any traffic in a protocol- or application-agnostic manner and steer the encrypted traffic over the tunnel. Over the last couple of decades, numerous enhancements were developed to support multipoint or any-to-any kind of traffic as well. A quick comparison between different protocols is shown in Figure 3-1.

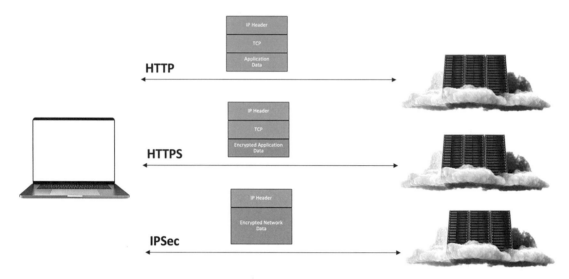

Figure 3-1. *Comparison between different protocols*

While IPSec and HTTPS help encrypt and protect the data, there are different types of attacks or potential information gathering kinds of attacks during the pre-traffic steering stage itself. For example, any end client is required to resolve the domain name to get the reachable IP address to create the connection or exchange the data. The Domain Name System (DNS) was introduced in 1983 through RFC1034. The malicious hackers take advantage of various vulnerabilities in the name resolution system to poison the record and resolve any genuine domain to bogus or malicious IP address and thereby steer all the traffic to the malicious server. These name resolution requests and replies are traditionally exchanged between the client and the server as plain text that makes it very easy to sniff the traffic and look into the domains visited by any user. Such user privacy compromise was addressed by encrypting the name resolution request and reply by sending them over HTTPS (DNS over HTTPS). This mechanism leverages the security offered by the SSL/TLS extension of HTTPS to obfuscate the domain name and related details carried in the DNS request and the response packet.

We will dig into some of these protocol captures and see how to decrypt the secure applications such as secure DNS or HTTPS traffic and dissect the data for network forensic analysis.

Capturing and Analyzing HTTPS

In this section, we will discuss the basics of the HTTPS protocol and how to capture and analyze HTTPS traffic. This section will primarily focus on HTTP2 where HTTP traffic is secured using the TLS layer and transported over the TCP protocol. In the next section, we will discuss about HTTP3.

Basics of HTTPS

Using HTTP as the protocol to request or send any data is done using GET and POST messages in plain text, thereby making it vulnerable for any malicious user to simply capture the data exchange and use the information. Figure 3-2 shows an example capture of an HTTP packet.

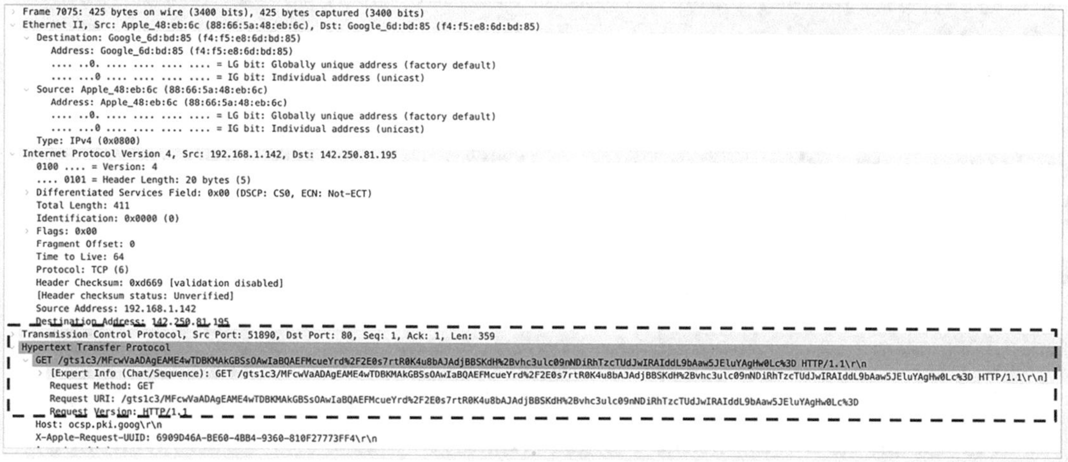

Figure 3-2. *Wireshark capture of an HTTP packet*

The capture shown in Figure 3-2 is an HTTP of version 1.1, GET message sent a specific URI defined in the capture. The IT operation team may use the relevant Wireshark filters during the traffic capture or after the capture to list the HTTP traffic and take necessary course of actions. The following are a few HTTP-specific filters that can be used to narrow down the HTTP packets in a large PCAP file.

To filter using a TCP destination port matching 80

```
tcp.dstport == 80
```

To filter all HTTP traffic

http

To filter all HTTP request traffic

http.request

To filter all HTTP GET messages

http.request.method == GET

As the HTTP protocol was evolving through versions, Transport Layer Security was introduced to encrypt the HTTP payload and obfuscate the information from any malicious users. HTTPS leverages the public key encryption concept that produces two keys as public and private keys as a pair. The public key is shared with the remote party by cryptographically signed SSL/TLS certificates. This key is used to encrypt the data, and the encrypted data can only be decrypted using the paired private key. The private key will not be shared with anyone and is stored locally. HTTPS was originally introduced by RFC2818 and was later obsoleted by RFC9110. By default, HTTPS works with TCP port 443, and any website that uses HTTPS must prefix the URI with https instead of http as shown in the following:

https://<domain-name>/<object>

Note   While HTTPS uses TCP port 443 by default, any application could also be used to customize the application to use a different port for HTTPS. So capturing and analyzing such a custom application may require knowledge about the custom port used.

The HTTPS sessions are established between the client and the server and secured by exchanging encryption keys using a TLS handshake. The basic workflow of HTTPS traffic is shown in Figure 3-3.

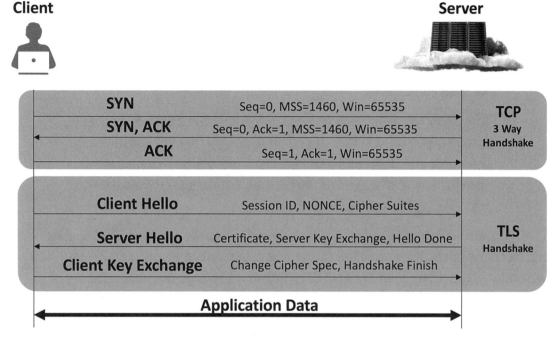

Figure 3-3. *TCP+TLS session establishment*

Once the TCP session is established between the client and the server, the TLS handshake will get kicked in to verify each party and to exchange the keys. It goes as follows:

- The client sends a **CLIENT HELLO** message as the first message to trigger the TLS handshake. This message carries different details such as Session ID, NONCE, and Cipher Suites. The Session ID is used to uniquely identify the session between the client and the server. The NONCE is a client-generated random value used to generate the master key. The Cipher Suites is a list of cryptographic options supported by the client along with the preference.

- The server will respond back with a **SERVER HELLO** message carrying details that are used to agree upon the algorithm to use for encryption. The HELLO messages will also carry additional extensions such as the Server Certificate and the Server Key Exchange. The Server Certificate is a mandatory object that must be sent by the server to the client whenever the key exchange method uses certificates for authentication. The Server Key Exchange message which is carried as an extension will include the public key for encryption. The server will also include a HELLO DONE extension to indicate that the server has exchanged all the relevant information to the client that are required for establishing this secured connection.

- The client will reply back with a **CLIENT KEY EXCHANGE** message to share the public key for the server to encrypt the application data. The client will then send a HELLO DONE extension to indicate that the client has exchanged all the relevant information required for establishing the secured connection.

Upon successful establishment of the secured connection, the application data will be encrypted by the shared public key which in turn can be decrypted only by the private key. Optionally, the CHANGE CIPHER SPEC message can be used to signal the transition in ciphering strategies and notify that the subsequent data will be exchanged by encrypting using the new algorithm and the associated keys. The CLOSE NOTIFY message is used to notify the remote party that there won't be any more data exchanged over this secured connection.

The peers use TLS Alert messages to signal any protocol failures. While CLOSE NOTIFY is one type of alert message, there are other types of alert messages such as UNEXPECTED MESSAGE or DECRYPTION FAILED that are used to signal the relevant cause of the protocol failures to the peer. Capturing such alert messages will help in analyzing and performing the root cause analysis for protocol failures.

Capturing and Filtering HTTPS Traffic

In this section, we will discuss the filtering options to capture only HTTPS traffic or to filter the HTTPS packets from a capture file.

HTTPS Traffic – Capture Filter

By default, HTTPS traffic uses TCP port 443, and this can be used to filter the packet during capture or during the analysis. As explained in Chapter 2, Wireshark allows us to capture the traffic by applying certain filters. We can use the same to instruct Wireshark to filter and capture only the HTTPS traffic as shown in Figure 3-4.

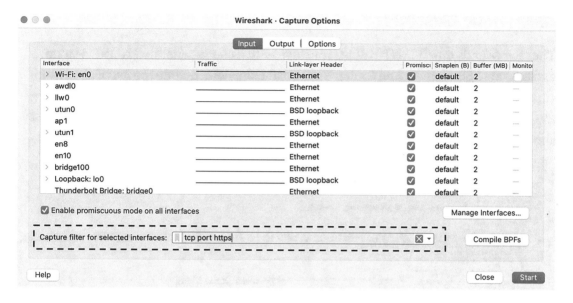

Figure 3-4. *Wireshark Capture Options for HTTPS*

Alternately, the CLI-based capture can use the following command to filter the capture to HTTPS traffic:

```
sudo tcpdump -i <interface> port 443 -w <filename>
```

Note   By default, a MacBook may not permit the user to capture the traffic from the Wireshark tool directly. The user may need to change the permission using "*sudo chown <user-id>:admin bp**" under the */dev* folder.

The preceding methods will create a file and store only the HTTPS traffic captured from the mentioned interface(s). This filtered capture is an efficient way of capturing traffic specific to the application that is required for analysis.

Analyzing HTTPS Traffic

In this section, we will analyze the steps involved in negotiating the encryption keys and establishing the TLS connection for secured application data transfer between the client and the server.

Client Hello Message

The client sends the CLIENT HELLO message with a client-generated NONCE value and a unique Session ID. The Cipher Suites extension will include the list of algorithms supported by the client. The algorithms are ordered based on the preference by setting the first preferred algorithm in the Cipher Suite right after the GREASE reserved field as shown in Figure 3-5.

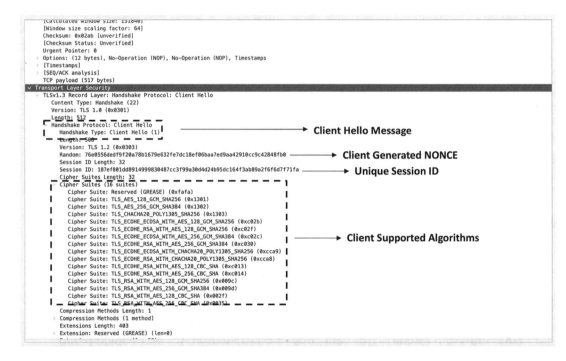

Figure 3-5. *Wireshark capture for TLS Client Hello*

The algorithm preferred by the client in the preceding capture is TLS_AES_128_GCM_SHA256, which is a 128-bit based Advanced Encryption Standard (AES) in Galois/Counter Mode (GCM). The CLIENT HELLO message also includes the Key Share Extension that includes the public key generated and signed by the client as shown in Figure 3-6.

```
∨ Extension: key_share (len=43)
     Type: key_share (51)
     Length: 43
   ∨ Key Share extension
       Client Key Share Length: 41
     ∨ Key Share Entry: Group: Reserved (GREASE), Key Exchange length: 1
         Group: Reserved (GREASE) (39578)
         Key Exchange Length: 1
         Key Exchange: 00
     ∨ Key Share Entry: Group: x25519, Key Exchange length: 32
         Group: x25519 (29)
         Key Exchange Length: 32
         Key Exchange: db7d2b29959f7d2ddac67742488124d2bb725c0ab8f1c9c19cca9014e4031963
```

Figure 3-6. *TLS key exchange extensions*

Note   The reserved value GREASE included as part of the Cipher Suite is not an algorithm. GREASE stands for **Generate Random Extensions and Sustain Extensibility** which is used to ensure that the remote party is handling the unknown value correctly by ignoring. More details about GREASE are available in RFC8701.

Server Hello Message

The server sends a SERVER HELLO message only as a response to any incoming CLIENT HELLO message. The server will include a locally generated NONCE value used to generate the master key. An example SERVER HELLO message is shown in Figure 3-7.

```
∨ Transport Layer Security
    ∨ TLSv1.3 Record Layer: Handshake Protocol: Server Hello
        Content Type: Handshake (22)
        Version: TLS 1.2 (0x0303)
        Length: 122
      ∨ Handshake Protocol: Server Hello
          Handshake Type: Server Hello (2)
          Length: 118
          Version: TLS 1.2 (0x0303)
          Random: 688a4e5552af6a0e7e5b5687c89389dee28f41eba2040c1c6c010e7de2860d11
          Session ID Length: 32
          Session ID: 187ef801dd8914999830487cc3f99a30d4d24b95dc164f3ab89a2f6f6d7f71fa
          Cipher Suite: TLS_AES_128_GCM_SHA256 (0x1301)
          Compression Method: null (0)
          Extensions Length: 46
        ∨ Extension: key_share (len=36)
            Type: key_share (51)
            Length: 36
          ∨ Key Share extension
            ∨ Key Share Entry: Group: x25519, Key Exchange length: 32
                Group: x25519 (29)
                Key Exchange Length: 32
                Key Exchange: d0203f13008c0d8026f9e77e5f1ec99a327eebc7ddeb4e60baa748e5e90c6c1b
        ∨ Extension: supported_versions (len=2)
            Type: supported_versions (43)
            Length: 2
            Supported Version: TLS 1.3 (0x0304)
          [JA3S Fullstring: 771,4865,51-43]
          [JA3S: eb1d94daa7e0344597e756a1fb6e7054]
    ∨ TLSv1.3 Record Layer: Change Cipher Spec Protocol: Change Cipher Spec
        Content Type: Change Cipher Spec (20)
        Version: TLS 1.2 (0x0303)
        Length: 1
        Change Cipher Spec Message
```

Figure 3-7. *TLS Server Hello Message*

The Cipher Suite will carry the algorithm selected by the server based on the preference received in the inbound CLIENT HELLO message. The SERVER HELLO message also includes the Key Share Extension that includes the public key generated and signed by the server. This key is used by the client to encrypt any data sent toward the server.

The SERVER HELLO message will also include certificates used to sign the public key shared to the client. Once the public keys are exchanged between the client and the server, the subsequent traffic will be encrypted using the keys and make it obfuscated to the transit user. Let us take an example capture as shown in Figure 3-8.

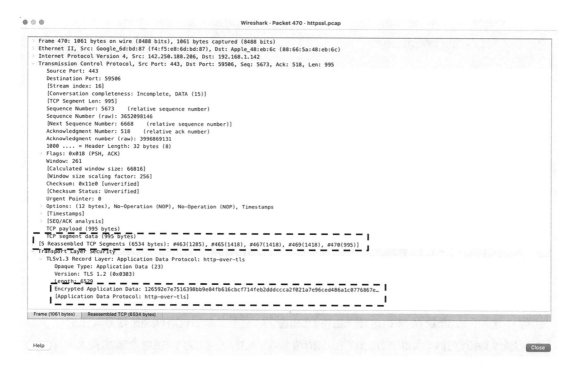

Figure 3-8. *Encrypted TLS packet*

Frame 470 shown in Figure 3-8 is a reassembled TCP segment that includes five frames numbered 463, 465, 467, 469, and 470. While Wireshark classified the above as HTTP-over-TLS data, it could be noted that the application data is not plain text. In the next section, we will see how to decrypt the TLS traffic for additional analysis.

Decrypting TLS Traffic Using Wireshark

In order to decrypt the TLS frames in Wireshark, we need the SSL key used for the respective session from the client and feed the same to Wireshark.

Collecting the SSL Key

The following is the procedure to collect the SSL key from a macOS-based machine:

1. All the browsers must be closed before collecting the SSL key. To avoid any background process stopping the SSL key collection, it is advisable to "***Force Quit***" all the web browser processes.

2. Open a new terminal window and export the SSL key using the following command:

```
Export SSLKEYLOGFILE="<path-to-store-the-file>/<file-name>"
```

3. Open the web browser from the same terminal using the CLI command as follows:

```
Open /Application/chrome.app
```

4. Open the Wireshark tool and start the packet capture from the respective interface to capture the HTTPS/SSL traffic.

5. Open any HTTPS website from the web browser to trigger the application traffic.

Note   If the web browser is already opened or if the web browser is opened manually without opening from the same terminal window where the SSL key is being logged, the keys will not be captured. It is critical that the web browser is closed prior to step 2.

With the preceding set of simple procedure, the SSL key for the respective session will be captured in the file mentioned in step 2. Any session from the same browser will use the same SSL key and can be decrypted by using the collected SSL key.

The following is the procedure to collect the SSL key from a Windows-based machine:

1. All the browsers must be closed before collecting the SSL key. Open the "***Advanced System Settings***" option from the Control Panel.

2. Click the "***Environment Variable***" option from this window.

3. Click "***New***" to add a user variable.

4. Use "***SSLKEYLOGFILE***" as Variable Name and specify the path to save the file.

Decrypting the HTTPS Traffic

By using the procedure explained in the previous section, we will now have the HTTPS/
SSL traffic captured using the Wireshark tool and the associated SSL key for the session
captured in the respective file. The SSL key can be fed to the Wireshark by selecting any
TLS frame from the capture file and following the options as shown in Figure 3-9.

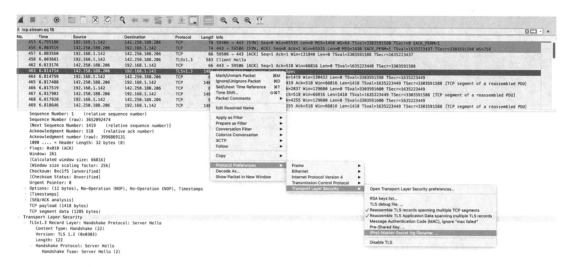

Figure 3-9. *Wireshark frame option for the SSL key*

The preceding selection will pop open the option to feed the SSL key file in the
"(Pre)-Master-Secret log filename" field where the captured SSL key file must be
uploaded. An example snapshot of the option field is shown in Figure 3-10.

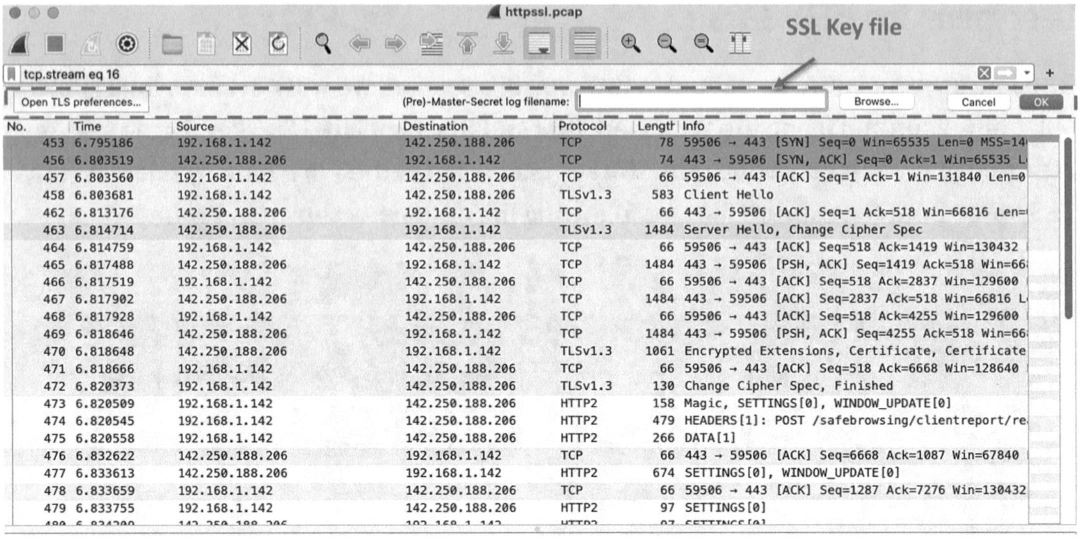

Figure 3-10. *SSL key feed*

Alternately, the Wireshark preference section can be opened to choose the TLS protocol by using the ***Preference ➤ Protocol ➤ TLS*** option as shown in Figure 3-11.

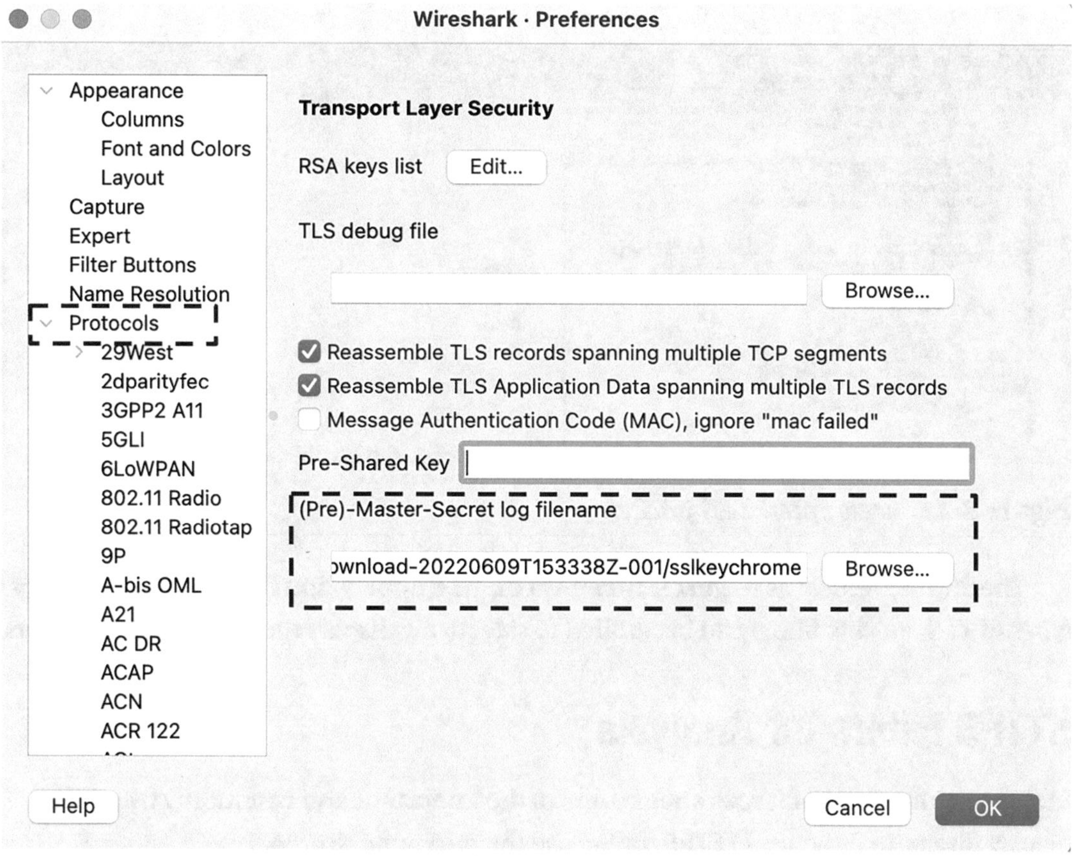

Figure 3-11. *Wireshark preference option for the SSL key*

Using any of the preceding approaches, the SSL key can be uploaded to Wireshark for decrypting the traffic. Upon uploading the SSL key file, Wireshark will be able to decrypt the HTTPS traffic for additional analytics. It could be noticed that Frame 470 which was earlier exhibiting the application payload as "Encrypted Application Data" before uploading the SSL key will now have the payload decrypted using the SSL key as shown in Figure 3-12.

```
> Frame 470: 1061 bytes on wire (8488 bits), 1061 bytes captured (8488 bits)
> Ethernet II, Src: Google_6d:bd:87 (f4:f5:e8:6d:bd:87), Dst: Apple_48:eb:6c (88:66:5a:48:eb:6c)
> Internet Protocol Version 4, Src: 142.250.188.206, Dst: 192.168.1.142
  Transmission Control Protocol, Src Port: 443, Dst Port: 59506, Seq: 5673, Ack: 518, Len: 995
  [5 Reassembled TCP Segments (6534 bytes): #463(1285), #465(1418), #467(1418), #469(1418), #470(995)]
  Transport Layer Security
    ∨ TLSv1.3 Record Layer: Handshake Protocol: Multiple Handshake Messages
        Opaque Type: Application Data (23)
        Version: TLS 1.2 (0x0303)
        Length: 6529
        [Content Type: Handshake (22)]
      ∨ Handshake Protocol: Encrypted Extensions
          Handshake Type: Encrypted Extensions (8)
          Length: 11
          Extensions Length: 9
        ∨ Extension: application_layer_protocol_negotiation (len=5)          Decrypted
            Type: application_layer_protocol_negotiation (16)                Application
            Length: 5                                                        Data
            ALPN Extension Length: 3
          ∨ ALPN Protocol
              ALPN string length: 2
              ALPN Next Protocol: h2
      > Handshake Protocol: Certificate
      > Handshake Protocol: Certificate Verify
      ∨ Handshake Protocol: Finished
          Handshake Type: Finished (20)
          Length: 32
          Verify Data
```

Figure 3-12. *Decrypted TLS packet*

The SSL key allows us to look further into the TLS application field, and so additional types of TLS-specific filters can be applied to selectively display the relevant TLS packets.

HTTPS Filters for Analysis

In this section, we will discuss about some of the important and commonly used TLS display filters. To filter any HTTPS traffic, use the port matching 443:

tcp.dstport == 443

To filter all HTTPS using TCP transport, use the following simple filter:

http2

To filter all TLS handshake, use the following filter:

tls.handshake

Additional filters can be used to selectively filter the TLS packets based on the message types. Table 3-1 lists a few examples to filter packets based on the TLS message types.

Table 3-1. *TLS Message Display Filter Options*

TLS Protocol Messages	Handshake Messages	• tls.handshake • tls.handshake.cert_type
	Cipher Suite/Change Messages	• tls.handshake.cipherspec • tls.change_cipher_spec
	Alert Messages	• tls.alert_message • tls.alert_message.desc • tls.alert_message.level
	Application Data	• tls.app_data • tls.app_data_proto

For more detailed filters, please refer to the following Wireshark reference: `www.wireshark.org/docs/dfref/t/tls.html`

HTTP2 Statistics Using Wireshark

While the readers might be aware that Wireshark allows us to display the statistics of different types of protocol packets, the accurate statistics of HTTPS using TLS can be listed only when the SSL key is loaded. As TLS encrypted the application data, the type of application data is not accessible by Wireshark without the SSL key. The statistics of HTTPS traffic using TLS can be listed using the option shown in Figure 3-13.

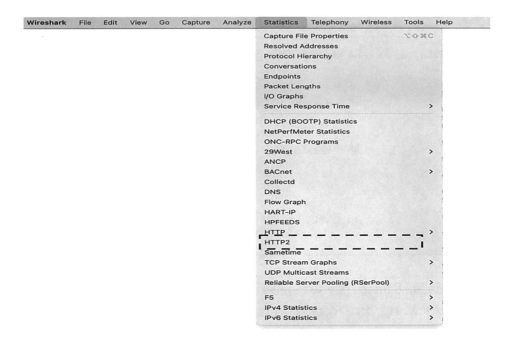

Figure 3-13. *Wireshark HTTPS statistics option*

Without the SSL key loaded to Wireshark, the statistics will simply show the count as 0. Once the SSL key is loaded, Wireshark will be able to identify the accurate statistics as shown in Figure 3-14.

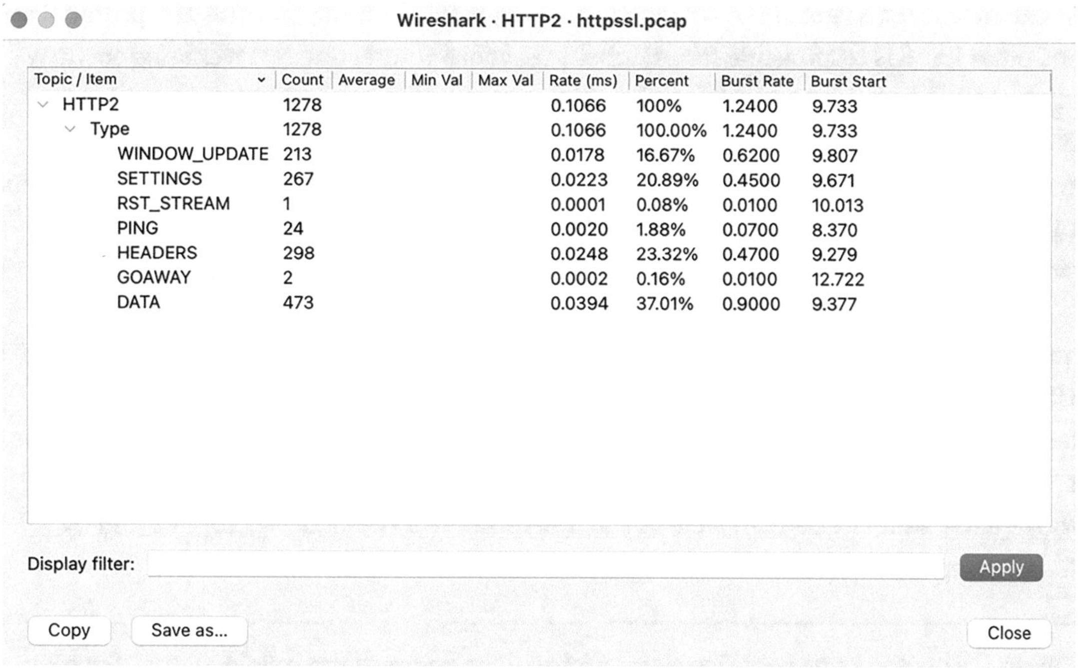

Topic / Item	Count	Average	Min Val	Max Val	Rate (ms)	Percent	Burst Rate	Burst Start
⌄ HTTP2	1278				0.1066	100%	1.2400	9.733
⌄ Type	1278				0.1066	100.00%	1.2400	9.733
WINDOW_UPDATE	213				0.0178	16.67%	0.6200	9.807
SETTINGS	267				0.0223	20.89%	0.4500	9.671
RST_STREAM	1				0.0001	0.08%	0.0100	10.013
PING	24				0.0020	1.88%	0.0700	8.370
HEADERS	298				0.0248	23.32%	0.4700	9.279
GOAWAY	2				0.0002	0.16%	0.0100	12.722
DATA	473				0.0394	37.01%	0.9000	9.377

Display filter: _____ Apply

Copy   Save as...   Close

Figure 3-14. *Wireshark HTTPS statistics*

This section explained how to capture the SSL key exchanged between the client and the server and load the same to Wireshark and decrypt the TLS application data.

Capturing and Analyzing QUIC Traffic

In this section, we will discuss the basics of the Quick UDP Internet Connection (QUIC) protocol and how to capture and analyze application traffic using QUIC as the transport protocol. Any HTTP traffic using QUIC as the transport protocol is referred to as HTTP3.

Basics of QUIC

As we discussed in the previous section, the notion of HTTP2 refers to the use of TLS over TCP to encrypt the application data where each protocol has their own set of characteristics to manage the connection at different layers. To be more specific, the TCP protocol is responsible for establishing reliable transport layer connection by leveraging the connection-oriented characteristics such as payload segmentation, segment loss detection and retransmission, congestion control, etc. The TLS protocol on the other hand is responsible for establishing secure connection by leveraging security characteristics such as encryption algorithm negotiation, key exchange, encryption and decryption, etc. In short, there are different protocols with their own set of responsibilities introducing operational challenges to manage and troubleshoot different protocols. This leads to the study in an attempt to simplify the message chattiness and protocols for operational simplification.

RFC9000 introduces a new Internet connection standard that merges the transport and session layer functions for secure and reliable transport of Internet traffic using UDP. As the readers might be aware, UDP is a connectionless transport protocol that lacks any reliability components such as packet loss detection and recovery, congestion control, session establishment, etc. The lack of these reliability components due to the replacement of TCP with UDP as the transport layer protocol is compensated by introducing these capabilities directly in the session layer functionalities.

Note   The use of the session layer protocol for some of the reliability functionality is not new, and the Trivial File Transport Protocol (TFTP) is one good example. TFTP uses UDP as the transport layer protocol and is used for large file transfers with additional semantics at the application layer for loss recovery.

QUIC leverages TLS for secure session establishment over the UDP transport layer that improves the performance without compromising the security. A quick comparison of HTTP over TCP+TLS and QUIC is shown in Figure 3-15.

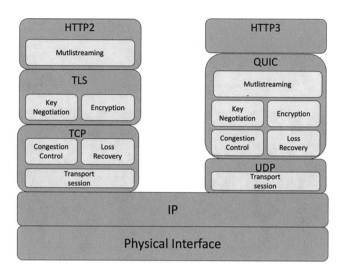

Figure 3-15. *TCP/TLS vs. QUIC/TLS comparison*

As it could be noted in the figure, reliability components such as congestion control and loss recovery along with the security components of TLS such as key negotiation and encryption that spread across different stack while using TCP+TLS are merged into QUIC, making it easy to operate and manage. QUIC possesses a combination of unique connection identifiers assigned by each endpoint to identify the connection between the client and the server. Multiple streams can be multiplexed within the same QUIC connection between the client and the server by assigning a unique stream ID for each stream. The basic workflow is as shown in Figure 3-16.

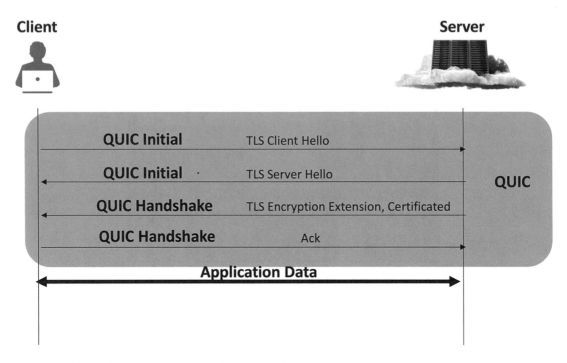

Figure 3-16. *QUIC session establishment*

Unlike TCP, there is no transport layer connection handshake, and the session establishment starts with the QUIC handshake as follows:

- The client assigns a unique destination connection ID (DCID) and sends a QUIC Initial packet including a TLS Client Hello message. This TLS message will carry the TLS-specific details such as the NONCE, Cipher Suite, etc.

- The server upon receiving the message will assign a locally unique source connection ID (SCID) and replies back with a QUIC Initial packet including a TLS Server Hello message.

- Followed by the Server Hello message, the server will send a QUIC handshake message including TLS encryption–specific details such as the keys, certificates, etc.

- The handshake is concluded by the client sending a QUIC Initial packet with the Ack frame.

Upon successful establishment of the secured QUIC connection, the application data will be encrypted by the negotiated key and transferred as a stream over the QUIC connection.

Capturing and Filtering QUIC Traffic

In this section, we will discuss the filtering options to capture only QUIC traffic or to filter the HTTPS packets from a capture file.

QUIC Traffic – Capture Filter

By default, QUIC traffic uses UDP port 443 which is like the port number used by TLS for TCP. By setting "*udp port 443*" in the Wireshark capture option field, the QUIC traffic can be filtered during the capture as shown in Figure 3-17.

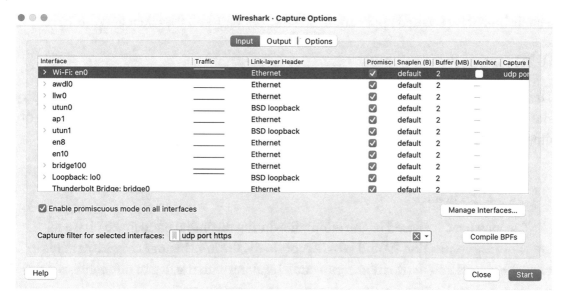

Figure 3-17. *Wireshark HTTPS capture filter*

Alternately, the CLI-based capture options can be used to filter the capture to QUIC traffic using the following command:

```
sudo tcpdump -i <interface> port 443 -w <filename>
```

Note   While different applications are being developed with QUIC as the transport protocol, the Google Chrome browser is a simple way of generating QUIC traffic. The Google Chrome browser uses QUIC as the default transport and session protocol, and simply visiting few websites in Chrome will generate QUIC traffic for capture and analysis.

Any of the preceding filtering methods allows us to filter QUIC traffic during the capture. As QUIC uses TLS, we need the SSL key captured using the procedure mentioned in the previous sections to decrypt the traffic for analysis.

Analyzing QUIC Traffic

In this section, we will analyze the steps involved in a QUIC handshake for connection establishment for secured application data transfer between the client and the server.

QUIC Header

The QUIC protocol evolved over a period by optimizing the format based on the industry standardization. The current version of QUIC as defined in RFC9000 supports the use of different types of QUIC header as follows:

- Long header
- Short header

The long header is used by the endpoints during the initial handshake phase to negotiate the connection ID and keys. Accordingly, the long header comprises fields to carry the source and destination connection ID along with the flag to differentiate if this is a long or short header. A sample capture is shown in Figure 3-18.

```
> Frame 233: 1292 bytes on wire (10336 bits), 1292 bytes captured (10336 bits)
> Ethernet II, Src: Apple_48:eb:6c (88:66:5a:48:eb:6c), Dst: Google_6d:bd:85 (f4:f5:e8:6d:bd:85)
> Internet Protocol Version 4, Src: 192.168.1.142, Dst: 172.253.115.95
> User Datagram Protocol, Src Port: 58646, Dst Port: 443
v QUIC IETF
  > QUIC Connection information
    [Packet Length: 1250]
    1... .... = Header Form: Long Header (1)
    .1.. .... = Fixed Bit: True
    ..00 .... = Packet Type: Initial (0)
    .... 00.. = Reserved: 0
    .... ..00 = Packet Number Length: 1 bytes (0)
    Version: 1 (0x00000001)
    Destination Connection ID Length: 8
    Destination Connection ID: 9eeceabf736bccc4
    Source Connection ID Length: 0
    Token Length: 0
    Length: 1232
    Packet Number: 1
    Payload: 0daaf1d334e563b252f2fa77a3cc1a563584506f8e763ad0273da31fb9fead5a73d9ff32...
  > PING
  > PADDING Length: 226
  > PING
  > PADDING Length: 419
  > PING
  > PING
  > PING
  > PADDING Length: 188
  > PING
  > PADDING Length: 46
  > CRYPTO
  > PING
  > PADDING Length: 9
  > CRYPTO
```

Figure 3-18. *Wireshark capture for a QUIC long header*

The most significant bit is used to define the header format. A value set to 1 identifies the header as a long header, and the rest of the bits are interpreted accordingly.

The packet type is a 2-bit-sized field that identifies the type of QUIC packet exchanged between the client and the server. A value of 00 indicates this packet as a QUIC Initial packet. A value of 01 indicates this as an RTT packet, and a value of 10 indicates this as a QUIC handshake packet.

The presence of the source and destination connection ID is defined using the respective connection ID length in bytes. In the preceding figure, the destination connection identifier (DCID) size is set to 8, which indicates that the size of the DCID is 8 bytes. On the other hand, the source connection identifier (SCID) length is set to 0, indicating that there is no SCID. Once the initial handshake is done, the endpoints will use the short header for actual payload transaction.

Short headers are a simplified version of the QUIC header and are used for stream and payload transmission after the initial handshake is done. A sample capture is shown in Figure 3-19.

```
> Frame 242: 610 bytes on wire (4880 bits), 610 bytes captured (4880 bits)
> Ethernet II, Src: Apple_48:eb:6c (88:66:5a:48:eb:6c), Dst: Google_6d:bd:85 (f4:f5:e8:6d:bd:85)
> Internet Protocol Version 4, Src: 192.168.1.142, Dst: 172.253.115.95
> User Datagram Protocol, Src Port: 58646, Dst Port: 443
  QUIC IETF
    v QUIC Connection information
        [Connection Number: 2]
      [Packet Length: 568]
      v QUIC Short Header DCID=9eeceabf736bccc4 PKN=5
          0... .... = Header Form: Short Header (0) ──────────► Header Type
          .1.. .... = Fixed Bit: True
          ..0. .... = Spin Bit: False
          ...0 0... = Reserved: 0
          .... .0.. = Key Phase Bit: False
          .... ..00 = Packet Number Length: 1 bytes (0)
          Destination Connection ID: 9eeceabf736bccc4 ─┼───────► Connection ID
          Packet Number: 5
          Protected Payload: 9f61f67943b45eaee9ad64a7b6e6d51b05fec179f4b03b2d21506c04856f79a799d142bb…
    > ACK
    > STREAM id=2 fin=0 off=41 len=9 dir=Unidirectional origin=Client-initiated
    > STREAM id=10 fin=0 off=0 len=351 dir=Unidirectional origin=Client-initiated
    > STREAM id=0 fin=1 off=0 len=166 dir=Bidirectional origin=Client-initiated
> Hypertext Transfer Protocol Version 3
> Hypertext Transfer Protocol Version 3
> Hypertext Transfer Protocol Version 3
```

Figure 3-19. *Wireshark capture for a QUIC short header*

The most significant bit is set to 0 to indicate that this header is a short header format. The other fields in the short header include the destination connection identifier and the packet sequence number. The sequence number is used for packet reordering or loss detection and recovery.

Note   During the time of this book authoring, the Chrome browser extension does not support the header format as defined in RFC9000. So, the readers may see a difference in their capture. The captures in this chapter are based on version 8 of the QUIC IETF draft (draft-ietf-quic-transport-08).

QUIC Initial Message – TLS Client Hello

The QUIC protocol reuses the TLS extensions, and so the client hello messages exchanged are similar to TCP+TLS except that, this time, the negotiation happens over the QUIC protocol. This being a QUIC Initial packet, the header format is set to long header. As the client will act as the destination for the traffic, it generates a locally unique destination connection identifier and includes the same in the QUIC header.

The client sends the TLS CLIENT HELLO message encapsulated within the QUIC packet including the Cipher Suite extensions for algorithm negotiation as shown in Figure 3-20.

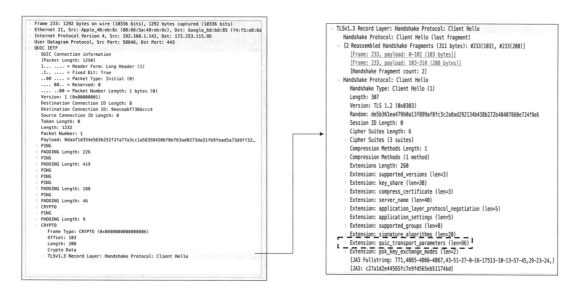

Figure 3-20. *QUIC TLS Client Hello message*

The client also includes QUIC-specific parameters in the TLS CLIENT HELLO message that are specific to the QUIC connection between the client and the server. A sample capture is shown in Figure 3-21.

```
∨ Extension: quic_transport_parameters (len=96)
     Type: quic_transport_parameters (57)
     Length: 96
  > Parameter: initial_max_streams_uni (len=2) 103
  > Parameter: initial_max_streams_bidi (len=2) 100
  > Parameter: initial_max_stream_data_bidi_local (len=4) 6291456
  > Parameter: max_datagram_frame_size (len=4) 65536
  > Parameter: initial_max_data (len=4) 15728640
  > Parameter: max_udp_payload_size (len=2) 1472
  > Parameter: max_idle_timeout (len=4) 30000 ms
  > Parameter: initial_max_stream_data_uni (len=4) 6291456
  > Parameter: Unknown 0xff73db (len=12)
  > Parameter: google_initial_rtt (len=4) 24625 us
  > Parameter: initial_max_stream_data_bidi_remote (len=4) 6291456
  > Parameter: google_quic_version (len=4)
  > Parameter: initial_source_connection_id (len=0)
  > Parameter: GREASE (len=4)
```

Figure 3-21. *QUIC transport parameters*

The preceding extension is used by the client to send the QUIC parameters such as the maximum unidirectional and bidirectional streams supported, window size, idle timer, etc. As it could be noted, all these transport layer reliability–specific details and the session layer encryption–specific details are shared in the initial packet itself to the server.

QUIC Initial Message – TLS Server Hello

The server upon receiving the QUIC Initial packet from the client with the CLIENT HELLO message will respond back with a QUIC Initial packet using long header format. As the server will act as the source, it generates a locally unique source connection identifier and includes the same in the QUIC header. A sample capture is shown in Figure 3-22.

```
> Frame 234: 1292 bytes on wire (10336 bits), 1292 bytes captured (10336 bits)
> Ethernet II, Src: Google_6d:bd:85 (f4:f5:e8:6d:bd:85), Dst: Apple_48:eb:6c (88:66:5a:48:eb:6c)
> Internet Protocol Version 4, Src: 172.253.115.95, Dst: 192.168.1.142
> User Datagram Protocol, Src Port: 443, Dst Port: 58646
v QUIC IETF
  > QUIC Connection information
    [Packet Length: 1250]
    1... .... = Header Form: Long Header (1)
    .1.. .... = Fixed Bit: True
    ..00 .... = Packet Type: Initial (0)
    .... 00.. = Reserved: 0
    .... ..00 = Packet Number Length: 1 bytes (0)
    Version: 1 (0x00000001)
    Destination Connection ID Length: 0
    Source Connection ID Length: 8
    Source Connection ID: 9eeceabf736bccc4
    Token Length: 0
    Length: 1232
    Packet Number: 1
    Payload: c2dbe498c3a8f2501e850fd1f7ebcfb27ded7b509c46e30f0232062b2367d8ff8bf14dac…
  v ACK
      Frame Type: ACK (0x0000000000000002)
      Largest Acknowledged: 1                    QUIC Acknowledgement
      ACK Delay: 0
      ACK Range Count: 0
      First ACK Range: 0
  v CRYPTO
      Frame Type: CRYPTO (0x0000000000000006)
      Offset: 0
      Length: 90                                 QUIC TLS Server Hello
      Crypto Data
      TLSv1.3 Record Layer: Handshake Protocol: Server Hello
      v Handshake Protocol: Server Hello
          Handshake Type: Server Hello (2)
          Length: 86
          Version: TLS 1.2 (0x0303)
          Random: d0f530506c11e67e1805eae0ba42af8d8cedc85dc79f1f05642d34ea00a559ba
          Session ID Length: 0
          Cipher Suite: TLS_AES_128_GCM_SHA256 (0x1301)
          Compression Method: null (0)
          Extensions Length: 46
        v Extension: key_share (len=36)
            Type: key_share (51)
            Length: 36
          > Key Share extension
        v Extension: supported_versions (len=2)
            Type: supported_versions (43)
            Length: 2
            Supported Version: TLS 1.3 (0x0304)
          [JA3S Fullstring: 771,4865,51-43]
          [JA3S: eb1d94daa7e0344597e756a1fb6e7054]
  v PADDING Length: 1116
      Frame Type: PADDING (0x0000000000000000)
      [Padding Length: 1116]
```

Figure 3-22. *QUIC TLS Server Hello message*

The QUIC Initial packet from the server includes the following frames:

- QUIC Ack frame

- Encrypted TLS frame

The QUIC Ack frame is used to acknowledge the incoming frames received from the client. The "***Largest Acknowledged***" field is used to carry the packet number received from the remote endpoint.

The encrypted TLS frame is used to carry the TLS SERVER HELLO message carrying the encryption and other TLS-specific parameters agreed based on the inbound TLS CLIENT HELLO message received from the client. Normally, this packet sent from the server will not include any QUIC-specific parameters.

QUIC Handshake Message – TLS Server Hello

The server will immediately send a QUIC handshake message that includes QUIC-specific parameters as shown in Figure 3-23.

```
∨ TLSv1.3 Record Layer: Handshake Protocol: Multiple Handshake Messages
  ∨ Handshake Protocol: Encrypted Extensions
      Handshake Type: Encrypted Extensions (8)
      Length: 193
      Extensions Length: 191
    › Extension: server_name (len=0)
    › Extension: application_layer_protocol_negotiation (len=5)
    ∨ Extension: quic_transport_parameters (len=170)
        Type: quic_transport_parameters (57)
        Length: 170
      › Parameter: initial_max_streams_uni (len=2) 103
      › Parameter: max_datagram_frame_size (len=4) 65536
      › Parameter: initial_max_stream_data_uni (len=4) 131072
      › Parameter: max_idle_timeout (len=4) 240000 ms
      › Parameter: GREASE (len=10)
      › Parameter: initial_max_streams_bidi (len=2) 100
      › Parameter: initial_max_stream_data_bidi_local (len=4) 131072
      › Parameter: initial_max_stream_data_bidi_remote (len=4) 131072
      › Parameter: initial_source_connection_id (len=8)
      › Parameter: max_udp_payload_size (len=2) 1472
      › Parameter: initial_max_data (len=4) 196608
      › Parameter: stateless_reset_token (len=16)
      › Parameter: original_destination_connection_id (len=8)
      › Parameter: disable_active_migration (len=0)
      › Parameter: google_quic_version (len=25)
      › Parameter: Unknown 0xff73db (len=28)
```

Figure 3-23. *QUIC server parameters*

The QUIC handshake packet from the server may include multiple types of extension within the encrypted TLS frame. This includes the QUIC protocol–specific parameters for negotiating the reliability characteristics such as idle timer for loss detection or congestion window.

The QUIC handshake will be used to finish the handshake by exchanging the "Finished" extension between the client and the server.

QUIC Protected Payload

Upon successful negotiation of the handshake between the client and the server, the negotiated QUIC-specific parameters such as the number of unidirectional and bidirectional streams, stream ID, window size, etc. along with the encryption-specific parameters such as the encryption key are used to transfer the HTTP traffic over a secured QUIC connection. A sample capture of the QUIC protected payload from the server to the client is shown in Figure 3-24.

```
Frame 239: 103 bytes on wire (824 bits), 103 bytes captured (824 bits)
Ethernet II, Src: Google_6d:bd:87 (f4:f5:e8:6d:bd:87), Dst: Apple_48:eb:6c (88:66:5a:48:eb:6c)
Internet Protocol Version 4, Src: 172.253.115.95, Dst: 192.168.1.142
User Datagram Protocol, Src Port: 443, Dst Port: 58646
QUIC IETF
  QUIC Connection information
    [Connection Number: 2]                              QUIC Short Header
  [Packet Length: 61]
  QUIC Short Header PKN=5
      0... .... = Header Form: Short Header (0)
      .1.. .... = Fixed Bit: True
      ..0. .... = Spin Bit: False
      ...0 0... = Reserved: 0
      .... .0.. = Key Phase Bit: False
      .... ..00 = Packet Number Length: 1 bytes (0)
      Packet Number: 5                                              QUIC Stream
      Protected Payload: 38995b85318992a704d7780475c8e58565e34f79398e8e47b8dac56a1123f500dec3e889…
  STREAM id=3 fin=0 off=0 len=41 dir=Unidirectional origin=Server-initiated
    Frame Type: STREAM (0x0000000000000008)
      .... ...0 = Fin: False
      .... ..0. = Len(gth): False
      .... .0.. = Off(set): False
    Stream ID: 3
      .... .... .... .... .... .... .... .... .... .... .... .... .... ...1 = Stream initiator: Server-initiated (1)
      .... .... .... .... .... .... .... .... .... .... .... .... .... ..1. = Stream direction: Unidirectional (1)
    Stream Data: 00041d01800100000680010000074064c000000d83b4badec0000000e8c513aec0000001…
  Hypertext Transfer Protocol Version 3
    Stream Type: Control Stream (0x0000000000000000)
    Type: SETTINGS (0x0000000000000004)
    Length: 29
    Frame Payload: 018001000006800100000740640c000000d83b4badec0000000e8c513ae
  > Settings – Max Table Capacity: 65536
  > Settings – Max Field Section Size: 65536
  > Settings – Blocked Streams: 100                              QUIC Payload - HTTP
  > Settings – GREASE
    Type: Reserved (0x1e20f75dd)
    Length: 0
```

Figure 3-24. *Wireshark capture for QUIC payload*

As discussed earlier, the subsequent packets after the handshake will use the QUIC short header that only includes the connection identifier and the packet number indicating the sequence of the packet within the connection. The QUIC packet in turn may carry multiple stream frames.

Each stream will have its own unique identifier as shown in the example. It also includes additional details such as the direction of the stream and if the stream is server or client initiated. Finally, the QUIC will also include a frame carrying the actual HTTP or other application payloads.

It could be noted that the number of initial messages exchanged between the client and the server is not very chatty while comparing to the TCP+TLS and thereby makes it lot more easier to manage.

Unlike TCP where each stream will have its own TCP session, QUIC allows to multiplex the streams within the same connection, making it more efficient compared to its ancestor approaches.

Decrypting QUIC/TLS Traffic

As QUIC uses TLS to encrypt the payload, the SSL key is mandatory to decrypt the payload details in Wireshark. A sample capture will exhibit encrypted data carried over QUIC and will not be able to differentiate the type of frames carried over a QUIC packet. A sample encrypted QUIC capture is shown in Figure 3-25.

```
> Frame 137: 69 bytes on wire (552 bits), 69 bytes captured (552 bits)
> Ethernet II, Src: Google_6d:bd:87 (f4:f5:e8:6d:bd:87), Dst: Apple_48:eb:6c (88:66:5a:48:eb:6c)
> Internet Protocol Version 4, Src: 172.253.115.138, Dst: 192.168.1.142
> User Datagram Protocol, Src Port: 443, Dst Port: 64502
∨ QUIC IETF
  ∨ QUIC Connection information
      [Connection Number: 1]
    [Packet Length: 27]
  ∨ QUIC Short Header
      0... .... = Header Form: Short Header (0)
      .1.. .... = Fixed Bit: True
      ..0. .... = Spin Bit: False
    Remaining Payload: f2050042247f1a057cc069e8a4570fd3008b7be8e2a05b01fac8
```

Figure 3-25. *Wireshark capture for encrypted QUIC payload*

The procedure explained to log the SSL key in the earlier part of this chapter is required to capture the SSL keys for the respective QUIC session in order to decrypt the QUIC payload.

QUIC Filters for Analysis

In this section, we will discuss about some of the important and commonly used QUIC-specific display filters. To filter any QUIC traffic, use the port matching 443:

udp.dstport == 443

Alternately, all the QUIC traffic can be filtered using the following simple filter:

quic

As mentioned earlier, QUIC may be used for applications other than HTTP. To filter all HTTP traffic over QUIC, use the following filter:

http3

Additional filters can be used to selectively filter the QUIC packets based on various attributes, and the following link includes the comprehensive list of the display filters:

www.wireshark.org/docs/dfref/q/quic.html

Capturing and Analyzing Secure DNS

In this section, we will discuss the basics of the DNS protocol and the machinery by looking into some of the basic packet captures and further discuss about common attacks and how to use Wireshark and packet capture for the analysis.

Basics of DNS

DNS was introduced by RFC1034 in 1983 to simplify the use of the Internet using domain names instead of the IP address itself. DNS could be considered as the phonebook of the Internet where any Internet resource such as a business or entertainment application will be registered with their domain or host name and the associated IP address. Anyone can resonate based on their own experience how simple it is to type www.gmail.com in a browser to access Google emails instead of remembering the Gmail server's IP address. The basic machinery of DNS is as shown in Figure 3-26.

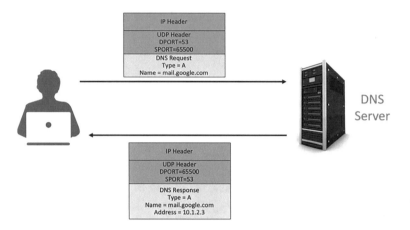

Figure 3-26. *Domain name resolution*

Any client will send a DNS Query message by encapsulating it in the UDP header with a destination port of 53 and send the request to the name server. The IP address of the name server is expected to be known to the client and normally will be pushed as part of the initial configuration. The Query message sent will carry the record type that describes the type of resource record and the Fully Qualified Domain Name (FQDN) which describes the name of the Internet resource being resolved. While there are different types of resource records available, we listed some of the most commonly used records as follows:

- A Record

- AAAA Record

- CNAME Record

- HTTPS Record

When the client is requesting the IPv4 address mapped to the resource name, the "Type" included in the Query message will be set to "A Record," and when the client is requesting the IPv6 address mapped to the resource name, the "Type" will be set to "AAAA Record." The "CNAME Record" is used to resolve the alias of one name to another. The type "HTTPS Record" helps resolve many resource-specific details associated to the resource name beyond the basic reachability information. The capture of the DNS Query message for type A record for the name "mail.google.com" is shown in Figure 3-27.

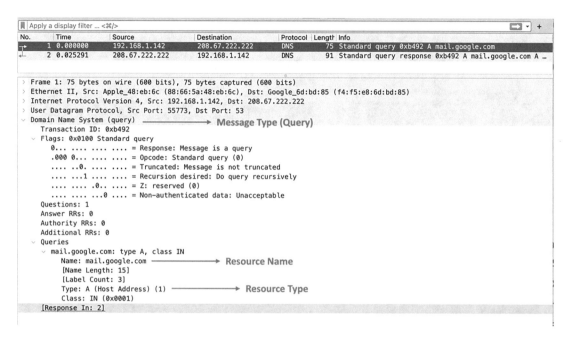

Figure 3-27. *DNS Query message*

The server upon receiving the request will perform a lookup in the cache or the domain name structure database, which is an inverted tree with multiple levels anchored on the root. An example of the DNS hierarchy is shown in Figure 3-28.

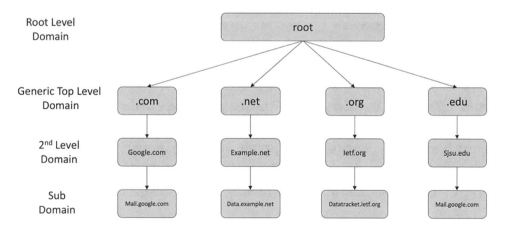

Figure 3-28. *DNS hierarchy*

Depending on the record type included in the incoming Query message, the respective record mapped to the resource name will be resolved and included in the DNS response back to the client as shown in Figure 3-29.

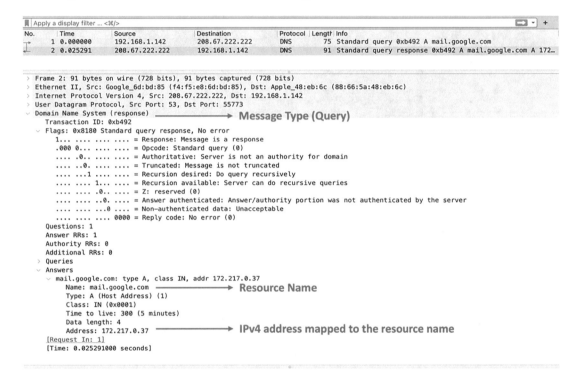

Figure 3-29. *DNS response*

As it could be noticed, DNS messages are plain text by default, thereby making it vulnerable for eavesdropping or tampering the request or response on the wire and thereby compromising the user privacy. Anyone with access to the network can simply capture all the DNS packets to observe the websites visited by the user. This information can in turn be used as a potential starting point to identify the social media used by the user and further hack the accounts. To address this challenge and preserve the user privacy, Secure DNS was introduced that obfuscates the DNS messages on the wire.

Secure DNS

Secure DNS was originally introduced around 2016 by making use of the Transport Layer Security (TLS) extensions. DNS over TLS (DoT) was defined in RFC7858 that establishes a secured TLS connection between the client and the name resolution server. Later, RFC8484 defines the protocol extension for DNS over HTTPS (DoH) that leverages the HTTPS protocol to encrypt and steer the DNS messages over HTTPS connection as shown in Figure 3-30.

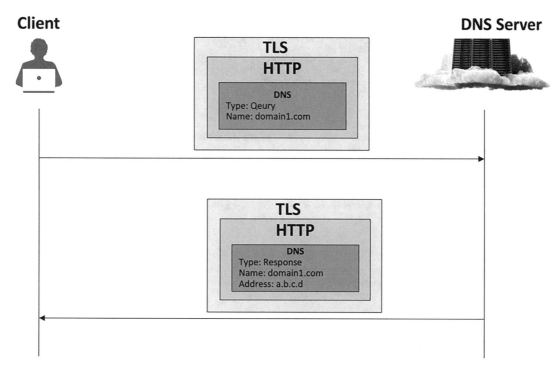

Figure 3-30. *Secure domain name resolution*

The traditional HTTP GET or POST methods are used to send the request and receive the response from the server. These methods collectively referred to as Secure DNS encrypt the DNS message and make it harder for any malicious users to eavesdrop or to manipulate the messages. The following is an example encoding of the DNS message using the HTTP GET method:

```
:method = GET
:scheme = https
:authority = <DNS Server Info>
:path = /dns-query?dns=<base 64 URL encoding>
:accept = application/dns-message
:user-agent = <browser>
```

The HTTP method used is GET, and the authority value is set to the DNS server information. The resource name that needs to be resolved is converted into base64 URL encoding and embedded within the GET payload. An example capture of the DoH frame is shown in Figure 3-31.

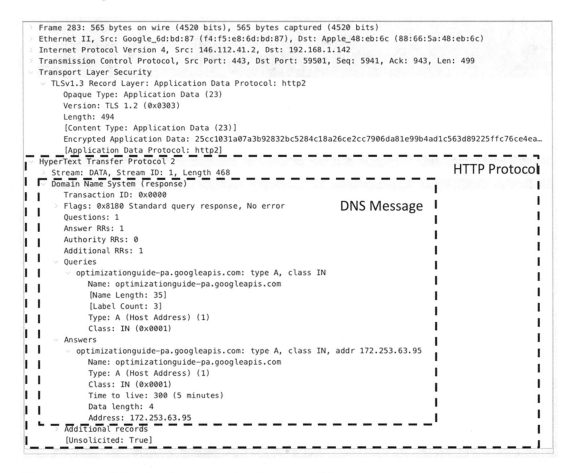

Figure 3-31. *Wireshark capture for Secure DNS*

Figure 3-31 is an example response from the DNS server where the DNS response message is encapsulated with an HTTP packet, which in turn is encrypted using TLS and forwarded to the client. Without the SSL key captured from the client, any malicious user cannot even identify what type of TLS traffic it is. This makes it really hard for the malicious users to track the browsing history or the sites of any legitimate users.

Summary

In this chapter, we discussed about the challenges associated to transferring critical data unencrypted and how the same can be used by malicious users to compromise the user privacy and security. We further discussed about the evolution of different security protocols and how the same helps encrypting the data in motion.

We further looked deep into capturing and analyzing Secure HTTP traffic over TCP and how to capture the relevant encryption keys to decrypt the traffic in Wireshark for analysis. We also looked into capturing and analyzing QUIC, which is another secure protocol for HTTP.

We also discussed about the challenges associated to resolving the domain name using traditional DNS using different captures and discussed how DNS over HTTP-based domain name resolution can help secure the user privacy.

References for This Chapter

[**RFC2818**] Rescorla, E., "HTTP Over TLS," RFC 2818, DOI 10.17487/RFC2818, May 2000, www.rfc-editor.org/ info/rfc2818

[**RFC9000**] Iyengar, J., Ed. and M. Thomson, Ed., "QUIC: A UDP-Based Multiplexed and Secure Transport," RFC 9000, DOI 10.17487/RFC9000, May 2021, www.rfc-editor.org/ info/rfc9000

[**RFC9001**] Thomson, M., Ed. and S. Turner, Ed., "Using TLS to Secure QUIC," RFC 9001, DOI 10.17487/RFC9001, May 2021, www. rfc-editor.org/info/rfc9001

[**RFC9110**] Fielding, R., Ed., Nottingham, M., Ed., and J. Reschke, Ed., "HTTP Semantics," STD 97, RFC 9110, DOI 10.17487/ RFC9110, June 2022, www.rfc-editor.org/info/rfc9110

CHAPTER 4

Capturing Wireless Traffic for Analysis

Wireless technology is one of the greatest inventions in the past century that help free the user and realize the actual benefit of "cablefree" without being attached to a string or cable for connection. The first ever wireless message was a morse code sent over a kilometer distance by the inventor of wireless technology Guglielmo Marconi. Fast forwarding 100+ years now, wireless is an integral part of our life with almost every connected device leveraging wireless technology in one form or the other and thereby making it lot easier for installation and management.

The breakthrough discovery of radio waves in 1880 paves the way for all the wireless communications that are currently being enjoyed by this and will be enjoyed by the future generations. While originally used for transmitting audio signals, the electromagnetic spectrum comprises various radiations such as microwave, infrared, and visible light that were explored further to encode data. The bandwidth and the coverage radius are determined by the selection of the radiation range within the spectrum.

Note While the electromagnetic spectrum spans across varying ranges, the primary focus of this chapter is on wireless LAN that ranges within 2.4 GHz to 6 GHz.

Basics of Radio Waves and Spectrum

Electromagnetic radiation is the flow of energy in the form of waves generated through a synchronized oscillation of electric and magnetic fields that can travel through any

© Nagendra Kumar Nainar and Ashish Panda 2023
N. K. Nainar and A. Panda, *Wireshark for Network Forensics*, https://doi.org/10.1007/978-1-4842-9001-9_4

medium or free space. While visible light is one form of electromagnetic radiation, the entire spectrum is categorized into seven different types that primarily vary based on the two main characteristics of the radiation known as wavelength and the frequency of the waveform as shown in Figure 4-1.

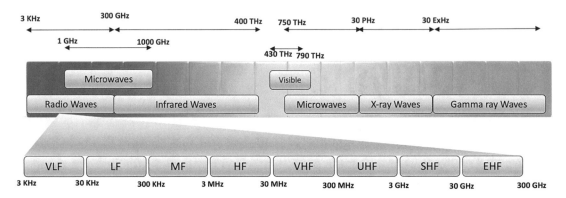

Figure 4-1. *Wireless spectrum*

The radiation travels at the speed of light in the form of sine waves in free space or in any medium. For better understanding, imagine you throwing a pebble into a still water, and you could notice the waves propagating outward in all direction as sine waves from the point where the pebble disturbed the still water. The radiation will travel in a similar manner from the source that generates the waves.

Following the basic physics definition, **wavelength** is the distance between peak points or adjacent crests of the sine waves and is measured in meters. On the other hand, **frequency** defines the number of wave cycles within a second and is measured in hertz (Hz). For example, a band with a frequency of 1 GHz represents 1 billion cycles per second. Both these important characteristics of electromagnetic radiations are related to each other using the following formula:

```
Wavelength = (speed of light)/(Frequency)
```

From the preceding formula, the speed of light is a constant value, and so, as the frequency goes higher, the wavelength will be reduced which indicates that lower frequency will be able to travel farther than the higher frequency waveforms. There is another interesting property of electromagnetic radiation known as **amplitude**. The wave amplitude is the power of the signal or the maximum displacement of the wave from its mean position. A pictorial representation of these radiation characteristics is shown in Figure 4-2.

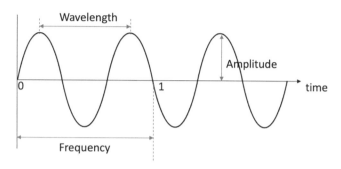

Figure 4-2. *Radio wave*

By modifying the amplitude (AM) or the frequency (FM) of the waves, data can be encoded and traversed from one point to another using the electromagnetic waves. This forms the basics of wireless communication technology.

Considering the range of spectrum available, there must be some form of regulatory body to regulate the allocation and licensing of the spectrum. The International Telecommunication Union (ITU) Radiocommunication Sector and the US Federal Communications Commission (FCC) took that responsibility to manage and regulate the frequency allocation and transmission methods. FCC grants the spectrum license to any entity by providing the exclusive rights to use the spectrum range for a period of time for a charge. Such licensed range can either be sublicensed or leased to other entities by the parent entity that owns the license but cannot be used by other entities without the consensus from the parent entity. In order to promote and drive innovation, FCC also assigns a range of spectrum as unlicensed which allows any entity to freely use this range without any charge.

Within the radio wave spectrum that spans from 3 KHz to 300 GHz, ITU reserves a range of frequency from radio waves internationally for industrial, scientific, and medical applications. This band is collectively referred to as the ISM band. FCC originally allocated three unlicensed frequency bands from ISM as 900 MHz, 2.4 GHz, and 5 GHz. Around 2020, FCC opens 6 GHz from the midband spectrum for unlicensed use by the public.

Note   The 900 MHz is a narrowband radio frequency primarily used for voice communication. For more details about the ISM band and the regulations, please refer to Article 5 of the ITU Radio Regulations, which is a document defined by ITU to regulate the radiocommunication services.

In the next section, we will further discuss about the unlicensed ISM band and how it is used for wireless LAN communication.

Basics of Wireless LAN Technology

A local area network (LAN) is a private collection of devices sharing the same subnet that either can reside within the same physical location or can span across regions using advanced technologies such as Virtual Extensible LAN (VxLAN) or Network Virtualization using GRE (NVGRE). Traditionally, all the devices within a LAN network are connected through wired Ethernet cable to layer 2 Ethernet switches. Connecting multiple devices to a shared medium raises different types of challenges such as defining a common and globally agreeable frame and header format, media access–specific challenges such as frame collision detection and avoidance, transmission error detection and correction, etc. To address these challenges, the Institute of Electrical and Electronics Engineers (IEEE) formed the 802 LAN/MAN Standards Committee around 1980 to develop and standardize OSI data link layer protocols and standards for LAN networks. IEEE 802.3 is the workgroup created for Ethernet-based LAN network. When the devices within the same LAN network are connected through a wireless medium instead of an Ethernet wired cable, the network is referred to as wireless LAN (WLAN).

Any wireless LAN network comprises a minimum of one wireless access point (AP) and one or more wireless endpoints or stations. The wireless AP acts as a central base station that is responsible for the following basic functionalities:

- Assign the endpoints to the respective wireless channels.

- Assign the IP address from the WLAN subnet.

- Transmit and receive wireless radio signals between each endpoint within the WLAN.

- Connect the endpoints within the WLAN to the wired network.

- The endpoints are any device such as laptops, mobile phones, or other smart-connected things that are capable of communicating via WLAN.

Note   Various taskforce and study groups were created under IEEE 802.3 to develop standards for different data rates such as 100 Gb Ethernet, 200 Gb Ethernet, 400 Gb Ethernet, etc. While IEEE primarily focused on developing standards for PHY and MAC layers, IETF created workgroups for upper layer protocols. IETF CAPWAP is one such workgroup chartered to develop upper layer protocols for WLAN.

Wireless LAN Channels

With the evolution of radio technologies and the release of unlicensed ISM bands by FCC, the IEEE 802.11 workgroup was created around 1985 in an attempt to develop and standardize PHY and MAC layer protocols. WLAN leverages unlicensed spectrum bands, and so most of (if not all) the standards are developed around 2.4 GHz and 5 GHz bands.

Note   With the recent release of 6 GHz from the midband as an unlicensed spectrum, new standards are being developed.

Within the 2.4 GHz band, there are a total of 14 equally spaced channels designated for WLAN usage as shown in Table 4-1.

Table 4-1. *2.4 GHz Frequency Channels*

Channel	Lower Frequency	Upper Frequency	Mid-frequency
1	2401	2423	2412
2	2406	2428	2417
3	2411	2433	2422
4	2416	2438	2427
5	2421	2443	2432
6	2426	2448	2437
7	2431	2453	2442
8	2436	2458	2447
9	2441	2463	2452
10	2446	2468	2547
11	2451	2473	2462
12	2456	2478	2467
13	2461	2483	2472
14	2473	2495	2484

Each channel within the 2.4 GHz range is 22 MHz in width and 5 MHz apart between each channel with some overlap between the channels with an exception for Channel 14. For example, Channel 1 ranges from a lower frequency of 2.401 GHz to a higher frequency of 2.423 GHz with a mid-frequency of 2.412 GHz, while Channel 2 ranges from a lower frequency of 2.406 GHz to a higher frequency of 2.428 GHz with a mid-frequency of 2.417 GHz. There is a significant overlap between these channels, and the use of such overlapping channels may cause network slowness and packet loss due to channel interference. To avoid any performance degradation, the best practice is to use non-overlapping channels. It could be noted from Table 4-1 that the upper frequency of Channel 1 is 2.423 GHz, while the lower frequency of Channel 5 is 2.421 GHz. So, Channel 1 overlaps with Channels 2, 3, 4, and 5. The lower frequency of Channel 6 is 2.426 GHz which does not overlap with Channel 1. Selecting such non-overlapping channels during the WLAN deployment will help avoid any channel interference and so improve the performance.

Note   In the 2.4 GHz band, Channels 12 and 13 are allowed to be used only in low-power mode. Channel 14 is not legally allowed to be used in the North America domain. This is to avoid interfering with the next licensed band that is used for satellite communication. So ideally, there are 11 channels available for use in 2.4 GHz.

Within the 5 GHz band, the US FCC defined four different Unlicensed National Information Infrastructure (U-NII) frequency bands that are used by WLAN vendors and different wireless service providers as shown in Table 4-2.

Table 4-2. *5 GHz Frequency Band*

Name	Frequency Range (GHz)	Bandwidth (MHz)
U-NII-1	5.150–5.250	100
U-NII-2A	5.250–5.350	100
U-NII-2B	5.350–5.470	120
U-NII-2C	5.470–5.725	255
U-NII-3	5.725–5.825	100

Each U-NII band within the 5 GHz band comprises multiple channels where each channel is of 20 MHz bandwidth. Multiple adjacent channels (more specifically 2, 4, or 8 adjacent channels) can be combined to form wider channels with 40 MHz, 80 MHz, and 160 MHz bandwidth, respectively. For example, Channel 36 from U-NII-1 has a bandwidth of 20 MHz with lower frequency of 5.170 GHz and upper frequency of 5.170 GHz. Channel 40 from U-NII-1 has a bandwidth of 20 MHz with lower frequency of 5.190 GHz and upper frequency of 5.210 GHz. Channel 38 combines Channels 36 and 40 to increase the bandwidth to 40 MHz with lower frequency of 5.170 GHz and upper frequency of 5.210 GHz. Unlike the 2.4 GHz band, 5 GHz can be used with a total of 25 non-overlapping channels.

Note   The U-NII-1 frequency band is to be used strictly for indoor purposes. The frequency band defined as U-NII-2B is currently not available for unlicensed use.

On the one hand, the lower frequency travels further but comprises smaller bandwidth, while on the other hand, the higher frequency comprises higher bandwidth but doesn't travel further. While both 2.4 GHz and 5 GHz are globally unlicensed, the speed and coverage range varies for both the bands. 2.4 GHz is primarily targeted to provide higher coverage with lower bandwidth, while 5 GHz is used to provide higher bandwidth.

Wireless LAN Topologies

Wireless LAN can be implemented and operated in different modes based on the service set configuration. A service set is a group of wireless network devices sharing a common wireless network identifier. There are different types of service sets defined in 802.11 standards as follows:

- Basic Service Set (BSS)

- Extended Service Set (ESS)

- Mesh Basic Service Set (MBSS)

Basic Service Set

The Basic Service Set (BSS) forms a group of wireless network endpoints sharing the same network identifier advertised by a wireless access point as shown in Figure 4-3.

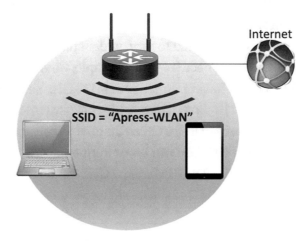

Figure 4-3. *Basic Service Set*

The network identifier is commonly referred to as the Service Set Identifier (SSID), which is a natural language label. This topology is referred to as an autonomous topology as they are stand-alone and fully functional service sets where the access point will allow the communication between the endpoints and beyond the wireless network. All the connected endpoints and the access point within the same BSS will use a single wireless LAN channel for sending and receiving radio signals.

Extended Service Set

As we discussed in the earlier part of the chapter, the wireless network coverage and the bandwidth availability are decided based on the band and the channel selection. So, it could be noted that the BSS is not sufficient to accommodate a lot of wireless network devices or to extend the coverage beyond what can be covered by a single wireless AP. The Extended Service Set (ESS) forms an extended group of service sets by connecting multiple wireless APs through wired infrastructure forming a larger wireless network as shown in Figure 4-4.

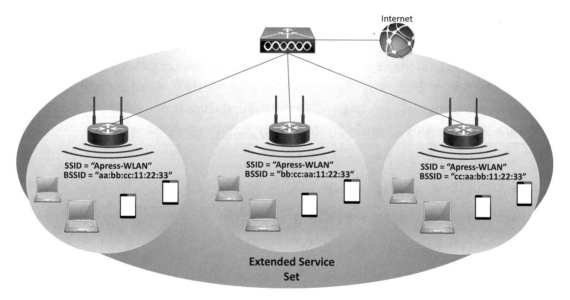

Figure 4-4. *Extended Service Set*

This topology leverages a common distribution system such as a wireless LAN controller that manages all the wireless AP configuration and inter-BSS communication between endpoints in different BSS. All the wireless APs within the ESS will advertise the same SSID, thereby allowing any wireless endpoint to seamlessly roam from one BSS to another BSS without service interruptions.

Note   In the ESS, we mentioned that all the wireless APs will advertise the same SSID which is the network name. To differentiate the wireless access point to which the endpoint is connected, each wireless AP will also advertise BSSID which is unique for each access point. BSSID is the MAC address of the advertising wireless AP.

Mesh Basic Service Set

The Mesh Basic Service Set (MBSS) forms a group of mesh stations sharing the same mesh profile to create a much larger wireless network (such as a community). Each AP within the mesh network will use radio antennas for both connecting the endpoints and backhauling the traffic toward other APs within the same mesh network.

Wireless LAN Encryption Protocols

The method of using radio waves to transmit data traffic makes it very attractive for malicious users to sniff the air traffic and misuse the information gathered. So, it is essential that the traffic exchanged over the wireless medium is highly encrypted to make it very challenging (if not impossible) for the malicious users to decrypt the data. There are different types of wireless LAN security introduced as follows:

- Wired Equivalent Privacy (WEP)

- Wi-Fi Protected Access (WPA)

- Wi-Fi Protected Access 2 (WPA2)

- Wi-Fi Protected Access 3 (WPA3)

The WEP protocol, originally standardized around 1999, uses a key value of size 40 bits along with a fixed-size initialization vector (IV) to generate a 64- or 128-bit-sized seed value that is used to encrypt the data before forwarding. The key used can be easily cracked, and so this approach is not very secured. The Wi-Fi Alliance officially decrypted this protocol around 2004, and it is not commonly used in the recent deployments.

The WPA protocol, originally standardized around 2003, leverages a much stronger mechanism referred to as the Temporal Key Integrity Protocol (TKIP) and Message Integrity Check (MIC). While MIC helps prevent man-in-the-middle attacks, TKIP dynamically changes the keys used to encrypt the data, thereby making it more challenging for the malicious users to decrypt the data exchanged over the wireless medium. The WPA can be implemented in two different modes. The personal mode, also referred to as WPA-PSK, leverages the preshared key to generate the encryption key, while the enterprise mode, also referred to as WPA-EAP, leverages an external authentication server to generate the encryption key based on the EAP parameters.

The WPA2 protocol, originally standardized around 2006, is far more advanced compared to the previous version WPA. WPA2 replaces TKIP with the Advanced Encryption Standard (AES) and Counter Mode Cipher Block Chaining Message Authentication Code Protocol (CCMP) to generate the encryption keys. Based on the combination of the preshared key associated to the wireless LAN network, the unique NONCE generated by the client, and the access point, a dynamic encryption key is generated which will be changed periodically to make it difficult for any malicious users to decrypt.

The WPA3 protocol is the most recent one and primarily being positioned for Wi-Fi 6. WPA3 leverages the Simultaneous Authentication of Equals (SAE)–based key establishment mechanism.

Setting Up 802.11 Radio Tap

In the previous chapters, we discussed about the use of tools such as tcpdump or natively using Wireshark to capture the packets. It could be noted that those captures are Ethernet, and so using the same option for a Wi-Fi interface will not help capture the frames with radio headers. Wireless network interface cards (NICs) that comprise the radio antenna can be configured to work in different modes. The following are the two modes that are commonly supported by many of the end-user devices:

- Managed mode

- Monitor mode

In the managed mode, the antenna will register with the base station as a traditional endpoint and consume the radio frames that are received from the respective channel allocated to the client. In the monitor mode, the antenna will be programmed to sniff any radio frames in the air.

In this section, we will discuss different options available for different operating systems to capture the wireless frames with radio headers for analysis.

Wireless Capture Using Native Wireshark Tool

This option works for all the operating systems that natively support the Wireshark tool. While this section was explained with captures from macOS, other operating systems support the same options.

In the Wireshark tool, open the "Capture Options" from Capture ➤ Options (or using shortcut keys such as "CMD+K" for macOS or "CTRL+K" for Windows). This will open the window to modify the capture options for all the interfaces as shown in Figure 4-5.

Figure 4-5. *Wireshark capture options*

It could be noted that by default, all the interfaces listed in the capture options are marked to capture incoming frames with the Ethernet header. An example output from a macOS with the default capture options for the Wi-Fi interface "en0" is shown in Figure 4-6.

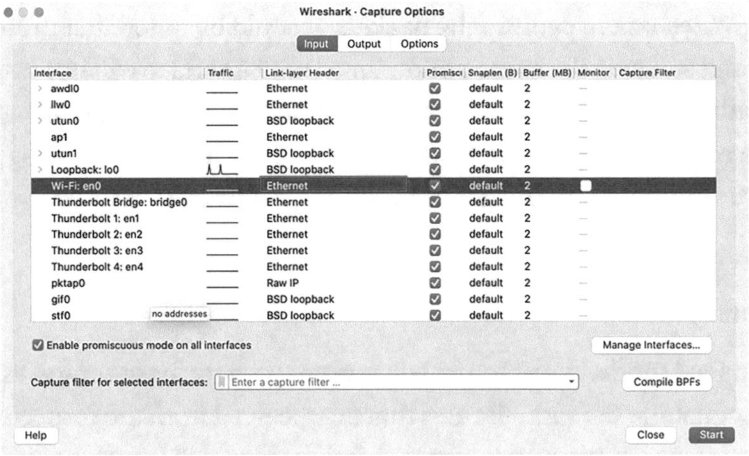

Figure 4-6. *Default capture options*

By enabling the "monitor" mode in the capture option, we can instruct the tool to capture radio headers for the Wi-Fi interface. An example output from a macOS with the monitor mode enabled in the options for the Wi-Fi interface "en0" is shown in Figure 4-7.

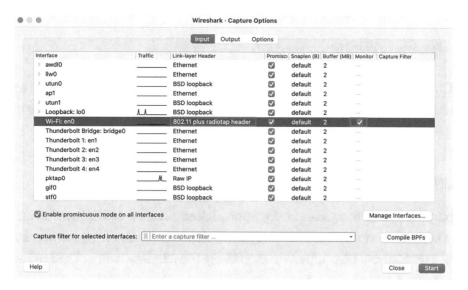

Figure 4-7. Monitor capture option

By starting the capture, we now can see that the tool captures frames with radio headers for analysis.

Note   When the radio antenna in the laptop is changed to be in monitor mode, it will capture all the radio frames in the air and not just the one targeted to the laptop. For security purposes, this feature may be disabled by the administrators.

Wireless Capture Using AirPort Utility

The AirPort Utility is a CLI-based tool that is available for macOS that was originally used to pull AirPort base station–specific information. This tool leverages the SNMP-based polling mechanism to graphically represent the Wi-Fi network and to make any changes. This tool comes with a sniffer option that can be used to capture wireless radio frames by specifying the channel where the frames need to be captured. An example is shown in Figure 4-8.

```
nagendrakumarnainar@Nagendras-MacBook-Pro ~ %
nagendrakumarnainar@Nagendras-MacBook-Pro ~ %
nagendrakumarnainar@Nagendras-MacBook-Pro ~ % airport en0 sniff 149
Capturing 802.11 frames on en0.
^CSession saved to /tmp/airportSniffoQI0bm.cap.
nagendrakumarnainar@Nagendras-MacBook-Pro ~ %
```

Figure 4-8. *AirPort Utility commands*

The CLI format as shown earlier will allow us to instruct the interface (en0 in this example) from where the radio frames must be captured and the channel (149 in this example) as well.

Wireless Capture Using Diagnostic Tool

In this option, we use a macOS-native graphical user interface tool known as the Wireless Diagnostic Tool that is available for wireless troubleshooting purposes natively in macOS. This tool can be popped up by clicking the wireless icon + "Option" key as shown in Figure 4-9.

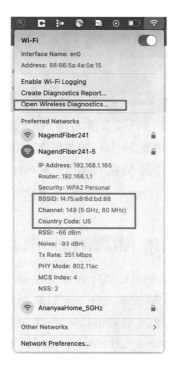

Figure 4-9. *Wireless Diagnostic Tool*

Now click the Window ➤ Sniffer option to pop open the wireless sniffer as shown in Figure 4-10.

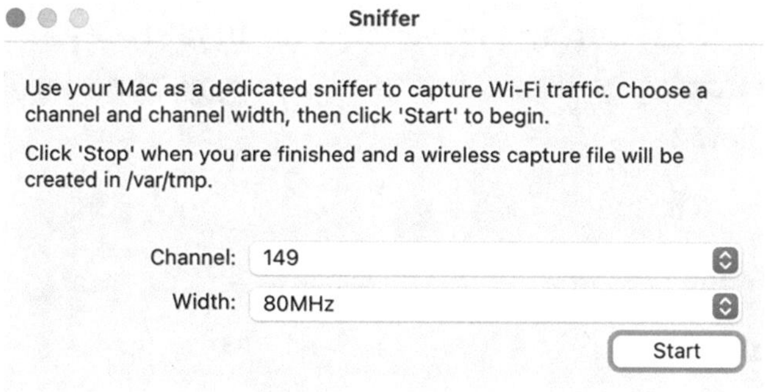

Figure 4-10. *Diagnostic sniffer configuration*

Note When the radio antenna in the laptop is programmed to be in monitor mode using any of the preceding options, the end-user device, such as a laptop, will stop working in managed mode and go offline, losing any Internet connectivity. Once the capture is stopped, the device doesn't move to managed mode and connect to the network by default. It may need to be done manually.

Wireless Operational Aspects – Packet Capture and Analysis

In this section, we will discuss various operational aspects of a wireless LAN network along with packet capture and analysis.

802.11 Frame Types and Format

The IEEE 802.11 frame format is defined in a way that any receiving antenna can use the information in the MAC sublayer to identify if the frame is destined for itself along with the type of the frame to process it further accordingly. There are three main types of 802.11 frames as follows:

- Management frame

- Control frame

- Data frame

The generic format of IEEE 802.11 frame is as shown in Figure 4-11.

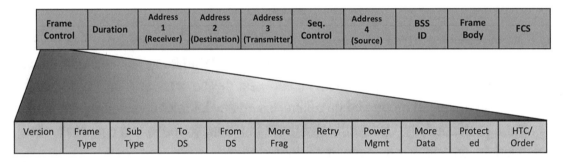

Figure 4-11. *IEEE 802.11 frame format*

The **Frame Control Field** is of 2-byte size that in turn encompasses subfields for control information and additional flags. The **Version** is a 2-bit-sized subfield with a value set to 00. The **Frame Type** and the **Sub-Type** subfields define the type of the frame. The **To DS** flag identifies the direction of the frame if it is going to the access point. The **From DS** flag identifies if the frame is coming from the access point. For any broadcast frames, both the To DS and From DS flags will be set to 0. The **More Frag** flag indicates that additional fragments of the frame will follow. The **Retry** flag indicates that this frame is a retransmission of a previous frame. The **Power Mgmt** flag indicates that the sender is in power-save mode. The **Protected** flag indicates that the frame is encrypted.

The **Duration** is of 2-byte size that serves two purposes based on the type of the frame. This field can be used to carry the Association ID when the frame type is control frames and the same field is used to carry time duration when the frame type is management or data. The duration value defined is the airtime reserved by the sending antenna for an acknowledgment before resending the frame.

The **Address 1 (Receiver)** is set to the MAC address of the receiver of the frame. The **Address 2 (Destination)** is set to the MAC address of the ultimate destination of the frame that will further process the upper layer payloads. The **Address 3 (Transmitter)** is set to the MAC address of the transmitting radio antenna. The **Address 4 (Source)** is set to the MAC address of the ultimate source that originated the frame.

The BSSID (as defined in the earlier section) is set to the MAC address of the access point.

One of the sample captures of the wireless management frame is shown in Figure 4-12.

```
>  Frame 3: 280 bytes on wire (2240 bits), 280 bytes captured (2240 bits)
>  Radiotap Header v0, Length 56
v  802.11 radio information
      PHY type: 802.11a (OFDM) (5)
      Turbo type: Non-turbo (0)
      Data rate: 6.0 Mb/s
      Channel: 149
      Frequency: 5745MHz              802.11 Radio specific Information
      Signal strength (dBm): -82 dBm
      Noise level (dBm): -93 dBm
      Signal/noise ratio (dB): 11 dB
      TSF timestamp: 1880407270
   >  [Duration: 324µs]
v  IEEE 802.11 Beacon frame, Flags: ........C
      Type/Subtype: Beacon frame (0x0008)
   v  Frame Control Field: 0x8000
         .... ..00 = Version: 0
         .... 00.. = Type: Management frame (0)
         1000 .... = Subtype: 8
      v  Flags: 0x00
            .... ..00 = DS status: Not leaving DS or network is operating in AD-HOC mode (To DS: 0 From DS: 0) (…
            .... .0.. = More Fragments: This is the last fragment
            .... 0... = Retry: Frame is not being retransmitted
            ...0 .... = PWR MGT: STA will stay up
            ..0. .... = More Data: No data buffered
            .0.. .... = Protected flag: Data is not protected
            0... .... = +HTC/Order flag: Not strictly ordered
      .000 0000 0000 0000 = Duration: 0 microseconds      IEEE 802.11 Frame
      Receiver address: ff:ff:ff:ff:ff:ff
      Destination address: ff:ff:ff:ff:ff:ff
      Transmitter address: f4:f5:e8:6e:5c:00
      Source address: f4:f5:e8:6e:5c:00
      BSS Id: f4:f5:e8:6e:5c:00
      .... .... .... 0000 = Fragment number: 0
      0001 1101 1000 .... = Sequence number: 472
      Frame check sequence: 0xcf188f5f [unverified]
      [FCS Status: Unverified]
>  IEEE 802.11 Wireless Management
```

Figure 4-12. *802.11 management frame*

The 802.11 radio information field includes the radio-specific details such as the spectrum band (2.4 GHz vs. 5 GHz), the channel on which the frame is captured, the data rate for this channel, the signal-to-noise ratio (SNR), signal strength, etc. This information is essential to troubleshoot any wireless failures or slowness-specific issues. For example, a minimum of 20 dB SNR value is recommended for the wireless network to function properly, and a value of around 40 dB is considered excellent.

The radiotap module also includes an additional metadata container to include other radio-specific details to the frame as shown in Figure 4-13.

```
∨ Radiotap Header v0, Length 56
    Header revision: 0
    Header pad: 0
    Header length: 56
  › Present flags
    MAC timestamp: 1881866236
  ∨ Flags: 0x12
      .... ...0 = CFP: False
      .... ..1. = Preamble: Short
      .... .0.. = WEP: False
      .... 0... = Fragmentation: False
      ...1 .... = FCS at end: True
      ..0. .... = Data Pad: False
      .0.. .... = Bad FCS: False
      0... .... = Short GI: False
    Data Rate: 6.0 Mb/s
    Channel frequency: 5745 [A 149]
  ∨ Channel flags: 0x0140, Orthogonal Frequency-Division Multiplexing (OFDM), 5 GHz spectrum
      .... .... .... ...0 = 700 MHz spectrum: False
      .... .... .... ..0. = 800 MHz spectrum: False
      .... .... .... .0.. = 900 MHz spectrum: False
      .... .... ...0 .... = Turbo: False
      .... .... ..0. .... = Complementary Code Keying (CCK): False
      .... .... .1.. .... = Orthogonal Frequency-Division Multiplexing (OFDM): True
      .... .... 0... .... = 2 GHz spectrum: False
      .... ...1 .... .... = 5 GHz spectrum: True
      .... ..0. .... .... = Passive: False
      .... .0.. .... .... = Dynamic CCK-OFDM: False
      .... 0... .... .... = Gaussian Frequency Shift Keying (GFSK): False
      ...0 .... .... .... = GSM (900MHz): False
      ..0. .... .... .... = Static Turbo: False
      .0.. .... .... .... = Half Rate Channel (10MHz Channel Width): False
      0... .... .... .... = Quarter Rate Channel (5MHz Channel Width): False
    Antenna signal: -45 dBm
    Antenna noise: -94 dBm
    Antenna: 1
  › Vendor namespace: 00:10:18-0
  › Vendor namespace: 00:10:18-3
```

Figure 4-13. *Radiotap metadata*

The radiotap header shown in Figure 4-13 is actually not part of the frame. But this is a metadata container added by the radiotap module while capturing the wireless frame. This metadata container includes frame- and channel-specific details such as the frequency, the frame timestamp, antenna signal, etc.

Wireless Network Discovery

Any wireless LAN access point will periodically send a management type of frame known as **beacons**. The beacons are used by the access points to advertise the capabilities and the availability of different SSIDs available for the endpoints to join. In a home network, it is very common to see multiple SSIDs listing due to the availability of multiple wireless LAN networks from neighboring homes. The user endpoints such as laptops or mobile phones capture and list these SSIDs based on the incoming beacons as shown in Figure 4-14.

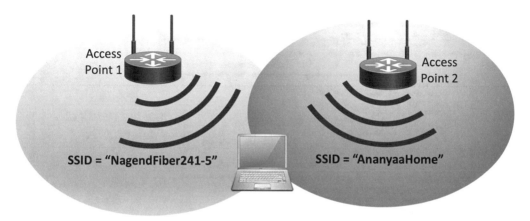

Figure 4-14. *802.11 SSID broadcast*

The endpoint station will continuously scan all the available channels to detect any new beacons and list the SSIDs for the user to connect. The received beacon management frame will include various essential details advertised by the access point that are required for the endpoint stations to join the network as shown in Figure 4-15.

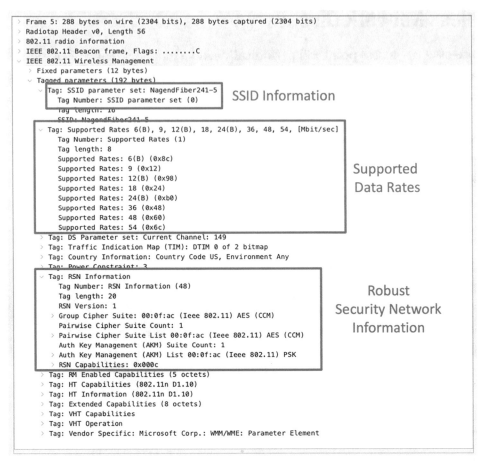

Figure 4-15. *802.11 beacon frame*

The SSID parameter will carry the SSID details configured for the advertising wireless access point. The frequency band and the channel information along with the SSID will be used by the endpoint while sending the request to join the network. The beacon also includes all the data rates supported by the access point. Depending on the type of the 802.11 standard configured on the access point, different data rates will be advertised. One of the data rates will be mandatory for the endpoint and the access point to negotiate and support the onboarding.

The Robust Security Network (RSN) parameter is an optional field included in the beacons advertising the encryption and authentication capabilities. Depending on the type of the group Cipher Suite, the respective keys will be negotiated to encrypt the payload. The **Authentication Key Management (AKM)** field is used to identify if the initial authentication is based on a preshared key or using the 802.1X method. In the preceding beacon frame, the AKM is set to PSK (Phase Shift Keying), which indicates that a preshared key is required to authenticate during the onboarding process.

Note   By continuously broadcasting the SSID, the network is vulnerable for malicious users to try hacking the network. For security purposes, most of the wireless access point vendors support the configuration option to disable the SSID broadcast. In such case, the user endpoint stations are required to be manually configured with the wireless network details.

Some of the useful filtering mechanisms to filter all the beacons or specific fields within the beacons are as follows.

To filter all the management frames

```
wlan.fc.type == 0
```

To filter all the management frames of subtype beacons

```
wlan.fc.type_subtype == 0x0008
```

To filter all the frames based on the BSSID

```
Wlan.bssid == aa:bb:cc:11:22:33
```

To filter all the beacons with RSN

```
Wlan.tag.number == 48
```

Note   For detailed filtering options specific to 802.11 frames, please visit www.wireshark.org/docs/dfref/w/wlan.html.

Wireless LAN Endpoint Onboarding

By simply scanning the wireless channels, any endpoint station will be able to identify all the available wireless LAN networks based on the received beacons. In this section, we will discuss the registration and user onboarding process to join the network.

The wireless LAN connection between an endpoint and the access point leverages different types of control frames as shown in Figure 4-16.

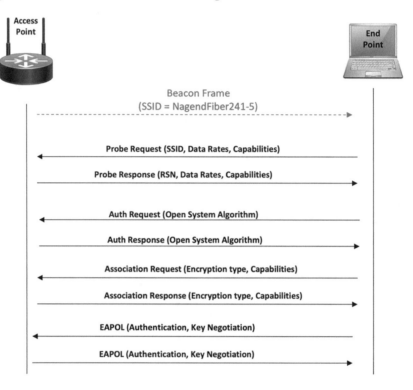

Figure 4-16. *Registration process*

In the following section, we will split the process into different phases and explain the same using 802.11 frame captures.

Probing Phase

The endpoint station will trigger the registration process by sending a Probe Request as a broadcast targeting all the access points. When there is more than one access point, the station can choose which access point to register during the association phase, based on the advertised capabilities, signal strength, etc. An example Probe Request frame is shown in Figure 4-17.

```
∨ IEEE 802.11 Probe Request, Flags: ........C
    Type/Subtype: Probe Request (0x0004)
  > Frame Control Field: 0x4000
    .000 0000 0000 0000 = Duration: 0 microseconds
    Receiver address: ff:ff:ff:ff:ff:ff
    Destination address: ff:ff:ff:ff:ff:ff
    Transmitter address: 88:66:5a:4a:0a:15
    Source address: 88:66:5a:4a:0a:15
    BSS Id: ff:ff:ff:ff:ff:ff
    .... .... .... 0000 = Fragment number: 0
    1100 1111 0101 .... = Sequence number: 3317
    Frame check sequence: 0x865e09f5 [unverified]
    [FCS Status: Unverified]
∨ IEEE 802.11 Wireless Management
  ∨ Tagged parameters (100 bytes)
    ∨ Tag: SSID parameter set: NagendFiber241-5
        Tag Number: SSID parameter set (0)
        Tag length: 16
        SSID: NagendFiber241-5
    ∨ Tag: Supported Rates 6, 9, 12, 18, 24, 36, 48, 54, [Mbit/sec]
        Tag Number: Supported Rates (1)
        Tag length: 8
        Supported Rates: 6 (0x0c)
        Supported Rates: 9 (0x12)
        Supported Rates: 12 (0x18)
        Supported Rates: 18 (0x24)
        Supported Rates: 24 (0x30)
        Supported Rates: 36 (0x48)
        Supported Rates: 48 (0x60)
        Supported Rates: 54 (0x6c)
    > Tag: HT Capabilities (802.11n D1.10)
    > Tag: Extended Capabilities (4 octets)
    > Tag: Interworking
    > Tag: VHT Capabilities
    > Tag: Vendor Specific: Apple, Inc.
    > Tag: Vendor Specific: Broadcom
```

Figure 4-17. *Probe Request frame*

During the troubleshooting or analysis, any Probe Request frames can be filtered using the following wireshark:

wlan.fc.type_subtype == 0x0008

The subtype of this frame is set to Probe Request, and this frame is sent from the endpoint station to the wireless access point. The source and the transmitter address are the same and are set to the sending endpoint station. The destination and the transmitter address are set to broadcast. The SSID is set to the tag of the wireless LAN network to which the endpoint is intending to join. While the SSID is set to the relevant name, the BSSID is set to broadcast as this frame is a broadcast and is not targeted to any specific wireless access point.

The wireless access point upon receiving the Probe Request frame will reply back with a Probe Response frame as shown in Figure 4-18.

```
> IEEE 802.11 Probe Response, Flags: ........C
∨ IEEE 802.11 Wireless Management
  ∨ Fixed parameters (12 bytes)
      Timestamp: 6673917235629
      Beacon Interval: 0.102400 [Seconds]
    ∨ Capabilities Information: 0x1111
        .... .... .... ...1 = ESS capabilities: Transmitter is an AP
        .... .... .... ..0. = IBSS status: Transmitter belongs to a BSS
        .... ..0. .... 00.. = CFP participation capabilities: No point coordinator at AP (0x00)
        .... .... ...1 .... = Privacy: AP/STA can support WEP
        .... .... ..0. .... = Short Preamble: Not Allowed
        .... .... .0.. .... = PBCC: Not Allowed
        .... .... 0... .... = Channel Agility: Not in use
        .... ...1 .... .... = Spectrum Management: Implemented
        .... .0.. .... .... = Short Slot Time: Not in use
        .... 0... .... .... = Automatic Power Save Delivery: Not Implemented
        ...1 .... .... .... = Radio Measurement: Implemented
        ..0. .... .... .... = DSSS-OFDM: Not Allowed
        .0.. .... .... .... = Delayed Block Ack: Not Implemented
        0... .... .... .... = Immediate Block Ack: Not Implemented
  ∨ Tagged parameters (186 bytes)
    > Tag: SSID parameter set: NagendFiber241-5
    > Tag: Supported Rates 6(B), 9, 12(B), 18, 24(B), 36, 48, 54, [Mbit/sec]
    > Tag: DS Parameter set: Current Channel: 149
    > Tag: Country Information: Country Code US, Environment Any
    > Tag: Power Constraint: 3
    ∨ Tag: RSN Information
        Tag Number: RSN Information (48)
        Tag length: 20
        RSN Version: 1
      > Group Cipher Suite: 00:0f:ac (Ieee 802.11) AES (CCM)
        Pairwise Cipher Suite Count: 1
      > Pairwise Cipher Suite List 00:0f:ac (Ieee 802.11) AES (CCM)
        Auth Key Management (AKM) Suite Count: 1
      > Auth Key Management (AKM) List 00:0f:ac (Ieee 802.11) PSK
      > RSN Capabilities: 0x000c
    > Tag: RM Enabled Capabilities (5 octets)
    > Tag: HT Capabilities (802.11n D1.10)
    > Tag: HT Information (802.11n D1.10)
    > Tag: Extended Capabilities (8 octets)
    > Tag: VHT Capabilities
    > Tag: VHT Operation
    > Tag: Vendor Specific: Microsoft Corp.: WMM/WME: Parameter Element
```

Figure 4-18. *Probe Response frame*

The Probe Response sent from the wireless access point is a unicast frame, and so the destination and the receiver address will be set to the MAC address of the endpoint station. The Capabilities Information field will include different types of capabilities of the access point. The ESS bit is set to 1 when the access point is configured to be part of the infrastructure network and not as an ad hoc network. The Privacy bit is set to 1 that mandates the use of security protocols to encrypt the data exchanged between the endpoint station and the access point.

It also includes the Robust Security Network information that instructs the type of authentication and encryption supported by the access point for secured onboarding and data privacy purposes.

Authentication Phase

The endpoint station upon receiving the Probe Response frame will send the Authentication frame which is a management frame for initial authentication. In this phase, the 802.11 layer 1 will be authentication, and, by default, the endpoint and the access point use Open System Authentication during this phase. Open System Authentication is equivalent to null authentication where there is no password or keys exchanged. Instead, the access point will check for BSS compatibility by comparing the received capabilities with its own. An example Authentication frame is shown in Figure 4-19.

```
IEEE 802.11 Authentication, Flags: ........C
   Type/Subtype: Authentication (0x000b)
   Frame Control Field: 0xb000
    .000 0000 0011 1100 = Duration: 60 microseconds
   Receiver address: f4:f5:e8:6d:bd:88
   Destination address: f4:f5:e8:6d:bd:88
   Transmitter address: 88:66:5a:4a:0a:15
   Source address: 88:66:5a:4a:0a:15
   BSS Id: f4:f5:e8:6d:bd:88
   .... .... .... 0000 = Fragment number: 0
   1100 1111 0110 .... = Sequence number: 3318
   Frame check sequence: 0x3c5e7768 [unverified]
   [FCS Status: Unverified]
IEEE 802.11 Wireless Management
   Fixed parameters (6 bytes)
      Authentication Algorithm: Open System (0)
      Authentication SEQ: 0x0001
      Status code: Successful (0x0000)
   Tagged parameters (11 bytes)
      Tag: Vendor Specific: Broadcom
         Tag Number: Vendor Specific (221)
         Tag length: 9
         OUI: 00:10:18 (Broadcom)
         Vendor Specific OUI Type: 2
         Vendor Specific Data: 020000100000
```

Figure 4-19. 802.11 Authentication frame

This management frame is unicasted from the endpoint station to the wireless access point. The Authentication Algorithm field is set to a value of 0 which indicates that the algorithm is Open System. The Status code is set to "Successful" in this frame.

Note   While the figure and most of the standards indicate that the authentication request and response frames are exchanged, there is just a subtype that indicates the frame as an Authentication frame. The Authentication SEQ of 1 is considered as the request and 2 as the response. Both the frames will have the Status code set to "Successful."

Association Phase

Until the authentication phase, the endpoint station may in parallel communicate with multiple access points. But the association happens with just one access point. The endpoint can decide which access point to associate based on the capabilities advertised by the access point, signal strength, signal-to-noise ratio, etc. An example Association frame is shown in Figure 4-20.

```
>  IEEE 802.11 Association Request, Flags: ........C
∨  IEEE 802.11 Wireless Management
   ∨  Fixed parameters (4 bytes)
      >  Capabilities Information: 0x0111
         Listen Interval: 0x000a
   ∨  Tagged parameters (141 bytes)
      >  Tag: SSID parameter set: NagendFiber241-5
      >  Tag: Supported Rates 6(B), 9, 12(B), 18, 24(B), 36, 48, 54, [Mbit/sec]
      >  Tag: Power Capability Min: -7, Max: 20
      ∨  Tag: Supported Channels
            Tag Number: Supported Channels (36)
            Tag length: 10
         >  Supported Channels Set #1 First: 36, Range: 4
         >  Supported Channels Set #2 First: 52, Range: 4
         >  Supported Channels Set #3 First: 100, Range: 12
         >  Supported Channels Set #4 First: 149, Range: 4
         >  Supported Channels Set #5 First: 165, Range: 1
      >  Tag: RSN Information
      >  Tag: HT Capabilities (802.11n D1.10)
      >  Tag: VHT Capabilities
      >  Tag: Vendor Specific: Apple, Inc.
      >  Tag: Vendor Specific: Broadcom
      >  Tag: Vendor Specific: Microsoft Corp.: WMM/WME: Information Element
```

Figure 4-20. *802.11 Association Request frame*

The endpoint will unicast this management frame and will include only the capabilities that match the one advertised by the access point to which the endpoint is associating. In addition, the endpoint will include all the supported channels from the spectrum to let the access point choose the one supported.

The wireless access point will reply back with the Association Response management frame that is unicasted to the endpoint station. An example frame is shown in Figure 4-21.

```
∨  IEEE 802.11 Wireless Management
   ∨ Fixed parameters (6 bytes)
      > Capabilities Information: 0x1111
        Status code: Successful (0x0000)
        ..00 0000 0000 0010 = Association ID: 0x0002
   ∨ Tagged parameters (119 bytes)
      > Tag: Supported Rates 6(B), 9, 12(B), 18, 24(B), 36, 48, 54, [Mbit/sec]
      > Tag: HT Capabilities (802.11n D1.10)
      ∨ Tag: HT Information (802.11n D1.10)
           Tag Number: HT Information (802.11n D1.10) (61)
           Tag length: 22
           Primary Channel: 149
         > HT Information Subset (1 of 3): 0x05
         > HT Information Subset (2 of 3): 0x0004
         > HT Information Subset (3 of 3): 0x0000
         > Rx Supported Modulation and Coding Scheme Set: Basic MCS Set
      > Tag: VHT Capabilities
      > Tag: VHT Operation
      > Tag: Extended Capabilities (8 octets)
      > Tag: Vendor Specific: Microsoft Corp.: WMM/WME: Parameter Element
```

Figure 4-21. *802.11 Association Response frame*

The Status code in this frame is set to "Successful," indicating the successful association of the endpoint to the wireless LAN network. The wireless access point will include the channel details to which the endpoint is associated. In the preceding example, the primary channel is marked as 149, which is of 5.745 GHz frequency with a width of 20 MHz.

802.1X Exchange Phase

Once the endpoint station is associated, a four-way handshake is used to generate and exchange the relevant set of keys to encrypt the data exchanged between the devices over the wireless medium. The first important key is known as the Pairwise Master Key (PMK) that plays a vital role in generating the encryption key. When the mode is set to WPA or WPA2 personal (that uses PSK), the PMK is the passphrase configured with the wireless network.

The first EAPOL message is sent from the access point to the endpoint station as shown in Figure 4-22.

```
 ∨ 802.1X Authentication
      Version: 802.1X-2004 (2)
      Type: Key (3)
      Length: 95
      Key Descriptor Type: EAPOL RSN Key (2)
      [Message number: 1]
   ∨ Key Information: 0x008a
          .... .... .... .010 = Key Descriptor Version: AES Cipher, HMAC-SHA1 MIC (2)
          .... .... .... 1... = Key Type: Pairwise Key
          .... .... ..00 .... = Key Index: 0
          .... .... .0.. .... = Install: Not set
          .... .... 1... .... = Key ACK: Set
          .... ...0 .... .... = Key MIC: Not set
          .... ..0. .... .... = Secure: Not set
          .... .0.. .... .... = Error: Not set
          .... 0... .... .... = Request: Not set
          ...0 .... .... .... = Encrypted Key Data: Not set
          ..0. .... .... .... = SMK Message: Not set
      Key Length: 16
      Replay Counter: 1
      WPA Key Nonce: 271e6659947dcd7f3365ef5fdfa0e8c6262ea3df62830d35719a00bb91c343d5
      Key IV: 00000000000000000000000000000000
      WPA Key RSC: 0000000000000000
      WPA Key ID: 0000000000000000
      WPA Key MIC: 00000000000000000000000000000000
      WPA Key Data Length: 0
```

Figure 4-22. *First EAPOL frame*

The access point will generate a locally unique NONCE (referred to as aNONCE) value and include the same in the first EAPOL frame. The endpoint will generate a locally unique NONCE value (referred to as sNONCE) and use a combination of aNONCE, sNONCE, access point MAC address, and endpoint MAC address to generate a Pairwise Transient Key (PTK). This key is used to encrypt all the unicast traffic.

The end point will reply to the access point by sending the next EAPOL frame as shown in Figure 4-23.

```
∨  802.1X Authentication
      Version: 802.1X-2004 (2)
      Type: Key (3)
      Length: 117
      Key Descriptor Type: EAPOL RSN Key (2)
      [Message number: 2]
   ∨  Key Information: 0x010a
         .... .... .... .010 = Key Descriptor Version: AES Cipher, HMAC-SHA1 MIC (2)
         .... .... .... 1... = Key Type: Pairwise Key
         .... .... ..00 .... = Key Index: 0
         .... .... .0.. .... = Install: Not set
         .... .... 0... .... = Key ACK: Not set
         .... ...1 .... .... = Key MIC: Set
         .... ..0. .... .... = Secure: Not set
         .... .0.. .... .... = Error: Not set
         .... 0... .... .... = Request: Not set
         ...0 .... .... .... = Encrypted Key Data: Not set
         ..0. .... .... .... = SMK Message: Not set
      Key Length: 16
      Replay Counter: 1
      WPA Key Nonce: 22c58dbe9936f0581f4aca4bce8c791589210365a1eb77030ba050fc59b89389
      Key IV: 00000000000000000000000000000000
      WPA Key RSC: 0000000000000000
      WPA Key ID: 0000000000000000
      WPA Key MIC: f7e57db19628f31fbcf1238b253b4203
      WPA Key Data Length: 22
   >  WPA Key Data: 30140100000fac040100000fac040100000fac020c00
```

Figure 4-23. *Second EAPOL frame*

As shown in Figure 4-23, the End point will include the sNONCE value that can be used by the access point to generate the PTK to encrypt the unicast traffic. The endpoint also includes the MIC value that can be used by the access point to validate the integrity of the incoming EAPOL frame.

The third EAPOL message is sent by the access point to the endpoint station as shown in Figure 4-24.

```
∨ 802.1X Authentication
      Version: 802.1X-2004 (2)
      Type: Key (3)
      Length: 151
      Key Descriptor Type: EAPOL RSN Key (2)
      [Message number: 3]
    ∨ Key Information: 0x13ca
          .... .... .... .010 = Key Descriptor Version: AES Cipher, HMAC-SHA1 MIC (2)
          .... .... .... 1... = Key Type: Pairwise Key
          .... .... ..00 .... = Key Index: 0
          .... .... .1.. .... = Install: Set
          .... .... 1... .... = Key ACK: Set
          .... ...1 .... .... = Key MIC: Set
          .... ..1. .... .... = Secure: Set
          .... .0.. .... .... = Error: Not set
          .... 0... .... .... = Request: Not set
          ...1 .... .... .... = Encrypted Key Data: Set
          ..0. .... .... .... = SMK Message: Not set
      Key Length: 16
      Replay Counter: 2
      WPA Key Nonce: 271e6659947dcd7f3365ef5fdfa0e8c6262ea3df62830d35719a00bb91c343d5
      Key IV: 00000000000000000000000000000000
      WPA Key RSC: 0000000000000000
      WPA Key ID: 0000000000000000
      WPA Key MIC: ebccc05125cb1abb573176a5958cd0d8
      WPA Key Data Length: 56
      WPA Key Data: b06a838b3d5defa0777e5f4e3ffa19846005f022102a08fee8309d9c25984514b9e8099d…
```

Figure 4-24. *Third EAPOL frame*

The "Install" flag in Key Information is set to 1 that instructs the endpoint to install and use the PTK. The access point also generates a Groupwise Temporal Key (GTK) that is used to encrypt all the broadcast and multicast traffic. This key is normally shared by multiple devices associated to the same access point. The access point will generate this GTK, encrypt it with PTK, and send it over the third EAPOL frame.

The final EAPOL frame is sent as an acknowledgment by the endpoint station to the access point. The endpoint is now ready to send and receive wireless data traffic over the channel assigned.

Wireless LAN Data Exchange

The traffic exchanged over the wireless medium is encrypted using the keys negotiated during the registration process as defined in the previous section. Any Wireshark capture file will have the ability to read and analyze the radio and 802.11 header information, but the upper layer protocols will be encrypted. One of the encrypted frames is shown in Figure 4-25.

```
>  Frame 215: 136 bytes on wire (1088 bits), 136 bytes captured (1088 bits)
>  Radiotap Header v0, Length 56
∨  802.11 radio information
      PHY type: 802.11a (OFDM) (5)
      Turbo type: Non-turbo (0)
      Data rate: 6.0 Mb/s
      Channel: 149
      Frequency: 5745MHz
      Signal strength (dBm): -66 dBm
      Noise level (dBm): -97 dBm
      Signal/noise ratio (dB): 31 dB
      TSF timestamp: 1886652427
     [Duration: 132µs]
∨  IEEE 802.11 Data, Flags: .p....F.C
      Type/Subtype: Data (0x0020)
    ∨ Frame Control Field: 0x0842
         .... ..00 = Version: 0
         .... 10.. = Type: Data frame (2)
         0000 .... = Subtype: 0
       > Flags: 0x42
         .000 0000 0000 0000 = Duration: 0 microseconds
         Receiver address: ff:ff:ff:ff:ff:ff
         Transmitter address: f4:f5:e8:6d:bd:88
         Destination address: ff:ff:ff:ff:ff:ff
         Source address: 88:66:5a:4a:0a:15
         BSS Id: f4:f5:e8:6d:bd:88
         STA address: ff:ff:ff:ff:ff:ff
         .... .... .... 0000 = Fragment number: 0
         0000 1100 1100 .... = Sequence number: 204
         Frame check sequence: 0xbe7c233e [unverified]
         [FCS Status: Unverified]
     >  CCMP parameters
   Data (44 bytes)
      Data: 2b5f8e02adcaa0485491c321bb693cfb61e9ed086c257dc222d922eaf8ee0dee9ddd9b45…
      [Length: 44]
```

Figure 4-25. *802.11 encrypted data frame*

The Frame 215 shown in Figure 4-25 is an 802.11 Data frame broadcasted from the access point to all the endpoints in the WLAN network. It could be noted that the upper layer payload encapsulated by the 802.11 header is not plain text, making it hard for analysis.

Decrypting 802.11 Data Frame Payload

In order to decrypt the 802.11 Data frames in Wireshark, we need the encryption keys that are used by the access point and the endpoint to encrypt the payload.

Generating the WPA-PSK Key

To generate the WPA-PSK key, we need the SSID and the passphrase associated to the SSID. There are different tools that can be used to generate the WPA-PSK key. One simple option is to use the WPA PSK (Raw Key) Generator tool available in the Wireshark web page: `www.wireshark.org/tools/wpa-psk.html`.

By feeding the SSID and the passphrase, the tool will help us generate the associated PSK key as shown in Figure 4-26.

Figure 4-26. *Key generator tool*

The generated PSK key is now fed to the Wireshark for decryption by selecting the options as shown in Figure 4-27.

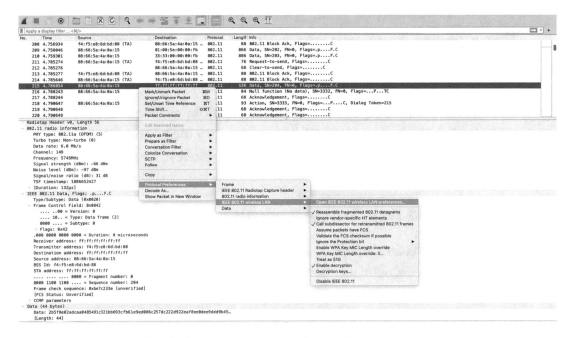

Figure 4-27. *Wireshark decryption key configuration*

The preceding selection will pop open the option to feed the WPA-PSK key file as shown in Figure 4-28.

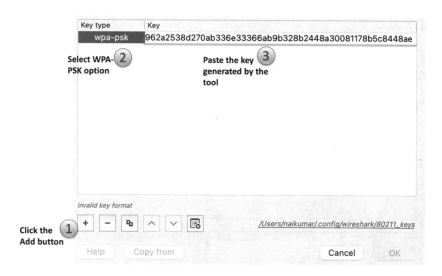

Figure 4-28. *Feeding the WPA-PSK key*

Once the key is fed, it could be noted that the Wireshark is now able to decrypt the 802.11 upper layer payload for additional analytics. The Frame 215 is decrypted to an ARP packet as shown in Figure 4-29.

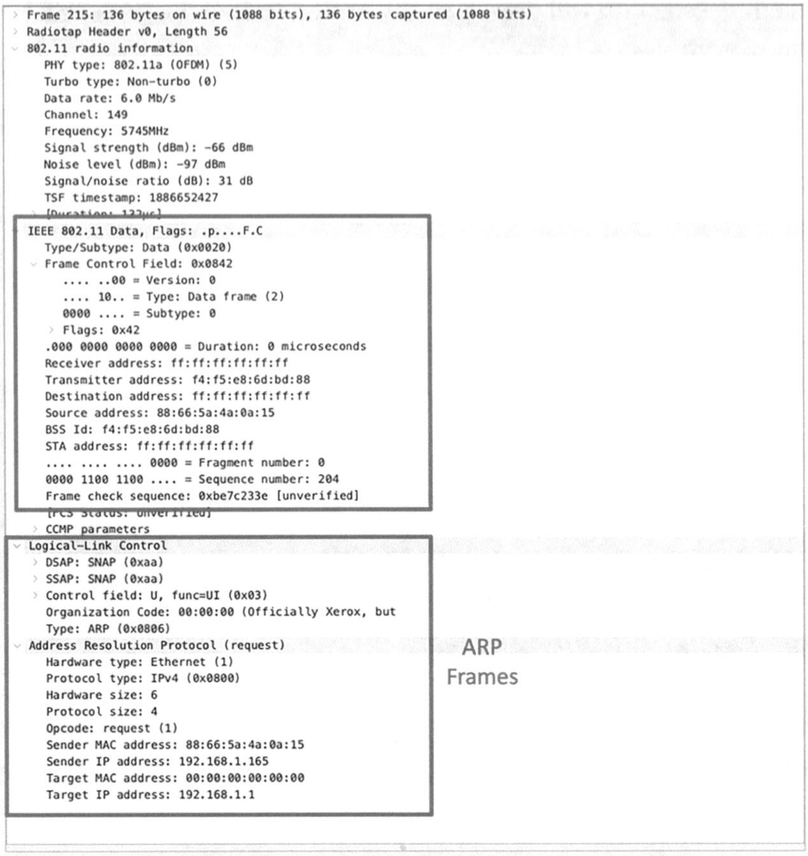

```
> Frame 215: 136 bytes on wire (1088 bits), 136 bytes captured (1088 bits)
> Radiotap Header v0, Length 56
v 802.11 radio information
    PHY type: 802.11a (OFDM) (5)
    Turbo type: Non-turbo (0)
    Data rate: 6.0 Mb/s
    Channel: 149
    Frequency: 5745MHz
    Signal strength (dBm): -66 dBm
    Noise level (dBm): -97 dBm
    Signal/noise ratio (dB): 31 dB
    TSF timestamp: 1886652427
   [Duration: 132µs]
  IEEE 802.11 Data, Flags: .p....F.C
    Type/Subtype: Data (0x0020)
  v Frame Control Field: 0x0842
      .... ..00 = Version: 0
      .... 10.. = Type: Data frame (2)
      0000 .... = Subtype: 0
    > Flags: 0x42
      .000 0000 0000 0000 = Duration: 0 microseconds
    Receiver address: ff:ff:ff:ff:ff:ff
    Transmitter address: f4:f5:e8:6d:bd:88
    Destination address: ff:ff:ff:ff:ff:ff
    Source address: 88:66:5a:4a:0a:15
    BSS Id: f4:f5:e8:6d:bd:88
    STA address: ff:ff:ff:ff:ff:ff
      .... .... .... 0000 = Fragment number: 0
      0000 1100 1100 .... = Sequence number: 204
    Frame check sequence: 0xbe7c233e [unverified]
   [FCS Status: Unverified]
  > CCMP parameters
v Logical-Link Control
  > DSAP: SNAP (0xaa)
  > SSAP: SNAP (0xaa)
  > Control field: U, func=UI (0x03)
    Organization Code: 00:00:00 (Officially Xerox, but
    Type: ARP (0x0806)
v Address Resolution Protocol (request)
    Hardware type: Ethernet (1)
    Protocol type: IPv4 (0x0800)
    Hardware size: 6
    Protocol size: 4
    Opcode: request (1)
    Sender MAC address: 88:66:5a:4a:0a:15
    Sender IP address: 192.168.1.165
    Target MAC address: 00:00:00:00:00:00
    Target IP address: 192.168.1.1
```

ARP

Frames

Figure 4-29. *802.11 decrypted data frame*

Note   During the time of this chapter authoring, decryption support for WPA3 is a work under progress. More support will be available in the future, which is currently outside the scope of this chapter.

Wireless LAN Statistics Using Wireshark

During any wireless LAN troubleshooting, it might be interesting to know the list of all the SSIDs and any relevant details such as the associated channels for those SSIDs or additional statistics such as the frame counts and types for each SSID. The Wireshark tool allows us to pull such statistics on a per-pcap file basis. The statistics for wireless LAN traffic can be listed using the option shown in Figure 4-30.

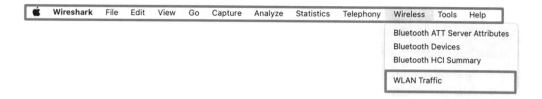

Figure 4-30. *WLAN statistics options*

The Wireshark tool will list the statistics of all the 802.11 frames on a per-SSID basis as shown in Figure 4-31.

BSSID	Channel	SSID	Percent Packets	Percent Retry	Retry	Beacons	Data Pkts	Probe Reqs	Probe Resp	Auths	Deauths	Other	Protection
00:25:00:ff:94:73		<Broadcast>	15.5	0.0	0	0	0	0	0	0	0	230	
1c:f2:9a:7e:15:2e	149	m@noy@$h	11.4	0.0	0	119	49	0	1	0	0	0	Unknown
1c:f2:9a:7e:29:d9	149	m@noy@$h	14.0	1.0	2	122	59	0	3	0	0	23	Unknown
1e:f2:9a:7e:15:2c	149	Manoyash_Guest	8.3	0.0	0	121	0	0	2	0	0	0	
1e:f2:9a:7e:15:2d		<Broadcast>	3.8	1.8	1	0	53	0	0	0	0	4	Unknown
1e:f2:9a:7e:29:d8	149	Manoyash_Guest	8.3	0.8	1	120	0	0	3	0	0	0	
1e:f2:9a:7e:29:d9	149	<Broadcast>	5.7	1.2	1	12	63	0	0	0	0	10	Unknown
86:2a:fd:65:e4:62		DIRECT-62-HP O...	8.4	0.0	0	122	0	0	2	0	0	0	
9a:7e:15:2d:1e:f2		<Broadcast>	0.1	0.0	0	0	1	0	0	0	0	0	Unknown
9a:7e:29:d9:1e:f2		<Broadcast>	0.4	16.7	1	0	6	0	0	0	0	0	Unknown
f4:f5:e8:6d:bd:88	149	NagendFiber241-5	13.8	4.4	9	120	62	0	6	2	4	10	CCMP
f4:f5:e8:6e:5c:00	149	VISAHOME	9.2	0.0	0	114	22	0	0	0	0	0	Unknown
ff:ff:ff:ff:ff:ff		Sonos_YPIWM4K...	0.6	0.0	0	0	0	9	0	0	0	0	
ff:ff:ff:ff:ff:ff		NagendFiber241-5	0.1	0.0	0	0	0	1	0	0	0	0	
ff:ff:ff:ff:ff:ff		777	0.1	0.0	0	0	0	2	0	0	0	0	
ff:ff:ff:ff:ff:ff		Nagendra Kumar...	0.1	0.0	0	0	0	2	0	0	0	0	
ff:ff:ff:ff:ff:ff		NagendraKumar ...	0.1	0.0	0	0	0	2	0	0	0	0	
ff:ff:ff:ff:ff:ff		<Broadcast>	0.1	0.0	0	0	0	2	0	0	0	0	

Figure 4-31. *WLAN statistics output*

Note   Additional statistics of WLAN traffic on a per-MAC address basis is also available in the same statistics window. By clicking the respective SSID/BSSID tab, we will be able to analyze the percentage of frames sent by each device on a per-MAC basis.

Summary

In this chapter, we discussed about the basics of the wireless spectrum along with the definitions of different radio spectrum characteristics and how they help us realize the cablefree world. We further discussed about different licensed and unlicensed bands, channel ranges for each of the bands, and how they can be used for wireless LAN deployments. We also discussed about different deployment topologies.

We further looked deep into capturing and analyzing 802.11 frames over the wireless medium. We discussed about different configuration options to set the radiotap in different operating systems and how to further dissect the fields. We discussed about different wireless security protocols and how they encrypt the data frames and also the options available in Wireshark to decrypt for analysis purposes.

References for This Chapter

IEEE 802.11: `www.ieee802.org/11/`

FCC 2.4 GHz: `https://transition.fcc.gov/Bureaus/Engineering_Technology/Orders/2000/fcc00312.pdf`

WPA3 Specification: `www.wi-fi.org/download.php?file=/sites/default/files/private/WPA3_Specification_v3.0.pdf`

Wireless LAN Display Filters: `www.wireshark.org/docs/dfref/w/wlan.html`

WPA-PSK Key Generator Tool: `www.wireshark.org/tools/wpa-psk.html`

CHAPTER 5

Multimedia Packet Capture and Analysis

In today's Internet, multimedia and streaming audio/video traffic dominate over other data traffic. According to some surveys, 60% of the overall web traffic belongs to digital audio/video and streaming applications, and it's growing.

Multimedia applications can be streaming stored audio/video content, or there can be a real-time audio/video call. Some of the traffic can be sensitive to delay jitter and network performance. Wireshark helps in troubleshooting and analysis of such application data transfer from a network perspective.

In this chapter, you will learn about how Wireshark helps capture and analyze various types of multimedia application traffic. The following is a summary of some of the important concepts that will be discussed in this chapter:

- Popular multimedia protocols in use

- Capturing multimedia objects (files, images, etc.) in a data stream

- Capture and analysis of streaming applications

- Capture and analysis of secure real-time audio/video applications

Multimedia Applications and Protocols

Multimedia applications may consist of multiple types of media like text, images, audio, and video, sometimes all together or any combination of these. For example, streaming Netflix multimedia content may have different audio, video, images, and text in the same stream.

N. K. Nainar and A. Panda, *Wireshark for Network Forensics*, https://doi.org/10.1007/978-1-4842-9001-9_5

Multimedia on the Web

Normally, the multimedia content over the Web is transported using HTTP or HTTPS using a TCP transport. But more and more implementations are moving toward HTTP/3 over QUIC, which uses the UDP transport.

The web multimedia content can be sourced as embedded files, stored locally, and played by the browser as most browsers with HTML5 support audio, video, and images natively without needing additional players. In some scenarios, specialized audio or video players may be requesting and receiving the content.

Audio and video files can have a specific format like WebM, MP3, MP4, etc. These are basically containers which define the structure and specification of how the embedded multimedia content is packaged. The container may have the following details.

- Metadata describing the title, length, etc.

- Text media which has text tracks for subtitles.

- The audio may have multiple audio tracks. The container format defines the type of audio codec or algorithm used to encode and decode the analog audio in digital format.

- Embedded video may have multiple video tracks encoded in the specific video codec.

An example of a container format is MP4 which packages video using H.264 video codec and audio in AAC or MP3 audio codec. WebM format packages video in VP8/9 video codec and audio in Vorbis or Opus audio codec.

Wireshark supports multiple codec formats and can decode captured data that is using a supported codec. The Supported codecs on your Wireshark installations can be found from the ***about Wireshark ➤ plugins*** screen.

Multimedia Streaming

Streaming involves delivering multimedia content in real time and playing the same in real time without storing locally. Streaming can be for live content (audio/video broadcast, webcasts) or stored content (movie, music, recordings, etc.).

Streaming Transport

The use of Wireshark capture can help identify the type of transport and encoding being used by the streaming providers. The transport protocols may vary from streaming provider to provider. A summary of some studies done for a few popular streaming implementations and providers is as follows:

- Netflix uses HTTP1.1 over TCP and can use up to ten parallel sessions.

- Amazon Prime uses HTTP/2 over a TCP transport and normally uses one session.

- YouTube uses a mix of DASH (Dynamic Adaptive Streaming over HTTP) over TCP (approx. 40%) and QUIC using UDP (approx. 60%). The TCP part can have up to six sessions.

- **RTSP**: Many streaming implementations may use RTSP (Real-Time Streaming Protocol). RTSP uses TCP for stream control (start, stop, play, etc.). The actual stream media delivery with RTSP normally uses RTP (Real-Time Transport Protocol) for content along with RTCP (Real-Time Control Protocol) for statistics and QoS. Some RTSP implementations may use other content delivery protocols as well apart from RTP/RTCP.

- **RTMP**: RTMP (Real-Time Messaging Protocol) is used in Flash Player–based media communication. It is a proprietary protocol with some specifications made open for public use by the owner Adobe. Though it's an aging protocol, many implementations still exist, mostly for source-to-server content distribution.

  RTMP uses multiple channels for session control and data transport multiplexed over the same TCP session. To facilitate real-time communication, it fragments data into default 64 bytes for voice and 128 bytes for video and can multiplex fragments of different channels into a single TCP session. There is a UDP variant (RTMFP) and a secure variant (RTMPE) of RTMP available for use.

Stream Encoding Format

A packet capture with Wireshark will help identify the exact streaming format. The media format may vary based on the device being used, content provider, and implementation. Also, the encoding type varies from bandwidth availability, requested resolution by the client, etc.

As an example, YouTube supports MP4, WebM, and HLS formats for most high bandwidth sessions and may use FLV, 3GP, etc. for low bandwidth, low-resolution sessions. Also, documentations suggest a movement toward AV1 format for better quality and bandwidth savings.

Real-Time Multimedia

With real-time communications like audio and video calls and conferencing, the content is played in real time and not stored locally similar to streaming media. Real-time media are susceptible to delay, jitter, and packet drops. Hence, UDP is preferred for transporting real-time media. However, HTTPS over TCP may be seen for audio/video signaling in some implementations. The following are some of the common protocols in use for real-time audio/video calls or conferencing.

Signaling

SIP

The Session Initiation Protocol works on UDP and is one of the widely used protocols for choice for signaling audio/video calls. SIP signaling between the endpoints and endpoints to the server makes an IP phone behave like a normal PSTN phone. SIP handles registering the endpoints with the media servers, responsible for dial tone generation, dialing numbers, ringtone, call accept, reject, call forwarding, call waiting, etc.

SDP

SIP works hand in hand with another signaling protocol called Session Description Protocol. SDP is included in the SIP packet payload itself. SDP helps endpoints to communicate their preference of the type of media or media attributes being used for the actual voice packets being transported. For example, the SDP header specifies media attributes like, codec type used, bit rate, transport protocol (RTP) etc.

Figure 5-1 shows the detailed headers of SIP and SDP.

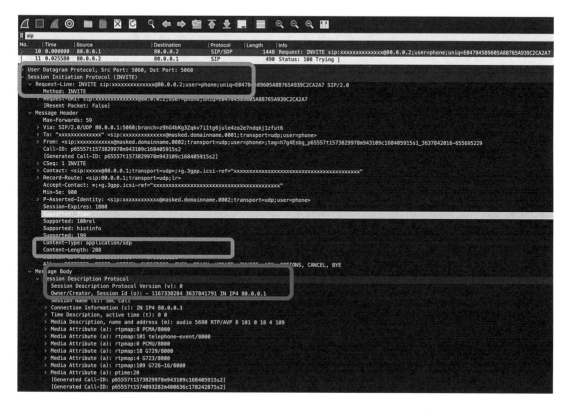

Figure 5-1. *SIP and SDP*

SIP over TLS (SIPS)

In the latest deployments, a secure version of SIP is preferred which uses SIP over TLS (Transport Layer Security), which provides encryption, authentication, and integrity protection. TLS was described in detail in Chapter 3. The updated version of RFC3261 describes both SIP and SIP over TLS. TLS standards are described in RFC5246 (TLS 1.2) and RFC8446 (TLS 1.3)

H.323

H.323 is the recommended protocol of choice by ITUT. Although not as popular as SIP, H.323 is normally seen with implementations where video calls are also in use. H.323 is a suite of protocols which has various individual protocols for each signaling aspect like registration, call signaling, call control, statistics, etc. The H.323 suite uses RTP for actual voice packet transport.

Media Transport

The multimedia transport protocols help transport actual voice packets over the IP network. UDP is the protocol of choice, but some implementations may have the option to switch to TCP in case UDP doesn't work due to infrastructures not allowing the same. The following are some of the popular protocols.

RTP

Real-Time Transport Protocol works on UDP and is the most popular protocol of choice. Once the signaling protocols SIP, H.323, etc. signal the session, voice packets start getting transported through RTP using the negotiated parameters like RTP UDP port, encoding, bitrate, etc. RTP is not connection oriented, but it maintains a packet sequence number and timestamp to help in the detection of packet loss, jitter, etc. However, RTP has no mechanism to detect losses. It uses RTCP for the same.

RTCP

The Real-Time Transport Control Protocol is sometimes known as the sister protocol of RTP and helps in statistics collection, packet loss, and jitter analysis. RTCP acts as feedback to the RTP endpoints and helps in improving the quality of the session.

RTP

```
> Frame 493: 214 bytes on wire (1712 bits), 214 bytes captured (1712 bits)
> Ethernet II, Src: 00:00:00_00:00:00 (00:00:00:00:00:00), Dst: 00:00:00_00:00:00 (00:00:00:00:00:00)
> Internet Protocol Version 4, Src: 80.0.0.3, Dst: 80.0.0.2
> User Datagram Protocol, Src Port: 40376, Dst Port: 8000
∨ Real-Time Transport Protocol
    > [Stream setup by SDP (frame 10)]
      10.. .... = Version: RFC 1889 Version (2)
      ..0. .... = Padding: False
      ...0 .... = Extension: False
      .... 0000 = Contributing source identifiers count: 0
      0... .... = Marker: False
      Payload type: ITU-T G.711 PCMA (8)
      Sequence number: 11331
      [Extended sequence number: 76867]
      Timestamp: 289878434
      Synchronization Source identifier: 0x58f33dea (1492336106)
      Payload: d55bd54556d454d556de515655d5d1d5d455515153d5515455d5564f5edec0dbdcc3dbd6…
```

RTCP

```
∨ Real-time Transport Control Protocol (Sender Report)
    > [Stream setup by SDP (frame 10)]
      10.. .... = Version: RFC 1889 Version (2)
      ..0. .... = Padding: False
      ...0 0001 = Reception report count: 1
      Packet type: Sender Report (200)
      Length: 12 (52 bytes)
      Sender SSRC: 0xd2bd4e3e (3535621694)
      Timestamp, MSW: 3314714324 (0xc59286d4)
      Timestamp, LSW: 4131758539 (0xf645a1cb)
      [MSW and LSW as NTP timestamp: Jan 14, 2005 17:58:44.962000000 UTC]
      RTP timestamp: 640
      Sender's packet count: 4
      Sender's octet count: 640
    ∨ Source 1
        Identifier: 0xd2bd4e3e (3535621694)
      ∨ SSRC contents
          Fraction lost: 0 / 256
          Cumulative number of packets lost: 0
        > Extended highest sequence number received: 262148
          Interarrival jitter: 0
          Last SR timestamp: 2262103621 (0x86d4f645)
          Delay since last SR timestamp: 1 (0 milliseconds)
∨ Real-time Transport Control Protocol (Receiver Report)
    > [Stream setup by SDP (frame 10)]
      10.. .... = Version: RFC 1889 Version (2)
      ..0. .... = Padding: False
      ...0 0001 = Reception report count: 1
      Packet type: Receiver Report (201)
      Length: 7 (32 bytes)
      Sender SSRC: 0xd2bd4e3e (3535621694)
    ∨ Source 1
        Identifier: 0x58f33dea (1492336106)
      ∨ SSRC contents
          Fraction lost: 0 / 256
          Cumulative number of packets lost: 0
        ∨ Extended highest sequence number received: 11332
            Sequence number cycles count: 0
            Highest sequence number received: 11332
          Interarrival jitter: 0
          Last SR timestamp: 2262103621 (0x86d4f645)
          Delay since last SR timestamp: 1 (0 milliseconds)
> Real-time Transport Control Protocol (Source description)
```

Figure 5-2. *RTP and RTCP*

SRTP and SRTCP

RTP packets can be easily decoded using specific codecs. With SRTP, the voice packets can be encrypted, which makes voice calls secure. To decrypt, the master key should be known, which was used to encrypt the packets. SRTP uses an AES default 128 key for encryption. Also, packet authentication and integrity are supported with the HMAC-SHA1 algorithm, which produces a 160-bit hash truncated to 32 bits to be tagged with each packet. Also, antireplay protection is done by tracking each sequence number, and if the same sequence number is seen again, it's dropped.

For session statistics collection and quality control, SRTP uses SRTCP which is the secure version of RTCP.

WebRTC

With peer-to-peer communications, evolving WebRTC (WebRTC) is becoming one of the most popular protocols that enable web browsers to establish a secure peer-to-peer real-time voice, video, or text messaging session. WebRTC is open source and thereby enables cross-app communication also. Most of the mobile voice/video messaging applications like Google Hangouts, WhatsApp, Facebook Messenger, and Cisco Webex are adopting WebRTC.

From a protocol perspective, WebRTC can use SIP, SIP with TLS, or any other signaling method. For media transportation, SRTP is used for secure communication. As the endpoints normally are behind NAT but their web browsers need to establish peer-to-peer sessions, they must discover their own and peer public IP. WebRTC uses external STUN or TURN servers to discover the same and establish peer-to-peer sessions.

How Can Wireshark Help

Wireshark can help with multimedia communication in many ways. The following are some of the important ones:

- Wireshark can simulate an application by reconstructing the content from the captures. For example, it can replay an RTP audio stream, extract file objects, etc. This comes in handy with forensic analysis.

- Wireshark captures help in application profiling, protocols in use, and understanding of the underlying multimedia communication.

- Wireshark capture can help find if the application is sending a multimedia packet with the right QoS and whether it is being given adequate priority in the network or not.

- Wireshark capture can help in capacity planning. If we do not know at what rate a stream is playing and to scale up such sessions how much bandwidth is needed, we can capture one session and analyze the same.

- Multimedia communications are sensitive to delay, jitter, and packet drop. A Wireshark packet capture and analysis can clearly show if the application is suffering due to any such issues in the network.

- Sometimes, a video or audio communication may break due to the application issues on any of the endpoints. A Wireshark packet capture can clearly establish whether it's an application issue or a network side issue.

Multimedia File Extraction from HTTP Capture

Web applications can have embedded multimedia objects like audio, images, or video. If the captured packets of the communication between the client and the server are stitched together with Wireshark, the objects can be reconstructed without having the end application running.

Wireshark as of version 3.6.7 supports extracting objects from an HTTP/1 stream. HTTP/2 and HTTP/3 are not supported yet. Refer to the Wireshark issue 16126, tracked through `https://gitlab.com/wireshark/wireshark/-/issues/16126`. For such objects which can't be done automatically by Wireshark, manual reassembly of packet payload needs to be done.

To start an extraction, follow the GUI menu *File ➤ export objects ➤ HTTP*.

This opens the following dialogue box which shows various objects detected in the HTTP stream. In our case, you can see multiple image objects. The filename is anonymized and shows as XXXX, but in the actual scenario, it shows the name.

Click the right file to export and hit save to save the file. The file can be opened in the relevant applications.

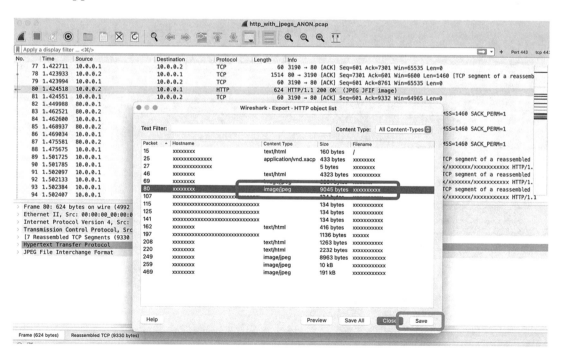

Figure 5-3. *HTTP multimedia file export*

Streaming RTP Video Captures

Unlike static files, a streaming audio/video is not completely saved on the client but played as it is received in chunks.

RTP is often used as the transport protocol for real-time audio and video. The following is a sample capture snapshot of an RTP stream transporting MPEG-2 formatted video content. If the stream uses nonstandard RTP ports, Wireshark has to be instructed to treat it as RTP. You can do so by right-clicking the stream, choosing *decode as*, and under the current column, choosing *RTP* as the protocol. Details about the format and encoding were discussed in the section "Stream Encoding Format."

Wireshark analysis of the capture can help with the encoding-related issues and packet drops. Even the stream can be replayed with a built-in RTP replay feature on Wireshark. We will discuss this in more detail in the upcoming section "RTP Stream Analysis."

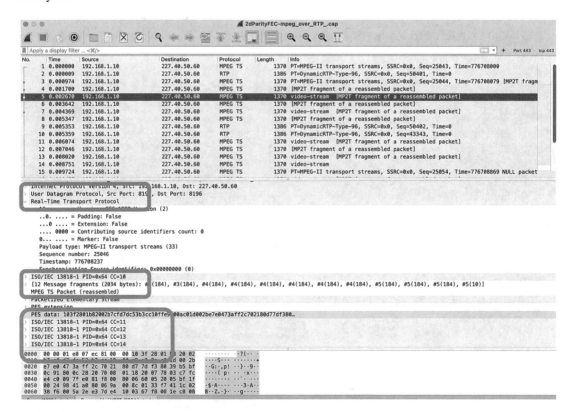

Figure 5-4. *Streaming MPEG-2 over RTP*

Real-Time Media Captures and Analysis

We had a detailed discussion on real-time multimedia communications in the section "Real-Time Multimedia." In this section, we will learn about the features available in Wireshark to capture and analyze audio/video calls with RTP, SIP, and SRTP-based communications.

Most of the modern implementations including WebRTC are using secure signaling (SIP with TLS) and secure transport (with SRTP) for real-time multimedia.

This section focuses on secure SIP (SIP with TLS) and secure RTP with SRTP. However, all discussions remain applicable to SIP/SDP and RTP/RTCP except the decryption part.

Decrypting Signaling (SIP over TLS)

Signaling in real-time applications and telephony handles the session initiation, maintenance, and termination aspects. SIP is the most common UDP-based signaling protocol in use, and with modern implementations, SIP is being replaced with SIP over TLS (also known as SIPS) based on TCP transport. The updated version of RFC3261 describes both SIP and SIP over TLS. TLS standards are described in RFC5246 (TLS 1.2) and RFC8446 (TLS 1.3).

Wireshark supports decrypting SIP over TLS if the key is known. A key can be obtained easily from the application side on the server or on the client. We are not specifying the exact method of key extraction as it can vary from application to application, but details on the same can be found on `https://wiki.wireshark.org/TLS`.

TLS can have two popular choices of key exchange, that is, **RSA** and **DHE** or its better variant **ECDHE** (Diffie-Hellman key exchange/Elliptic-Curve DHE).

The server hello packet shows the key exchange type and the Cipher Suite in use. Details can be seen from Figure 5-9.

153

Depending on whether it's an RSA key or a DHE type key exchange, the Wireshark can be fed with the key for decrypting the TLS packet in a flexible way. The following methods are supported by Wireshark:

- Method 1: Premaster keylog file

   This is the same process as the one discussed in Chapter 3 at the TLS decryption section. It supports both RSA and DHE key exchange types of the keys. The dialogue can be launched by navigating through the menu **Wireshark ➤ Preferences ➤ Protocols ➤ TLS**.

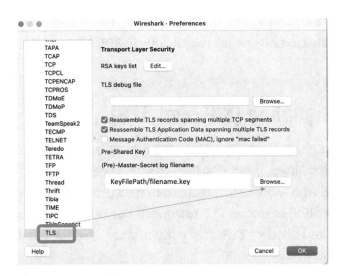

Figure 5-5. *Premaster keylog file*

- Method 2: RSA keys dialogue [all packets]

   - The dialogue can be launched by navigating through the menu **Wireshark ➤ Preferences ➤ RSA keys**.

   - The capture file should be closed and opened for the keys to take effect.

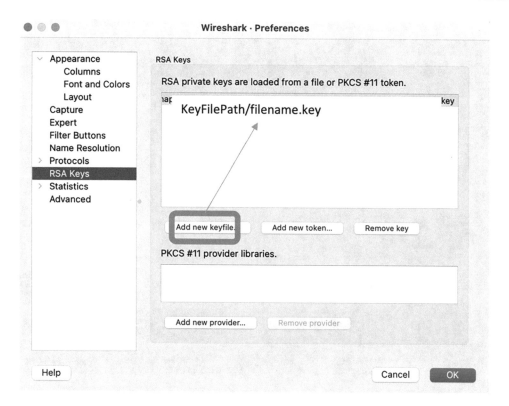

Figure 5-6. *RSA keys dialogue for all packets*

- Method 3: RSA keys list dialogue [specific to connection]

  - The dialogue can be launched by navigating through the menu **Wireshark ➤ Preferences ➤ Protocols ➤ TLS**.

  - Method 2 is recommended over method 3 as it is being deprecated in the future.

  - Both methods 2 and 3 do not support TLS 1.3 yet as of the writing of this book.

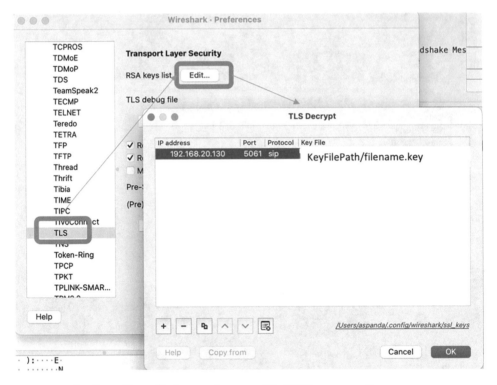

Figure 5-7. *RSA keys lists dialogue for specific TCP connection*

- Method 4: Right click, protocol preference dialogue

    - The dialogue can be launched by clicking the desired packet being displayed and clicking the menu item "protocol preferences," navigating through the menu **Wireshark ➤ Preferences ➤ Protocols ➤ TLS**.

    - An appropriate option in the same menu can be chosen.

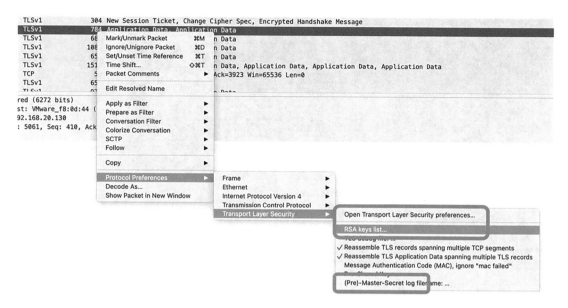

Figure 5-8. *TLS packet protocol preference*

Packets before decryption can be seen as encrypted application data, but post decryption, SIP-related detailed packet structure can be seen. If the packet is not getting decoded properly, the decode as SIP portion can be tried after right-clicking the specific packet.

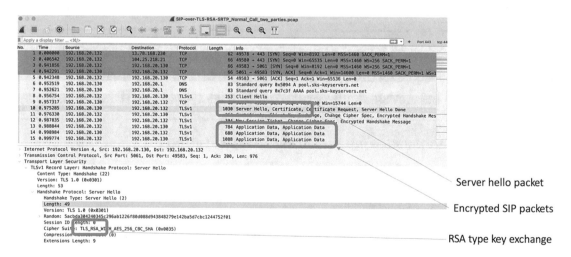

Figure 5-9. *SIP over TLS packets – encrypted*

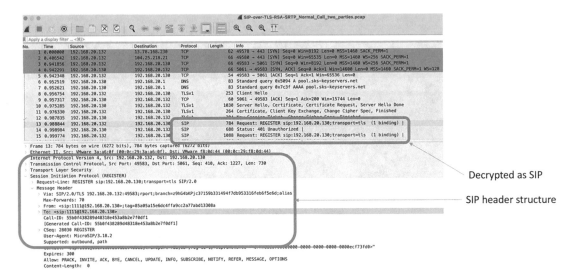

Figure 5-10. *SIP over TLS packets – decrypted*

Decrypting Secure RTP

SRTP payload is encrypted using a key received through the SDP packet as part of SIP signaling. SDP (Session Descriptor Protocol) defines the parameters for the SRTP session, in this case, the secure key. If SIP over TLS is used for signaling, then the SDP packet has to be decrypted first to extract the key that is used for SRTP.

Wireshark (3.6.7) doesn't have the capability to decode SRTP packets as of writing this book. This section describes the use of the open source utility **libsrtp** in conjunction with the Wireshark utility **text2pcap** to decrypt the SRTP packets.

The following are the steps involved in the decryption of SRTP:

- Extract the SRTP encryption key from SDP.

- Filter SRTP-only packets.

- Feed the key and SRTP packets to libsrtp.

- Convert text format to pcap with text2pcap and add the missing UDP header.

Extract the SRTP Encryption Key from SDP

The SIP over TLS packets first need to be decrypted using steps described in the section "Decrypting Signaling (SIP over TLS)."

- Then filter SDP packets and look for the packet from the server, which shows **Status OK**.

- From the crypto media attribute, copy the value of the key string after character "**inline**". This is a base64-encoded key, but no need to decode as libsrtp supports in the same format.

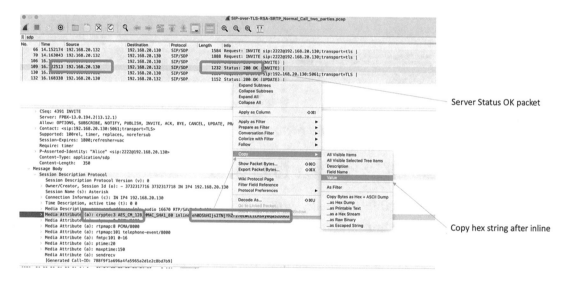

Figure 5-11. *Extracting the SRTP encryption key*

Filter SRTP-only Packets

The libsrtp utility does not work well when there are SRTP and mixed type packets in the pcap file. To work around this, the SRTP packets can be filtered with a simple display filter matching "rtp."

It can be seen from the figure that the SRTP frames have the payload in the encrypted format. The selected frames can be exported into a single file by navigating to the menu **File ➤ Export specified packets**.

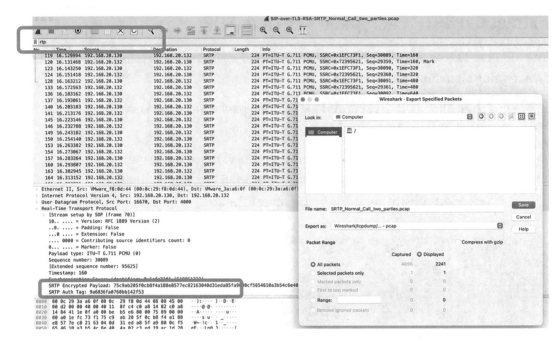

Figure 5-12. *Filter SRTP packets and export*

Feed the Key and SRTP Packets to Libsrtp

Libsrtp is an open source utility originally written by Cisco engineer David McGrew but has got good community contribution. The package, if not installed, can be cloned from the GitHub repo (https://github.com/cisco/libsrtp) and compiled before execution:

```
% git clone https://github.com/cisco/libsrtp.git
% cd libsrtp
% ./configure
% make
<SNIP>
Build done. Please run
% cd test
user@host/libsrtp/test % ./rtp_decoder -a -t 10 -e 128 -b
ehODSbHIjs2TNjYhZrz7ecWCLiLRskyOqaS2bOGU * < SRTP_Call_capture.pcap | more
Using libsrtp2 2.5.0-pre [0x2050000]
security services: confidentiality message authentication
setting tag len 10
```

```
set master key/salt to 7a1d0349b1c88ecd9336362166bcfb79/
c5822e22d1b24cb4a9a4b66ce194
Starting decoder
00:00.000000
0000 80 00 75 89 00 00 00 a0 1e fc 73 f1 ff ff ff ff
0010 ff ff ff ff ff ff ff ff ff ff ff ff ff ff ff ff
0020 ff ff ff ff ff ff ff ff ff ff ff ff ff ff ff ff
0030 ff ff ff ff ff ff ff ff ff ff ff ff ff ff ff ff
0040 ff ff ff ff ff ff ff ff ff ff ff ff ff ff ff ff
0050 ff ff ff ff ff ff ff ff ff ff ff ff ff ff ff ff
0060 ff ff ff ff ff ff ff ff ff ff ff ff ff ff ff ff
0070 ff ff ff ff ff ff ff ff ff ff ff ff ff ff ff ff
0080 ff ff ff ff ff ff ff ff ff ff ff ff ff ff ff ff
0090 ff ff ff ff ff ff ff ff ff ff ff ff ff ff ff ff
00a0 ff ff ff ff ff ff ff ff ff ff ff ff
00:00.013256
```

> **Note**   Libsrtp decrypts the payload and strips off all headers including Ethernet,
> IP, and the UDP header. When there is silence, the RTP packet payload can be seen
> as all FF.

Convert Text Format to pcap and Add the Missing UDP Header

Libsrtp dumps the decrypted SRTP payload (which is RTP) in text format as simple RTP
packets with no other header. As RTP uses the UDP transport, without that packets can't
be dissected properly. Hence, a dummy Ethernet, IP, and UDP header can be added
while converting from text to pcap with the **text2pcap** utility. Text2pcap comes by
default along with all Wireshark installations.

Note   Libsrtp decrypt and text2pcap conversion can be combined and executed as a single command by piping libsrtp output to text2pcap as shown in the following:

```
test %./rtp_decoder -a -t 10 -e 128 -b
ehODSbHIjs2TNjYhZrz7ecWCLiLRskyOqaS2bOGU * < SRTP_Call_
capture.pcap | text2pcap -t "%M:%S." -u 10000,10000 - - >
SRTP_decoded.pcap
Using libsrtp2 2.5.0-pre [0x2050000]
security services: confidentiality message authentication
setting tag len 10
set master key/salt to
7a1d0349b1c88ecd9336362166bcfb79/c5822e22d1b24cb4a9a4b66ce194
Starting decoder
Input from: Standard input
Output to: Standard output
Output format: pcap
Generate dummy Ethernet header: Protocol: 0x800
Generate dummy IP header: Protocol: 17
Generate dummy UDP header: Source port: 11000.
Dest port: 11000
Wrote packet of 214 bytes.
Wrote packet of 214 bytes.
Wrote packet of 214 bytes.
Read 1118 potential packets, wrote 1118 packets (257164 bytes).
test %
```

Explanation of Options Used Previously

For libsrtp and text2pcap, the meaning of each option can be verified with the -h option. The ones used in the preceding example are described as follows.

For SRTP Decode

As we can see from Figure 5-11, the Cipher Suite used in the SRTP packets is **AES_CM_128_HMAC_SHA1_80**. This means

-**e** = The key length for AES encryption is 128 bytes.

-**b** = The key supplied is in base64 or ASCII type and not in hex or binary.

-**a** -**t** = The authentication and antireplay tag (hash) length is 80 bits = 10 bytes.

For text2pcap

-**t** = Timestamp format to be added in the packet **"%H:%M:%S."**.

-**u 11000, 11000** = Add a UDP header (source and destination port 11000 in this case) with a new related IP and Ethernet header.

If any nonstandard RTP port is used like 11000 in this case, Wireshark won't be able to dissect the packet as RTP. In this case, after opening the pcap file, right-click the packet and choose the menu item *Decode as* and specify RTP.

Telephony and Video Analysis

Wireshark packet capture and analysis can help troubleshoot any application or network issues affecting the audio and video quality. Wireshark has got good built-in tools for SIP, RTP, and other protocol analyses. The following section describes some of the tools, techniques, and analysis approaches.

Wireshark Optimization for VoIP

The default Wireshark display and UDP decode approach can be slightly tweaked to have a quick analysis:

- **Displaying source and destination ports**: Wireshark by default doesn't show source and destination transport ports in the display. Although absolutely not necessary, it may help in identifying some streams with port numbers that are not decoded by Wireshark. The dialogue box can be launched from **Wireshark Preferences ➤ Appearances ➤ Columns**, and add the entries as shown in Figure 5-13.

- **Heuristic RTP decodes:** RTP stream UDP ports in use can use a range of nondefault ports. What port is currently in use is announced by SIP Session Descriptor Protocol (SDP) packets at the start of the session. But if we do not have the SDP packets captured in the same file, Wireshark can't interpret the packet with a nondefault UDP port as RTP.

    - Wireshark has an automated workaround and when enabled tries to treat every nondefault UDP packet as RTP. If the decode is successful, it will decode as RTP, and if not successful, it will leave it as an unknown UDP packet. This option can be enabled by launching the dialogue from **Analyze ➤ Enabled Protocols ➤** search for **RTP ➤** tick/select the **rtp_udp** option available under RTP.

Figure 5-13. Wireshark optimization for audio/video analysis

QoS and Network Issues

Real-time communication needs priority treatment at the network over any other data packets. Without this, they may get affected due to congestion, buffering delays, packet drops, etc. QoS values (CoS, ToS, DSCP) are marked either by the source applications or at the edge of the network by the networking equipment like routers or switches. All other devices in the network are configured to give priority treatment for the assigned QoS markings.

However, if some applications don't mark the packet properly (mismatch on the network config and application markings), the markings can be cross-checked with Wireshark packet captures. ToS/DSCP markings can be verified on the IP header and CoS on the dot1q header.

If the issue is isolated to a particular network device, the packet capture at the input and output of the device can be compared to see QoS values (from the packet header), packet drops, jitter (RTP analysis), and throughput (I/O graphs). Corrective action can be taken accordingly.

```
> Frame 47: 528 bytes on wire (4224 bits), 528 bytes captured (4224 bits)
> Ethernet II, Src: VMware_3a:a6:0f (00:0c:29:3a:a6:0f), Dst: VMware_f8:0d:44 (00:0c:29:f8:0d:44)
v Internet Protocol Version 4, Src: 192.168.20.132, Dst: 192.168.20.130
    0100 .... = Version: 4
    .... 0101 = Header Length: 20 bytes (5)
  > Differentiated Services Field: 0x00 (DSCP: CS0, ECN: Not-ECT)
    Total Length: 514
    Identification: 0x7de4 (32228)
  > Flags: 0x40, Don't fragment
    ...0 0000 0000 0000 = Fragment Offset: 0
    Time to Live: 128
    Protocol: TCP (6)
    Header Checksum: 0x0000 [validation disabled]
    [Header checksum status: Unverified]
    Source Address: 192.168.20.132
    Destination Address: 192.168.20.130
> Transmission Control Protocol, Src Port: 49560, Dst Port: 5061, Seq: 5110, Ack: 5175, Len: 474
> Transport Layer Security
> Session Initiation Protocol (ACK)
v Session Initiation Protocol (SIP as raw text)
    ACK sip:2222@192.168.20.130;transport=tls SIP/2.0
    Via: SIP/2.0/TLS 192.168.20.132:49560;rport;branch=z9hG4bKPjc34df8d445174e65880a8d64a1d7b09c;alias
    Max-Forwards: 70
```

Figure 5-14. *QoS markings*

Analyzing VoIP Streams and Graph

VoIP packets can be captured at the source, destination, or anywhere in the path the packets take in the network. All the techniques discussed in Chapters 1 and 2 can be used to capture and filter the required packets.

When we have SIP, SDP, RTP, and RTCP packets captured in the same file, Wireshark can automatically detect the VoIP streams, populate call flow diagrams and statistics, and replay the calls. All related menus are located under the telephony menu.

Figure 5-15. *VoIP analysis menu items*

Call Flow and I/O Graph

Wireshark can automatically detect all calls in a capture. We can launch the same with the menu **Telephony ➤ VoIP calls**. As you can see in Figure 5-16, three call flows are detected. Two of them use SIP, and one uses MGCP-based signaling. The corresponding call status can also be seen based on the last signaling status.

To plot the call flow sequence ladder diagram automatically, we can choose the flow and click the Flow Sequence button.

Also, using the **Prepare Filter** button, relevant call-related signaling and transport packets can be copied. Using the packets in the flow, if the **Statistics ➤ Flowgraph** menu is triggered, it results in a ladder diagram like the flow sequence diagram but has more details related to RTP communication.

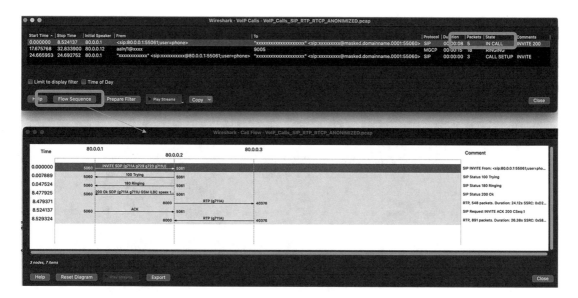

Figure 5-16. *VoIP calls and call flow sequence ladder diagram*

Analyzing SIP and SDP

If the intention is to only analyze the signaling, relevant packets can be filtered with the display filter "sip." A similar result can be achieved by triggering through the **Telephony ➤ SIP flows** menu. In case of call setup issues, the call flow sequence diagram can be plotted, or individual packets can be analyzed further.

SIP statistics can be launched through the **Telephony ➤ SIP**.

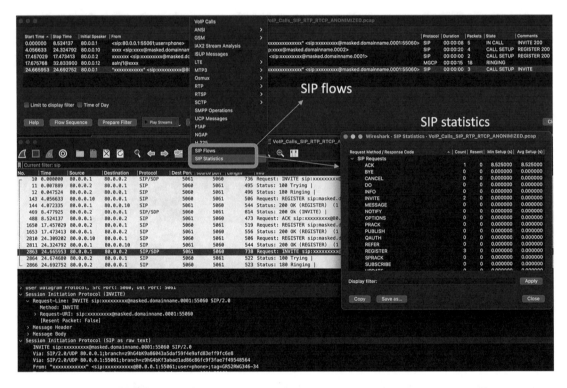

Figure 5-17. *SIP flows and statistics*

RTP Stream Analysis

Like SIP, all RTP streams captured in the pcap file can be found in a tabular manner by launching the **Telephony ➤ RTP ➤ RTP streams** dialogue.

It can be seen from Figure 5-18 that five RTP streams are detected.

Summary statistics (packet drop, min and max jitter, delay, codec in use, etc.) related to each stream is calculated and shown in the tabular format for each flow.

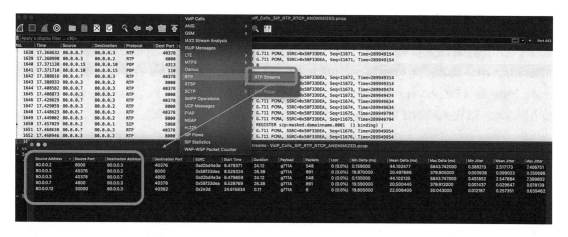

Figure 5-18. *RTP streams*

RTP Statistics, Packet Loss, Delay, and Jitter Analysis

Normally, the acceptable one-way delay is around 150ms and jitter around 40ms.
Beyond this, the audio quality may suffer. RTP per-packet detailed analysis can also
be done by launching the ***Telephony ➤ RTP ➤ RTP stream analysis*** dialogue menu.
This output shows the per-packet time delta, jitter, overall loss, and clock drift statistics.
Any issues seen here can help identify the network or application issues discussed in
previous sections.

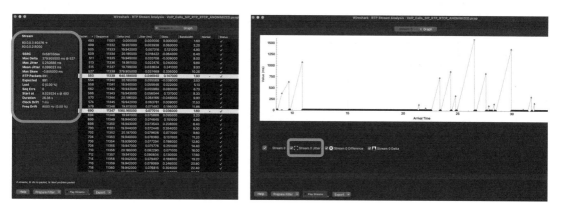

Figure 5-19. *RTP detailed stats, jitter, and drops*

Replaying RTP Payload

RTP encodes the digital voice as per certain encoding algorithms. The encoding algorithm type or codec type is carried in the RTP header ***Payload Type*** value. Wireshark has a built-in RTP player for some of the supported codecs. The list of supported codecs can be seen in the ***About Wireshark ➤ Plugins ➤ codec*** (drop-down) menu.

Figure 5-20. *Codec types*

The RTP player can be triggered from the RTP streams (as shown in Figure 5-18) tabular summary menu by choosing the desired stream. Also, the same can be triggered directly by clicking the desired RTP packet in the packet display window and then triggering the ***Telephony ➤ RTP ➤ RTP player*** menu. This dialogue box shows the voice graphs and some details about the stream. There are buttons to play, stop, and pause the voice replay. The graph is good for troubleshooting the call issues, as we can hear the exact voice replay of what an actual caller can hear.

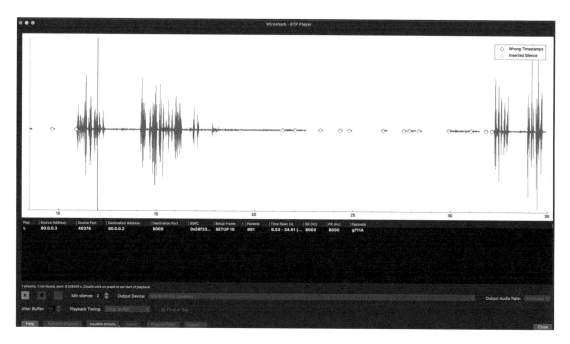

Figure 5-21. *RTP player voice graph*

Summary

This chapter is all about how Wireshark can help with multimedia application and protocol analysis. We learned about

- Various multimedia applications like web-based, streaming, and real-time multimedia

- The signaling and transport protocols associated with each type of multimedia and various encoding algorithms and formats

- How Wireshark helps in the capture and analysis of various multimedia types

- Decoding secure SIP and secure RTP packets

- How Wireshark helps in deep-dive analysis of SIP and RTP-based real-time communications like VoIP and video

References for This Chapter

Sample captures: Wireshark.org

Multimedia embedding: Developer.mozilla.org

Libsrtp: `https://github.com/cisco/libsrtp`

CHAPTER 6

Cloud and Cloud-Native Traffic Capture

The term "cloud computing" in the Information Technology (IT) world refers to the ability to run virtual instances of compute resources in a centralized data center with racks of physical servers and machines managed and offered as multitenant services by third parties. This new endowment to spin up on-demand compute resources in the cloud powered many businesses to host applications in a matter of minutes (if not seconds) at scale with the minimal skill set required to manage the resources yet without compromising resiliency. The term "cloud native" refers to the framework and architecture that introduces the ability of the applications to be hosted in such cloud environments to realize the maximum benefits offered by cloud computing.

In this chapter, we will start by sprucing up the readers' knowledge about the virtualization concept and explaining various capture techniques in different cloud environments. We would like to highlight that this chapter is not about control or management plane captures to debug cloud-native deployments but to capture the traffic from instances hosted as virtual machines and containers.

Evolution of Virtualization and Cloud

Virtualization is one of the greatest inventions in the past century that acts as a driving factor for other technology revolutions by drastically changing the way compute resources are available for anyone on an on-demand basis. With the invention of transistors by Bell Labs, the evolution of the computer quantum leaped from room-sized machines built with a few thousand vacuum tubes to palm-sized devices built with tiny transistors. Since the early 1990s, the demand for computing resources has constantly been rising due to the proliferating Internet-based businesses demanding digital transformation. While the advancement in transistor-based processors allowed

© Nagendra Kumar Nainar and Ashish Panda 2023
N. K. Nainar and A. Panda, *Wireshark for Network Forensics*, https://doi.org/10.1007/978-1-4842-9001-9_6

the industry to introduce cost affordable computers and servers with varying degrees of compute power and memory capacity, the amplifying expansion of business applications and the associated use cases introduced other sets of challenges such as capacity management, cost optimization, demanding operational skills, etc. Let us take an example of a business-critical application that requires high compute power. Based on the resource requirement and the capacity planning, it is identified that a server with 24 core CPU will be able to serve the application for 10k sessions. Now imagine that the customer base is evolving due to the attractive nature of the application and is becoming more and more critical. For resiliency and load distribution, multiple instances of the server will be required to be implemented in different parts of the world. This involves high capital expenditure (CAPEX) in procuring the hardware and installing the operating system, relevant binaries, and libraries and additional operational cost involving managing the servers across the world. Adding a new server or migrating the application from one server type to another will involve multiple months of engagement. As a best practice, it is common to see that the loads are distributed to each server in a way that the resource utilization is not more than 60–70% to have room for any unexpected surge or behavior. These challenges can be simplified into the following queries:

- Can we simplify the implementation of compute resources?

- Can we optimize the resource utilization without compromising resiliency?

- Can we optimize the cost of the resources and bring down the server when not in need?

While the preceding queries are explained with compute resources, these are all applicable for storage and network resources as well. Such CAPEX and OPEX challenges identified and raised by the IT professionals introduced the need for the new virtualization concept.

Basics of Virtualization

The concept of virtualization is the ability to abstract the physical characteristics of the underlying hardware to create a virtual environment and allow the user to instantiate virtual entities such as servers to utilize the available resources efficiently. The evolution of virtualization is as shown in Figure 6-1.

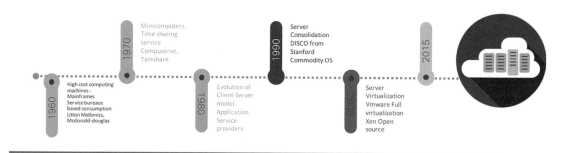

Figure 6-1. *Evolution of computing technology*

Note   While the concept of virtualization became very popular in the last couple of decades, the technique was explored in the early 1960s by the development of a virtualization hypervisor called Control Program by IBM.

In the early 1990s, Stanford University experts proposed the concept of running multiple operating systems sharing the same underlying hardware resources. In the late 1990s, VMware introduced a fully developed hypervisor that allows users to instantiate virtual machines running any guest operating system. This revolutionary introduction of hypervisor opened the gate for more innovation and development. Architecturally, virtualization can be classified into the following four types:

- Paravirtualization

- Full virtualization

- Hardware-assisted full virtualization

- Nested virtualization

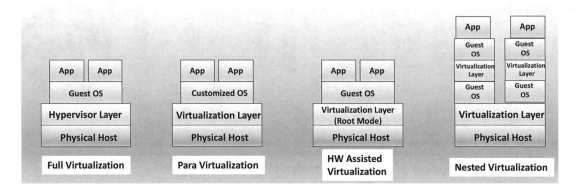

Figure 6-2. *Types of virtualization*

Paravirtualization is the technique used earlier that requires customizing the operating system to be hosted as virtual machines. The customized operating system is capable of making custom resource requests to the underlying hardware. As it could be noted, this is not a scalable approach as this requires customizing every operating system and making it compatible with different types of underlying hardware resources.

Full virtualization, on the other hand, introduces the hypervisor that acts as a medium between the guest operating system and the underlying hardware resources. Full virtualization eliminates the need for customizing the operating system and drastically improves the types of OS hosted as virtual machines.

The **hardware-assisted full virtualization** approach introduces the capability of natively supporting the virtualization by the processors that significantly improve the performance of the hosted virtual machines. Most of the recent processors, including the latest Apple processors, support hardware-assisted full virtualization.

Nested virtualization is an approach that allows the installation of a hypervisor layer on top of an existing virtual machine, thereby enabling the users to host virtual machines on a virtual machine.

Note   Some of the processors may require additional firmware upgrades or patches to support hardware-assisted full virtualization. When a virtual machine is instantiated on a host without hardware assistance, the performance is degraded, resulting in a poor user experience.

Hypervisor – Definition and Types

The hypervisor is a layer of software that abstracts the underlying hardware and partitions the resources such as CPU, memory, and storage into an isolated virtual environment and associates the same to different hosted virtual machines. The physical machine where the hypervisor is installed is commonly referred to as the host machine. The virtualization stack comprises multiple components with its unique functionality, such as

- Managing the underlying hardware and emulating virtual instances of CPU (vCPU), memory (vMem), and storage (vStorage)

- Managing the hypercall request for underlying hardware resources from the guest operating system

- Managing and scheduling the work on virtual processors across the host

In short, the hypervisor will emulate the virtual resources and manage the hypercalls from the hosted guest operating system to the underlying hardware to execute the relevant functionalities. There are two different types of hypervisors as follows:

- Type 1 Hypervisor (native)

- Type 2 Hypervisor (hosted)

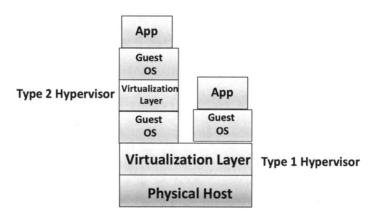

Figure 6-3. *Hypervisor types*

Type 1 Hypervisor, also known as the **native** or **bare-metal hypervisor**, is a software or firmware that is directly installed on top of the bare metal. As Type 1 Hypervisor does not require any operating system and runs directly on top of bare metal, it offers better performance compared to its counterpart. Linux KVM is one such Type 1 Hypervisor that is open source and so developed and managed by the open community.

Type 2 Hypervisor, also known as **hosted hypervisor**, is a software installed on a physical or a virtual machine with a guest operating system. This hypervisor leverages the nested virtualization concept and allows to host virtual entities on top of another virtual entity. VirtualBox and VMware Fusion are a few such Type 2 Hypervisors.

Note   There were some discussions to embed the hypervisor within the system BIOS itself. This type of hypervisor is referred to as Type 3.

Virtualization – Virtual Machines and Containers

In this section, we will spruce up the readers' knowledge about different virtualization by-products, such as virtual machines and containers.

Virtual Machines

The virtual machine (VM) is a type of server virtualization that allows the user to instantiate a server on top of the hypervisor. Multiple virtual machines can be hosted with their own share of underlying hardware resources, as shown in Figure 6-4.

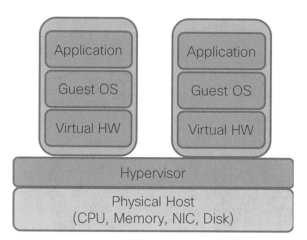

Figure 6-4. *Virtual machines*

This introduces the concept of offering Infrastructure as a Service (IaaS) by different cloud service providers (CSP). Each CSP offers different types of hardware resource configuration and a catalog of operating systems to choose and host the VM based on the business and user needs. The IaaS offered by Amazon Web Services (AWS) is referred to as Elastic Compute Cloud (EC2) instances. An example of EC2 instance hosting is shown in Figure 6-5.

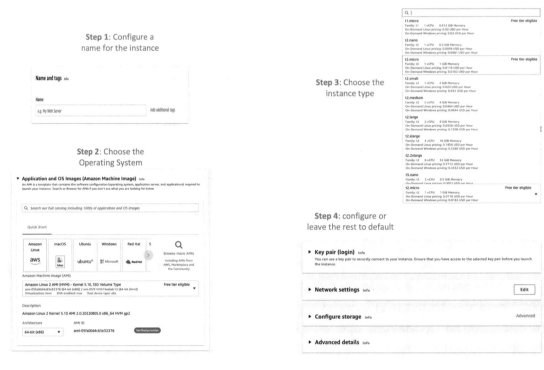

Figure 6-5. *EC2 instance hosting in AWS*

Containers

A container is another type of server virtualization that allows the user to host a lightweight compute entity comprising a package of binaries and libraries to host the relevant service. Unlike the virtual machine, containers do not have its own guest operating system. Instead, they share the underlying guest operating system as shown in Figure 6-6.

Containers

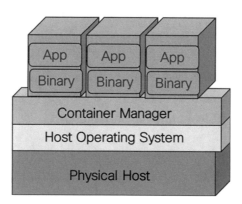

Figure 6-6. *Containers*

The container engine or the manager that is responsible for hosting and managing the containers in the user space. The kernel features such as cgroup and namespace are used to provide isolation and privacy between the containers that are sharing the same operating system. Docker and LXC are well-known container platforms used in the industry. While LXC is used only to Linux containers, the Docker platform is OS agnostic and can be used in different types of applications as containers.

Note   Different cloud service providers have different portals to configure and host the virtual machines. This book or chapter does not intend to help the readers learn each such portal and assume that the readers are familiar with the portal to perform the capture in machines hosted in different provider environments.

In the subsequent sections, we will discuss how to capture the traffic in different cloud environments, such as AWS and GCP, and cloud-native environments, such as Docker and Kubernetes.

Traffic Capture in AWS Environment

When one or more EC2 instances are hosted in the AWS environment, there are different options to capture the traffic. While one simple option is to use the native way of logging in to the EC2 instance and leverage the native tools such as tcpdump to capture the traffic, it is not different from how we capture in a physical server. However, such native option requires per-instance configuration to capture the traffic and does not provide a holistic view of the entire network. If the requirement is to capture the traffic to more than one instance in the same virtual private cloud (VPC), this native option is not sufficient.

In this section, we will discuss the traffic mirroring ability introduced in the AWS portal to configure the capture, the source, and the target along with the filters to specifically capture the traffic from one or more instances.

VPC Traffic Mirroring

One of the services offered by AWS is the virtual private cloud (VPC), which allows the user to isolate a group of EC2 instances. This is analogous to a group of physical servers connected to the same layer 2 subnet. In our setup, we have three EC2 instances connected to the same VPC as shown in Figure 6-7.

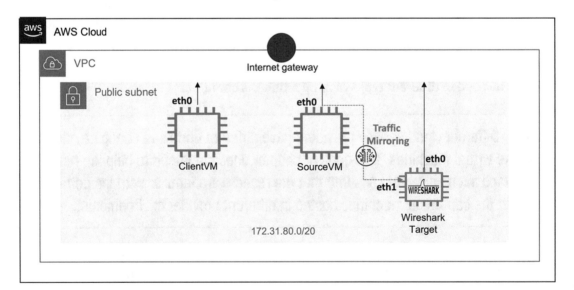

Figure 6-7. *AWS VPC example setup*

The SourceVM is hosted with one interface eth0 with Internet access. This is the interface from which bidirectional traffic is required to be captured. The ClientVM is hosted in the same VPC with one interface eth0, with Internet access. In our example, we use this VM to generate ICMP traffic to the SourceVM. The WiresharkTarget is the target VM to which the traffic from eth0 of SourceVM will be mirrored and captured. This VM is hosted with two interfaces where eth0 is with Internet access, while eth1 is used as the target interface to which the mirrored traffic from SourceVM will be replicated. Let us now look into the configuration and procedure to mirror the traffic in this scenario.

In the AWS console portal, hover over the **Services ➤ VPC** page, where "Traffic Mirroring" is a configuration option available under VPC as shown in Figure 6-8.

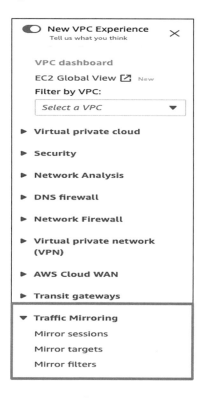

Figure 6-8. *VPC traffic mirroring configuration option*

From this option, configure the "Mirror targets" by specifying the target interface to which the traffic should be mirrored. In our example scenarios, eth1 of WiresharkTarget VM is the interface marked as **eni-0ba536f1e8dcf344b**. This interface is set to the target as shown in Figure 6-9.

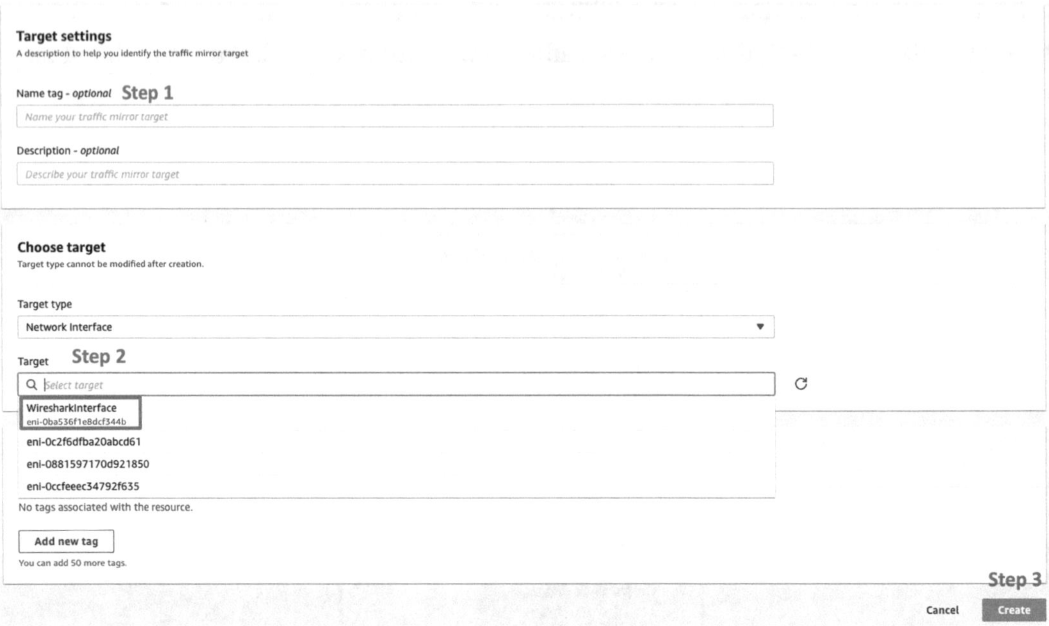

Target settings
A description to help you identify the traffic mirror target

Name tag - *optional*   **Step 1**

> Name your traffic mirror target

Description - *optional*

> Describe your traffic mirror target

Choose target
Target type cannot be modified after creation.

Target type

> Network Interface   ▼

Target   **Step 2**

> Q Select target   ⟳

> **WiresharkInterface**
> eni-0ba536f1e8dcf344b
>
> eni-0c2f6dfba20abcd61
>
> eni-0881597170d921850
>
> eni-0ccfeeec34792f635

No tags associated with the resource.

Add new tag
You can add 50 more tags.

Step 3

Cancel   Create

Figure 6-9. *VPC traffic mirroring – mirror target*

All the traffic mirror targets created are listed in the "Traffic mirror targets" page. In our example scenario, we created the target with a name "WiresharkTarget" as shown in Figure 6-10.

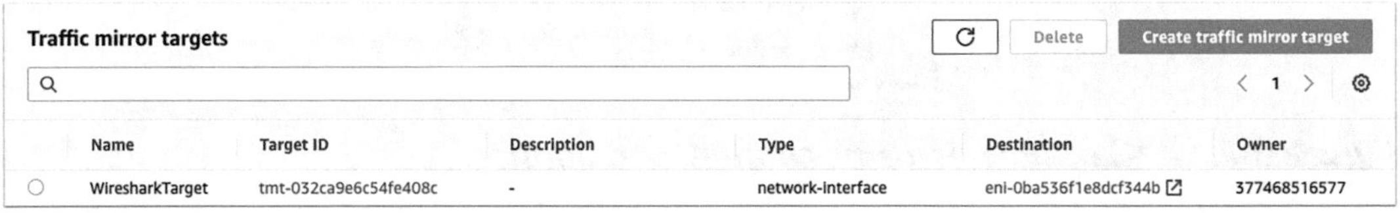

	Name	Target ID	Description	Type	Destination	Owner
○	WiresharkTarget	tmt-032ca9e6c54fe408c	-	network-interface	eni-0ba536f1e8dcf344b ⧉	377468516577

Traffic mirror targets   ⟳ Delete   Create traffic mirror target

⟨ 1 ⟩   ⚙

Figure 6-10. *VPC traffic mirroring – mirror target*

The next step is to create the mirror filter to specify the type of traffic to be captured. This allows the user to filter and capture selective traffic if the troubleshooting is focused on a specific TCP or UDP flow. Alternately, the filter can be created to capture all types of traffic as well. An example configuration is shown in Figure 6-11.

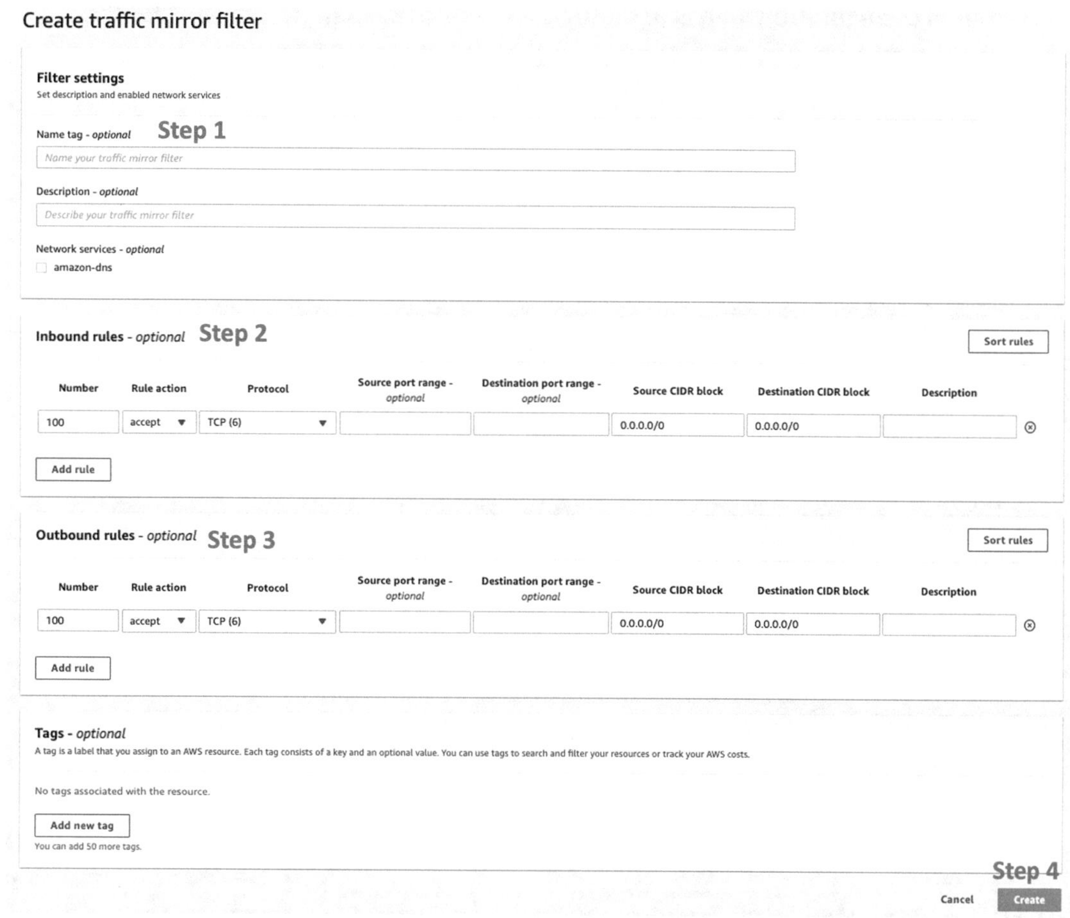

Create traffic mirror filter

Filter settings
Set description and enabled network services

Name tag - *optional*   **Step 1**

> Name your traffic mirror filter

Description - *optional*

> Describe your traffic mirror filter

Network services - *optional*
☐ amazon-dns

Inbound rules - *optional* **Step 2**   [Sort rules]

Number	Rule action	Protocol	Source port range - optional	Destination port range - optional	Source CIDR block	Destination CIDR block	Description	
100	accept ▼	TCP (6) ▼			0.0.0.0/0	0.0.0.0/0		⊗

[Add rule]

Outbound rules - *optional* **Step 3**   [Sort rules]

Number	Rule action	Protocol	Source port range - optional	Destination port range - optional	Source CIDR block	Destination CIDR block	Description	
100	accept ▼	TCP (6) ▼			0.0.0.0/0	0.0.0.0/0		⊗

[Add rule]

Tags - optional
A tag is a label that you assign to an AWS resource. Each tag consists of a key and an optional value. You can use tags to search and filter your resources or track your AWS costs.

No tags associated with the resource.

[Add new tag]
You can add 50 more tags.

Step 4

Cancel   [Create]

Figure 6-11. *VPC traffic mirroring – mirror filter*

All the traffic mirror filters created are listed in the "Traffic mirror filter" page. In our example scenario, we created the target with a name "TrafficFilter" as shown in Figure 6-12.

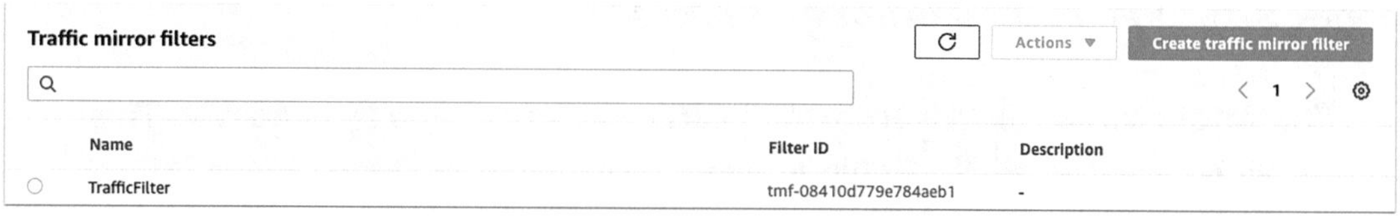

Traffic mirror filters   [⟳] [Actions ▼] [Create traffic mirror filter]

🔍   ⟨ 1 ⟩ ⚙

	Name	Filter ID	Description
○	TrafficFilter	tmf-08410d779e784aeb1	-

Figure 6-12. *VPC traffic mirroring – filter configuration*

The final configuration step is to configure the mirror session from the "Mirror Session" page. The configuration option is as shown in Figure 6-13.

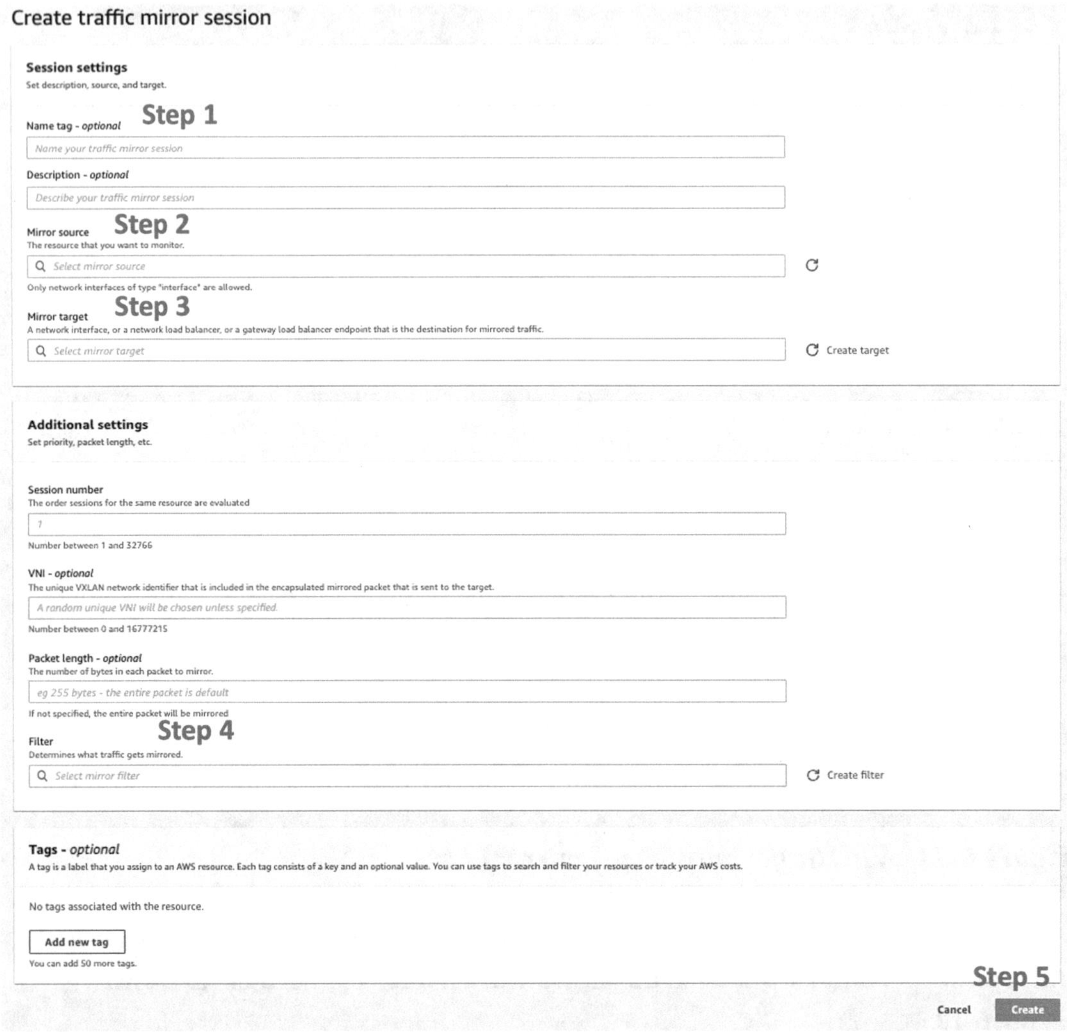

Figure 6-13. *VPC traffic mirroring – mirror session*

The "Mirror source" field is set to the interface ID of the eth0 of SourceVM. This is the interface from where the traffic should be mirrored and captured. The "Mirror target" field is set to the ID of the ***WiresharkTarget*** that we created in the previous step while creating the mirror target. The "Filter" field is set to the ID of the ***TrafficFilter*** that we created in the previous step while creating the mirror filter. The output after the configuration is as shown in Figure 6-14.

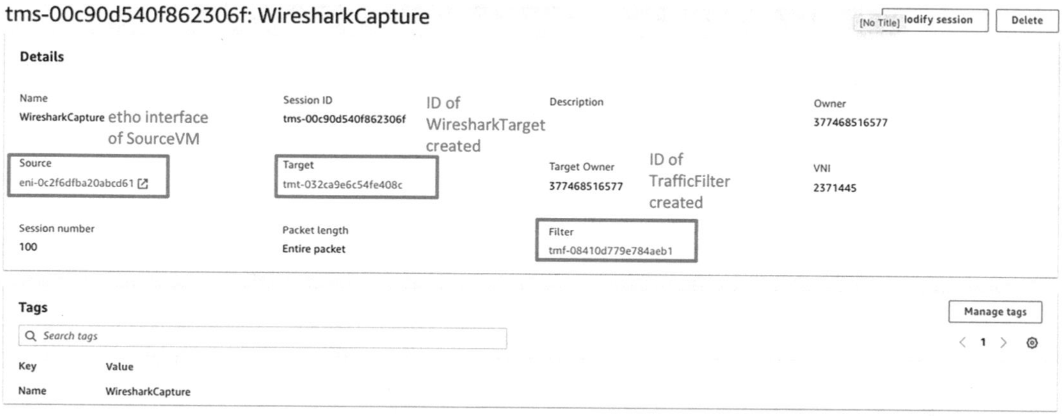

tms-00c90d540f862306f: WiresharkCapture

[No Title] **lodify session**   **Delete**

Details

Name
WiresharkCapture etho interface
of SourceVM

Session ID
tms-00c90d540f862306f

ID of
WiresharkTarget
created

Description

Owner
377468516577

Source
eni-0c2f6dfba20abcd61 ☑

Target
tmt-032ca9e6c54fe408c

Target Owner
377468516577

ID of
TrafficFilter
created

VNI
2371445

Session number
100

Packet length
Entire packet

Filter
tmf-08410d779e784aeb1

Tags

Manage tags

🔍 Search tags

< 1 > ⚙

Key
Name

Value
WiresharkCapture

Figure 6-14. *VPC traffic mirroring – mirror session configuration*

Now the setup is ready to mirror the traffic from the eth0 interface of SourceVM and mirror the traffic to eth1 of WiresharkTarget VM. By logging in to WiresharkTarget VM and using the tcpdump tool, we will be able to capture the traffic from eth1 which is the mirrored traffic from eth0 of SourceVM.

While the preceding example scenario was explained with one source port, multiple ports can be configured to mirror the traffic to the same target port.

Note   The mirrored traffic from the VPC is encapsulated using UDP port 4789 before forwarding to the target port. So, it is essential to configure the relevant security group rules to allow this UDP port.

Traffic Capture in GCP Environment

Like AWS, Google Cloud Platform (GCP) is another cloud service provider that offers compute and other cloud services to the customers. In this section, we will discuss the packet mirroring ability introduced by the GCP portal to configure the capture, the source, and the target using the "packet mirroring" feature. The procedure to enable the packet mirroring capability involves the following simple steps:

- Identify the source compute instances from where the packet needs to be mirrored and captured.

- Create a new compute instance to act as the target machine with Wireshark installed.

- Create a new unmanaged instance group and associate the target machine.

- Create a new UDP load balancer with the packet mirroring flag set and associate the instance group as the backend.

- Create the packet mirroring policy by setting the source as the instances from where the traffic should be mirrored and the target as the load balancer.

To further explain this capability, we created a virtual private cloud (VPC) in the GCP as shown in Figure 6-15.

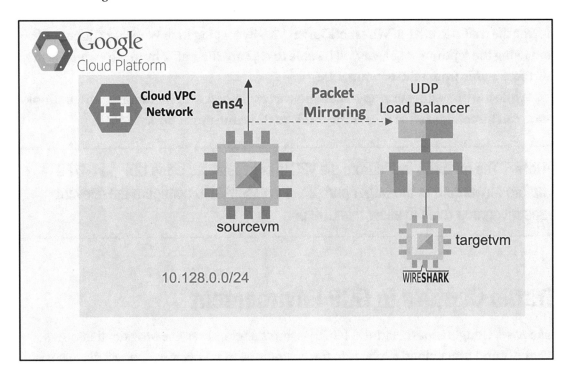

Figure 6-15. *GCP VPC example setup*

There are two Ubuntu-based compute instances created as part of the same VPC as sourcevm and targetvm. The sourcevm is used to generate traffic to the Internet, while the targetvm is used to capture the traffic for analysis. In the GCP portal, choose *Compute Engine ➤ Instance group* from the navigation menu and click the **Create Instance Group** option to go to the page as shown in Figure 6-16.

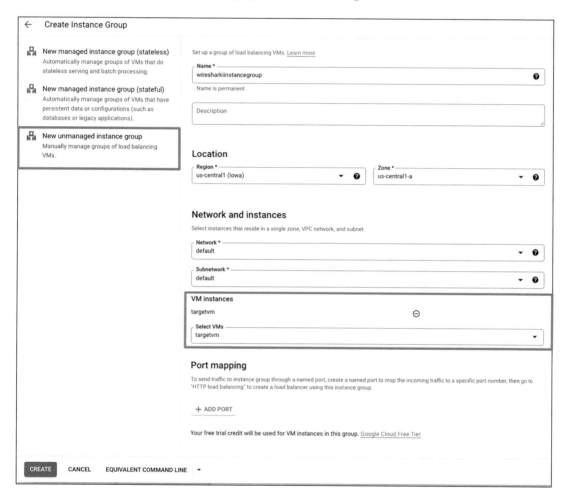

Figure 6-16. *VPC instance group configuration*

The instance group must be created as unmanaged by choosing the "New unmanaged instance group" option. Now, the targetvm is selected as the VM instance to be part of this group. The next step is to create the UDP load balancer to forward the mirrored traffic to the instance group configured as the backend for the load balancer.

The UDP load balancer is created by hovering to *Network Services* ➤ *Load balancing* from the navigation menu and clicking the **Create Load Balancer** to go to the page shown in Figure 6-17.

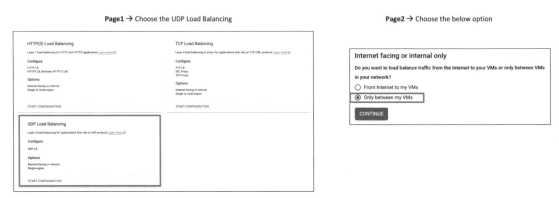

Figure 6-17. *VPC load balancing configuration*

Now, select **UDP Load Balancing** to create the load balancer to which the packet will be mirrored from the source instances. Since this load balancer is not expected to balance any Internet traffic, the Internet facing option is set to "Only between my VMs." This will take us to the next page to configure the frontend and the backend options as shown in Figure 6-18.

Figure 6-18. *VPC load balancer frontend and backend configuration*

The **Instance group** field in the backend is used to configure the unmanaged instance group we created and associated the targetvm. It is also essential to enable the **Packet Mirroring** flag in the frontend configuration. Without this flag, the load balancer will not be listed to be configured in the mirror policy section.

Note   All the network and subnet in our example configuration are left to default. If the network or the subnet differs in your scenarios or production environment, the relevant network and subnet must be chosen.

Once the UDP load balancer with packet mirroring is created, the final step is to configure the packet mirroring policy. The mirroring policy is created by hovering over to **VPC network ➤ Packet mirroring** from the navigation menu and choosing the Create Policy option to go to the page as shown in Figure 6-19.

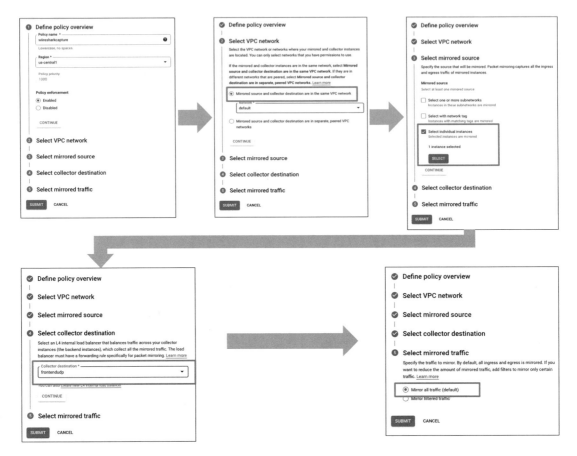

Figure 6-19. *VPC packet mirroring configuration*

In our example scenario, both the source and the target machines are in the same VPC network, and so the respective option is chosen to select the VPC network. The mirror source is set to the instance, and sourcevm is selected to mirror the traffic. The collector destination is set to the frontend created as part of the UDP load balancer, and finally the filter policies are created to choose all the traffic or selective traffic to be mirrored.

The setup is now ready to mirror the traffic from the sourcevm and replicate the traffic to the frontend of the load balancer which in turn will replicate it to the backend instance targetvm. By logging in to the targetvm and using the tcpdump tool, we will be able to capture the traffic from sourcevm.

Note   Most of the cloud providers such as AWS and GCP offer different types of third-party capturing tools as part of the marketplace. While in this book we used an Ubuntu instance as the target machine, any capturing tool and service such as Fortigate or Cisco Stealthwatch may be used as the target where the replicated traffic will be consumed for analytics purposes.

Traffic Capture in Docker Environment

Docker is a widely accepted container platform that is used to instantiate and manage container applications. Like any other container platform, Docker is a software that runs on top of an existing guest operating system, such as macOS, Linux, Windows, etc. To create an isolated network environment for the containers hosted in the guest OS, Docker offers three different types of networks as follows:

- Docker default bridge

- Docker user-defined bridge

- Host network

During the initial installation, Docker by default creates a bridge network as docker0 with a private range subnet used to assign the IP address to each hosted container. Any user can also create a user-defined bridge with its own subnet and policies. Alternately, Docker can host the container with a host network where the host interface will be shared by the containers. An example output of the default docker bridge is shown in Figure 6-20.

```
[ubuntu@ip-172-31-88-220:~$
[ubuntu@ip-172-31-88-220:~$ sudo docker network ls
 NETWORK ID       NAME       DRIVER      SCOPE
 6596cae657c2     bridge     bridge      local
 ab25df7067ef     host       host        local
 9da2b2f1f478     none       null        local
[ubuntu@ip-172-31-88-220:~$
[ubuntu@ip-172-31-88-220:~$ ifconfig docker0
docker0: flags=4163<UP,BROADCAST,RUNNING,MULTICAST>  mtu 1500
        inet 172.17.0.1  netmask 255.255.0.0  broadcast 172.17.255.255
        inet6 fe80::42:c8ff:fe24:8a8a  prefixlen 64  scopeid 0x20<link>
        ether 02:42:c8:24:8a:8a  txqueuelen 0  (Ethernet)
        RX packets 892  bytes 53203 (53.2 KB)
        RX errors 0  dropped 0  overruns 0  frame 0
        TX packets 1245  bytes 22748861 (22.7 MB)
        TX errors 0  dropped 0 overruns 0  carrier 0  collisions 0

[ubuntu@ip-172-31-88-220:~$
```

Figure 6-20. *Docker networks*

This bridge could be considered as a virtual switch that connects the containers to the host interface to reach the external network. An example topology of the docker default bridge network is shown in Figure 6-21.

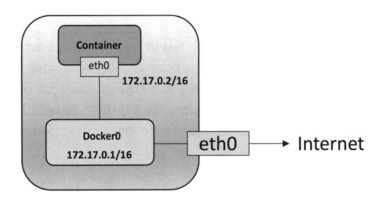

Figure 6-21. *Docker default bridge*

Each container will be assigned with a unique address from the subnet assigned to the docker0 interface. The host network is programmed to perform the Network Address Translation (NAT) operation for any traffic received from the Docker interface. Accordingly, the source address of the traffic will be changed to the host interface address. By simply using the docker0 interface as the capture interface, we will be able to capture all the packets destinated to the containers as shown in Figure 6-22.

194

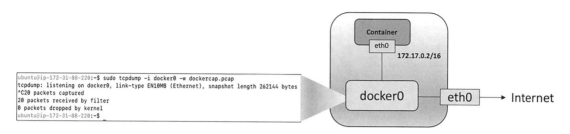

Figure 6-22. *Packet capture in the docker container*

Note   The traffic can also be captured from the host interface (eth0 in our example) using the same **tcpdump** command. But as mentioned in the preceding section, the source address of the traffic will be changed to the host interface address, and so it is hard to differentiate if the traffic is originally from the host or translated by the host. So, it is a lot easier to capture the traffic from the docker0 interface.

Traffic Capture in Kubernetes Environment

While Docker is the popular container platform to host application containers, the use of the command line to instantiate and manage applications on a per-container basis lacks dynamic lifecycle management of the application containers. For example, if one of the containers is stuck or down, manual intervention is required to identify the failed container instance and reinstantiate the application container. However, in a production-grade environment, it is common to run a voluminous number of containers running different applications, and it is humanly impossible to monitor and manually manage all such containers. What we need is a dynamic orchestration platform that can automate the deployment of containers, management, and scaling aspects with minimal or no manual intervention.

Kubernetes is a container orchestration platform that was originally introduced by Google and later opened to the community as an open source platform and now adopted by the Cloud Native Computing Foundation (CNCF). The basic architecture is shown in Figure 6-23.

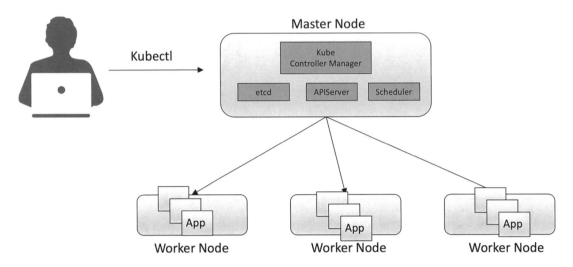

Figure 6-23. *Kubernetes architecture*

The Kubernetes architecture comprises a minimum of one master node and one or more worker nodes as control plane components, collectively referred to as a cluster. Within the cluster, any application is hosted as a Pod, which is a group of one or more containers. The ***init*** process or other ***service agents*** can be hosted as a container along with the application container within the Pod. The master node acts as the control plane component that manages all the worker nodes and then manages the Pod scheduling and scaling. In such container applications hosted as a Pod within the cluster, it is essential to perform traffic capture for various troubleshooting purposes. While one option to capture the traffic is to log in to each worker node and use the tcpdump command with the docker0 interface as input, this is already covered in the previous section. In this section, we will discuss another approach using the **ksniff** plugin that can be embedded within the ***kubectl***, which is the command-line interface for Kubernetes to host and manage the Pods.

The first step is to log in to the Kubernetes master node and make sure that the git module is installed. The command to install in a Linux-based master node is shown as follows:

```
nagendrakumar_nainar@cloudshell:~ (nyacorp)$ sudo apt-get install git

Reading package lists... Done
Building dependency tree... Done
Reading state information... Done
```

```
git is already the newest version (1:2.30.2-1).
0 upgraded, 0 newly installed, 0 to remove and 9 not upgraded.
nagendrakumar_nainar@cloudshell:~ (nyacorp)$
```

Once the git module is installed in the master node, the next step is to install *krew*, a kubectl plugin manager that helps the master node to discover the available kubectl plugins, install, and manage the plugins. The command to install the krew plugin is shown as follows:

```
nagendrakumar_nainar@cloudshell:~ (nyacorp)$ (
  set -x; cd "$(mktemp -d)" &&
  OS="$(uname | tr '[:upper:]' '[:lower:]')" &&
  ARCH="$(uname -m | sed -e 's/x86_64/amd64/' -e 's/\(arm\)\
  (64\)\?.*/\1\2/' -e 's/aarch64$/arm64/')" &&
  KREW="krew-${OS}_${ARCH}" &&
  curl -fsSLO "https://github.com/kubernetes-sigs/krew/releases/latest/
  download/${KREW}.tar.gz" &&
  tar zxvf "${KREW}.tar.gz" &&
  ./"${KREW}" install krew
)
```

The preceding command will install the plugin as follows:

```
++ mktemp -d
+ cd /tmp/tmp.L3pGB6nPFQ
++ uname
++ tr '[:upper:]' '[:lower:]'
+ OS=linux
++ uname -m
++ sed -e s/x86_64/amd64/ -e 's/\(arm\)\(64\)\?.*/\1\2/' -e 's/
aarch64$/arm64/'
+ ARCH=amd64
+ KREW=krew-linux_amd64
+ curl -fsSLO https://github.com/kubernetes-sigs/krew/releases/latest/
download/krew-linux_amd64.tar.gz
+ tar zxvf krew-linux_amd64.tar.gz
./LICENSE
```

```
./krew-linux_amd64
+ ./krew-linux_amd64 install krew
Adding "default" plugin index from https://github.com/kubernetes-sigs/krew-
index.git.
Updated the local copy of plugin index.
Installing plugin: krew
Installed plugin: krew
\
 | Use this plugin:
 |     kubectl krew
 | Documentation:
 |     https://krew.sigs.k8s.io/
 | Caveats:
 | \
 | | krew is now installed! To start using kubectl plugins, you
    need to add
 | | krew's installation directory to your PATH:
 | |
 | |    * macOS/Linux:
 | |      - Add the following to your ~/.bashrc or ~/.zshrc:
 | |          export PATH="${KREW_ROOT:-$HOME/.krew}/bin:$PATH"
 | |      - Restart your shell.
 | |
 | |    * Windows: Add %USERPROFILE%\.krew\bin to your PATH environment
    variable
 | |
 | | To list krew commands and to get help, run:
 | |    $ kubectl krew
 | | For a full list of available plugins, run:
 | |    $ kubectl krew search
 | |
 | | You can find documentation at
 | |    https://krew.sigs.k8s.io/docs/user-guide/quickstart/.
 | /
/
```

```
nagendrakumar_nainar@cloudshell:~ (nyacorp)$
```

Once the plugin manager is installed, set the export path to execute the plugin as follows:

```
nagendrakumar_nainar@cloudshell:~ (nyacorp)$
nagendrakumar_nainar@cloudshell:~ (nyacorp)$ export PATH="${KREW_ROOT:-
$HOME/.krew}/bin:$PATH"
nagendrakumar_nainar@cloudshell:~ (nyacorp)$ kubectl krew
krew is the kubectl plugin manager.
```

Now, use the plugin manager to install the ksniff plugin for kubectl as follows:

```
nagendrakumar_nainar@cloudshell:~ (nyacorp)$ kubectl krew install sniff
Updated the local copy of plugin index.
Installing plugin: sniff
Installed plugin: sniff
\
 | Use this plugin:
 |       kubectl sniff
 | Documentation:
 |       https://github.com/eldadru/ksniff
 | Caveats:
 | \
 | | This plugin needs the following programs:
 | | * wireshark (optional, used for live capture)
 | /
/
WARNING: You installed plugin "sniff" from the krew-index plugin
repository.
   These plugins are not audited for security by the Krew maintainers.
   Run them at your own risk.
nagendrakumar_nainar@cloudshell:~ (nyacorp)$
```

The cluster is now ready to capture the traffic to the Pod using the ksniff plugin installed within the cluster. The *kubectl sniff <Pod> -n <namespace> -o <outputfile>* command is used to capture the traffic from the respective Pod as shown in the following:

nagendrakumar_nainar@cloudshell:~ (nyacorp)$ **kubectl sniff nginx -n default -o k8s.pcap**

INFO[0000] using tcpdump path at: '/home/nagendrakumar_nainar/.krew/store/sniff/v1.6.2/static-tcpdump'

INFO[0000] no container specified, taking first container we found in pod.

INFO[0000] selected container: 'nginx'

INFO[0000] sniffing method: upload static tcpdump

INFO[0000] sniffing on pod: 'nginx' [namespace: 'default', container: 'nginx', filter: '', interface: 'any']

INFO[0000] uploading static tcpdump binary from: '/home/nagendrakumar_nainar/.krew/store/sniff/v1.6.2/static-tcpdump' to: '/tmp/static-tcpdump'

INFO[0000] uploading file: '/home/nagendrakumar_nainar/.krew/store/sniff/v1.6.2/static-tcpdump' to '/tmp/static-tcpdump' on container: 'nginx'

INFO[0000] executing command: '[/bin/sh -c test -f /tmp/static-tcpdump]' on container: 'nginx', pod: 'nginx', namespace: 'default'

INFO[0000] command: '[/bin/sh -c test -f /tmp/static-tcpdump]' executing successfully exitCode: '0', stdErr :''

INFO[0000] file found: ''

INFO[0000] file was already found on remote pod

INFO[0000] tcpdump uploaded successfully

INFO[0000] output file option specified, storing output in: 'k8s.pcap'

INFO[0000] start sniffing on remote container

INFO[0000] executing command: '[/tmp/static-tcpdump -i any -U -w -]' on container: 'nginx', pod: 'nginx', namespace: 'default'

^C

nagendrakumar_nainar@cloudshell:~ (nyacorp)$

The captured Wireshark file can be offloaded from the master node for analytics purposes.

Note   During the time of this chapter authoring, while ksniff is the better option to capture the traffic from the Pod, it is not officially managed by CNCF.

Summary

In this chapter, we spruced up the knowledge of the readers about virtualization and the evolution of cloud computing that is now offered as a new service by different cloud providers. We explained the different virtualization types and the hypervisor types to realize the benefits of virtualization.

We further discussed about different by-products of virtualization, such as virtual machines and containers, and the ability to orchestrate and manage those virtual entities.

With this background, we explained how to capture the traffic on different cloud providers with examples captured from virtual machines hosted on AWS and Google Cloud environments. We then explained how to capture the traffic from the Docker container platform and Kubernetes cluster.

References for This Chapter

Ramdoss, Yogesh, Nainar, Nagendra Kumar. *Containers in Cisco IOS-XE, IOS-XR, and NX-OS: Orchestration and Operations*, First Edition. Cisco Press, 2020.

https://kubernetes.io/docs/concepts/architecture/

https://kubesandclouds.com/index.php/2021/01/20/ksniff/

https://docs.docker.com/get-started/overview/

https://cloud.google.com/vpc/docs/packet-mirroring

https://docs.aws.amazon.com/vpc/latest/mirroring/what-is-traffic-mirroring.html

CHAPTER 7

Bluetooth Packet Capture and Analysis

Bluetooth is a very popular near-field wireless communication technology used extensively for gadgets that go cordless. Almost all modern audio/video and telephony equipment like wireless speakers, earphones, smartwatches, computer peripherals, and smartphones can use Bluetooth to communicate with external devices wirelessly. There are lots of other interesting use cases with Bluetooth Low Energy technology like indoor direction finding, inventory management, low-power data transfer, and near-field device networking. By 2021, the number of Bluetooth-enabled devices shipped annually touched one billion and is expected to reach seven billion by 2026.

In this chapter, you will learn how the Bluetooth packet capture over the air between a host and a peer device helps with the analysis of protocol communication and debug issues related to the same. The following is the summary of the important concepts covered:

- Evolution of Bluetooth standards

- Introduction to the Bluetooth protocol stack and filtering through Wireshark

- Wireshark tools required for Bluetooth capture (macOS, Windows, Linux)

- Wireshark Bluetooth packet capture analysis and troubleshooting scenarios

© Nagendra Kumar Nainar and Ashish Panda 2023
N. K. Nainar and A. Panda, *Wireshark for Network Forensics*, https://doi.org/10.1007/978-1-4842-9001-9_7

Introduction to Bluetooth

Bluetooth 1.0 was introduced in 1999 as a short-range packet-based wireless communication technology, and it has evolved since then to Bluetooth 5.3 released in 2021. Version 4.0 onward supports Bluetooth Low Energy (LE) technology, which uses less power and is in the range of 0.1–0.5 times the classic Bluetooth (before version 4).

Bluetooth was standardized by IEEE as 802.15.1 back in 2002, but since then all the development is controlled and maintained by the Bluetooth Special Interest Group (ISG), an industry-led group of 35,000+ companies. All Bluetooth products in the market should meet ISG standards.

Communication Models

Bluetooth Classic uses a hub and spoke communication model in which the hub (also known as the main) can communicate with up to seven spokes (also known as the follower). The main and followers can change roles based on agreement. Also, there is a Bluetooth mesh technology implementation which operates on a flood networking model (send the packet to all other peers except those who sent the packet to it). Bluetooth LE can operate in either of the models depending on the application profile. The device roles and negotiation can be tracked in the Wireshark Bluetooth captured packet type of HCI_CMD or HCI_EVT.

As seen in Figure 7-1, the laptop OS (host) sends instructions to the Bluetooth chip (controller) to connect to a pre-paired known headset with identifier *Plantron_a3:7b:19*. Also, the host specified in the command that the local device will be the master and won't accept a role switchover request.

```
> Frame 27: 16 bytes on wire (128 bits), 16 bytes captured (128 bits)
  Bluetooth
    [Source: host]
    [Destination: controller]
  Bluetooth HCI H1 Sent HCI Command
    [Direction: Sent (0)]
  Bluetooth HCI Command — Create Connection
  > Command  Opcode: Create Connection (0x0405)
    Parameter Total Length: 13
    BD_ADDR: Plantron_a3:7b:19 (bc:f2:92:a3:7b:19)
  > Packet Type: 0xcc18, DH5, DM5, DH3, DM3, DH1, DM1
    Page Scan Repetition Mode: R2 (0x02)
    Page Scan Mode: Mandatory Page Scan Mode (0x00)
    .000 0000 0000 0000 = Clock Offset: 0x0000 (0 msec)
    0... .... .... .... = Clock_Offset_Valid_Flag: false (0)
    Allow Role Switch: Local device will be master, and will not accept a master–slave switch request. (0x00)
    [Pending in frame: 28]
    [Command-Pending Delta: 4294967296ms]
    [Response in frame: 33]
    [Command-Response Delta: 562640715776ms]
```

Figure 7-1. *Bluetooth device role negotiation*

Radio and Data Transfer

The Bluetooth radios use an unlicensed but regulated spectrum at 2.40–2.483 GHz.
Bluetooth Classic (BR/EDR) uses 79 channels 1 MHz each, which includes 32 channels
for discovery purposes, whereas Bluetooth LE uses the same band with 40 channels,
each 2 MHz wide with only 3 channels for discovery. This makes discovery quicker in LE
as fewer channels to scan. The range, power output of the radios, modulation, and data
rate vary between Bluetooth versions (1–5) and standards (Classic/LE).

Table 7-1 and Figure 7-2 show some summary comparisons between various
specifications.

Figure 7-2. *Bluetooth Classic vs. LE*

Table 7-1. *Bluetooth Radio Specifications*

	Bluetooth Classic	Bluetooth Low Energy
Radio class	Type 1: 10–100 mW Type 2: 1–2.5 mW Type 3: 0.01–1 mW	Mostly Type 3 Consumption range 0.01–0.5 mW
Frequency band	2.4–2.483 GHz	2.4–2.483 GHz
Number of channels	79 total including 32 for discovery	40 total including 3 for discovery
Channel width	1 MHz	2 MHz
Modulation	BR: FSK/GFSK EDR2: π/4-DQPSK EDR3: 8 DQPSK HDR4: π/4-DQPSK HDR8: π/4-DQPSK	FSK/GFSK
Data rate	BR: 1 Mbps EDR2: 2 Mbps EDR3: 3 Mbps HDR4: 4 Mbps HDR8: 8 Mbps	125 Kbps to 2 Mbps
Range	Up to 100m depends on radio, data rate, and modulation	Up to 100m depends on radio, data rate, and modulation
Encryption	56/128-bit physical and application	AES 128-bit physical and application

BR: Basic rate

EDR: Enhanced data rate

HDR: High data rate

G/FSK: Gaussian/frequency-shift keying

PSK: Phase-shift keying

Bluetooth Protocol Stack

Bluetooth uses a completely different protocol stack specified and maintained by Bluetooth SIG standards. The protocols in the stack can be distributed across the hardware (controller) and software (host) portions of the device. The hardware or the Bluetooth chip is known as the controller and can be internal or external to the device. The software or OS is known as the host and runs the protocols that interact with the local controller and Bluetooth peer host.

Between the host and controller, there is a middle layer known as the Host Controller Interface (HCI) which provides a software interface to the host OS to interact with the controller hardware.

Note   In some implementations where both host and controller are integrated together (like an audio headset), HCI may be absent. But as a standard implementation, most vendors still retain the HCI layer in such scenarios.

Figure 7-3 shows a summary view of the Bluetooth protocol placement. The following section will discuss in detail each of these layers.

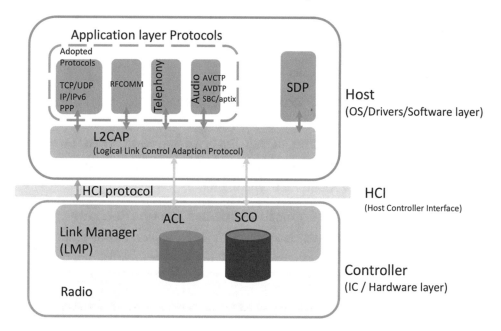

Figure 7-3. *Bluetooth protocol stack*

Controller Operations

The Bluetooth controller hardware normally takes care of the physical and data link layers of the communications. It has protocols running in the link manager and radio layers.

Radio and Baseband Processing

Bluetooth radio takes care of the modulation and demodulation of the baseband signal, transmission, and reception of the packets, synchronization through clocking, etc. Details on this were discussed in the "Radio and Data Transfer" section.

Link Management Protocol (LMP)

Before two devices can communicate, the link manager establishes a logical link between them through the Link Management Protocol. The LMP exchanges PDUs with the peer device to

- Collect device identification (like device name, MAC/hardware address)

- Negotiate authentication and encryption key

- Set up and tear down the link

- Negotiate link modes/types

    - **ACL**: Asynchronous Connection Less links are meant for packet-oriented communication and don't wait for any signaling or time slot to transmit the packet. For error detection, a CRC bit is appended along with actual data bits. Packets with CRC errors are retransmitted with an ACL type of link.

    - **SCO**: Synchronous Connection Oriented links are normally used for voice. The device must wait for its reserved time slot to transmit. SCO links support FEC, but no retransmissions are done.

LMP provides error detection through CRC check and error correction through forward error correction (FEC). Packets with CRC that are uncorrectable are retransmitted until an acknowledgment is received.

The **LELL** (Low Energy Link Layer) protocol is the simpler version of LMP used on Bluetooth LE devices.

HCI

HCI abstracts the underlying controller chip (any controller hardware) and presents it to the upper host layer as a software interface. HCI acts like a proxy between the hardware and software.

- All commands from the host to the controller are addressed to the HCI, and a response is sent from HCI to the host.

- All data communication through L2CAP also passes through HCI, and in the captured packets, you will see the HCI header.

On a hostless system where HCI is absent, data and control packets are directly handed off by L2CAP to the link layer.

The HCI frames can be filtered through the display filter "*hci_h4*" or "*hci_h1*" depending on the host HCI type.

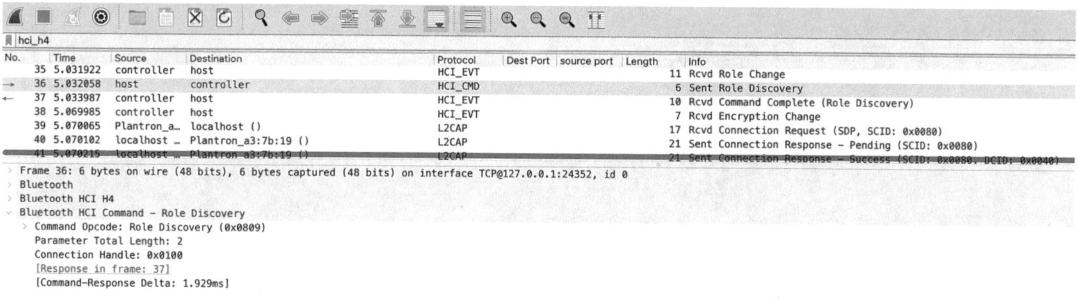

Figure 7-4. *HCI packet filter*

Host Layer Operation

L2CAP

L2CAP (Logical Link Control and Adaptation Protocol) operates on the host and is part of the data link layer that works with the LMP which is the controller part of the data link layer. Some of the important functions of L2CAP are

- Multiplexing multiple applications over a single link

  - All upper layer application, control, or discovery protocols data passes through L2CAP

- Fragmentation and reassembly of data

- Handling one to many replications (hub and spoke topology)

- Quality of service (QoS)

All L2CAP types of packets can be filtered using a display filter "*btl2cap*". Figure 7-5 shows SDP packets also as SDP is an upper layer protocol which hands over data to L2CAP to be sent on the link.

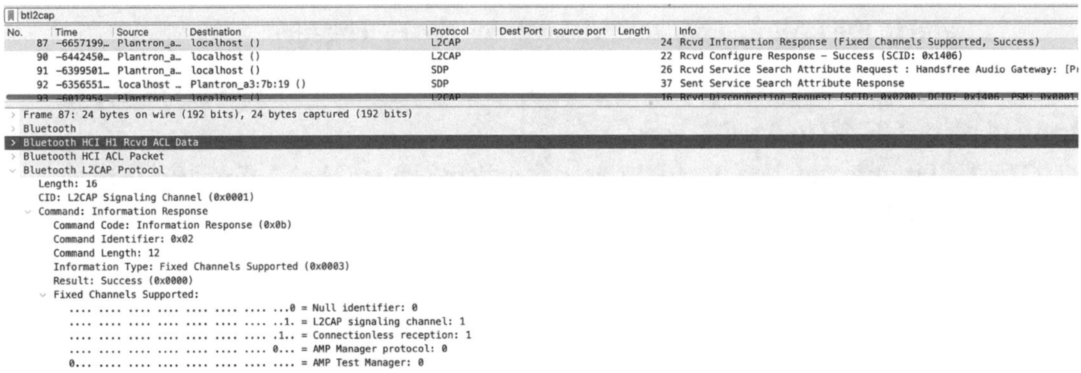

Figure 7-5. L2CAP packet filter

Application Profile–Specific Protocols

Bluetooth supports a wide variety of applications like telephony, audio/video, TCP/IP communication, medical or fitness equipment communication, computer I/O (mouse, keyboard, etc.), and many more. For every application, there is a standard protocol and parameter specifications defined by SIG, known as Bluetooth profiles.

The following are some of the protocols which run on top of L2CAP and help in application discovery and operation.

SDP

The Service Discovery Protocol (SDP) helps a Bluetooth-enabled device discover the service profile (the capabilities and services) offered by the peer device, for example, a Bluetooth-enabled mouse, keyboard, headset, etc. Also SDP specifies device-specific capabilities like, if it is an AV device, does it support an advanced audio distribution profile, or supports a hands-free profile or receiver-only profile, etc. After the connection is set up, SDP frames are exchanged between peer devices to agree on the profiles supported and what to use.

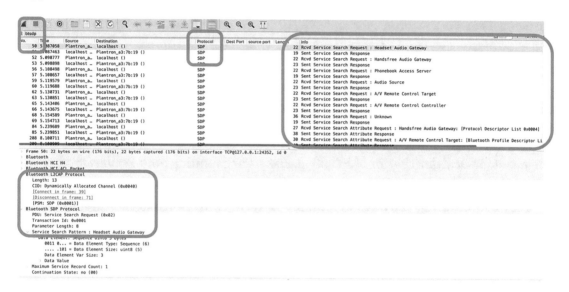

Figure 7-6. *Filtering SDP frames*

Telephony Control

The Telephony Control Protocol – Binary (TCS-Bin) takes care of use cases related to telephony control like answering a call, disconnecting a call, call volume control, etc. from a connected Bluetooth device.

Audio/Video Control and Transport

For audio control like music play, pause, forward, volume control, etc., a Bluetooth device uses the AVTCP (Audio Video Transport Control Protocol). For audio distribution, AVDTP (Audio Video Distribution Transport Protocol) is used by the A2DP profile.

RFCOMM

Radio Frequency Communication is a protocol used to emulate serial data connections the same as EIA-232/RS-232 over a radio link. Many protocols like Telephony Control can use RFCOMM to send control commands. Many other protocols also can use RFCOMM as it's natively available and simple to use.

Other Adopted Protocols

There are many protocols which are not native to Bluetooth but still have use cases and are being used. For example, PPP and TCP/IP-based protocols are foreign to Bluetooth. Still, they can be used and encapsulated over L2CAP and transported between peers.

Tools for Bluetooth Capture

All the popular operating systems don't support promiscuous mode (packets in the air not meant for local devices) for Bluetooth packets. For capturing promiscuous mode Bluetooth packet communication, an external Bluetooth sniffer like Ubertooth is required.

Only Linux natively provides support for capturing Bluetooth packets directly through Wireshark. For Windows and macOS, third-party tools are required.

Linux

Natively, Linux kernel supports Bluetooth captures through Wireshark with libpcap 0.9.6 onward (the latest libpcap is 1.9.1). To capture Bluetooth, Wireshark should be launched as root, or else the Bluetooth adapter is not seen in available adapters.

```
apress@apress-ubuntu:~$ sudo wireshark
 ** (wireshark:2592) 18:16:44.023135 [GUI WARNING] -- QStandardPaths: XDG_
RUNTIME_DIR not set, defaulting to '/tmp/runtime-root'
```

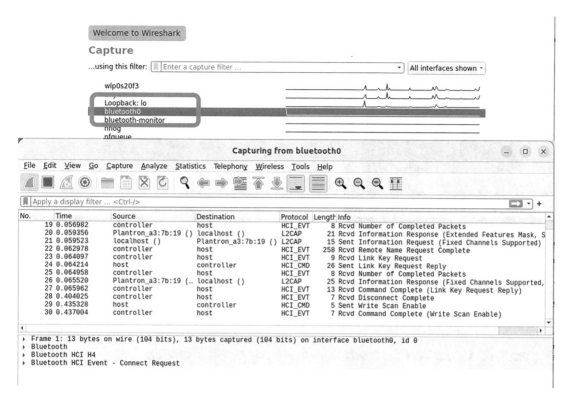

Figure 7-7. *Linux Wireshark Bluetooth packet capture*

Windows

On the Windows operating system, Wireshark cannot access the Bluetooth adapters directly. To capture Wireshark packets, the BTP (Bluetooth Test Platform) utilities provided by Microsoft are required. The BTP packages can be downloaded from Microsoft Through the link, `https://learn.microsoft.com/en-us/windows-hardware/drivers/bluetooth/testing-btp-setup-package`. The installer by default installs into the C:\BTP folder.

For capturing Bluetooth packets, from the command line, start the **BTVS** (Bluetooth Virtual Sniffer) utility within the BTP package.

- This opens a small GUI window which shows the packet statistics and a button to select the capture type (full packet/partial packet).

- If capture mode is defined as "**Wireshark**" (default mode), it automatically dumps the captured packets to a TCP pipe (port 24352 default) and starts Wireshark with the capture interface as the TCP pipe.

- In the following example, we have a specified mode and a non-default TCP port 23456.

- This may trigger a pop-up screen from Wireshark to allow the opening of the port.

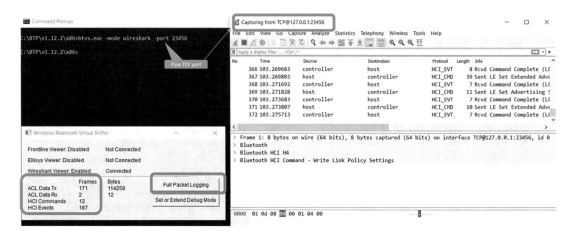

Figure 7-8. *Windows Bluetooth Wireshark capture with BTVS*

macOS

macOS also natively doesn't support Wireshark Bluetooth captures. However, the "packet logger" utility provided by Apple as part of the Xcode SDK can capture Bluetooth packets. Xcode is not required for the packet logger to work. The "additional tools for Xcode" package can be downloaded directly from the Apple website with this link, `https://developer.apple.com/download/all/?q=for%20Xcode`. There are several tools, which are part of the Xcode package but only the packet logger can be moved to the Application folder for use.

Figure 7-9. macOS packet logger Bluetooth capture

Note   Unlike Windows and Linux, live packet inspection cannot be done. The capture by "packet logger" can be exported to a file in *btsnoop* mode and inspected by Wireshark. The file extension may need to be manually changed to .pcap post export. The packet logger may truncate the payload portion of the packet if it's big.

Bluetooth Packet Filtering and Troubleshooting

Wireshark analysis of Bluetooth packets helps understand the communication at a very low level and also helps troubleshoot failure scenarios. The following section discusses some important scenarios where Wireshark may come in handy.

Controller-to-Host Communication

Sometimes, the local Bluetooth host or controller (Bluetooth hardware) may misbehave. Also, if there are interoperability issues with an external controller, for example, a Bluetooth dongle connecting the host through a USB, then Wireshark can be used.

All host-to-controller communication happens through the HCI. Inspecting the HCI messages can help in this case. Filtering HCI was discussed in the previous section "HCI."

No.	Time	Source	Destination	Protocol	Dest Port	source port	Length	Info
1	0.000000	controller	host	HCI_EVT			13	Rcvd Connect Request
2	0.000047	host	controller	HCI_CMD			11	Sent Accept Connection Request
3	0.003000	controller	host	HCI_EVT			7	Rcvd Command Status (Accept Connection Request)
4	0.031467	controller	host	HCI_EVT			14	Rcvd Connect Complete
5	0.031511	host	controller	HCI_CMD			6	Sent Read RSSI
6	0.032467	controller	host	HCI_EVT			30	Rcvd Vendor-Specific
7	0.033439	controller	host	HCI_EVT			10	Rcvd Command Complete (Read RSSI)
8	0.042292	host	controller	HCI_CMD			6	Sent Role Discovery
9	0.044455	controller	host	HCI_EVT			10	Rcvd Command Complete (Role Discovery)
10	0.044534	host	controller	HCI_CMD			8	Sent Write Automatic Flush Timeout
11	0.046451	controller	host	HCI_EVT			9	Rcvd Command Complete (Write Automatic Flush Timeout)
12	0.046597	host	controller	HCI_CMD			6	Sent Read Clock offset
13	0.048449	controller	host	HCI_EVT			7	Rcvd Command Status (Read Clock offset)
14	0.048610	host	controller	HCI_CMD			7	Sent Read Tx Power Level
15	0.049446	controller	host	HCI_EVT			8	Rcvd Read Clock Offset Complete
16	0.050519	controller	host	HCI_EVT			10	Rcvd Command Complete (Read Tx Power Level)
17	0.050669	host	controller	HCI_CMD			6	Sent Read Link Quality

***Figure 7-10.** Host and controller communication*

Pairing and Bonding

Pairing is used to authenticate a device and establish a bond by storing it as a known trusted device if the pairing is successful. Pairing normally requires a user to start the pairing process, but it can be done without user intervention also.

Once a device is paired and bonded, an authentication key is generated which is used to encrypt the communication data link. Once paired for subsequent attempts, no user intervention is required to connect two devices.

From Bluetooth 2.1 onward, Secure Simple Pairing (SSP) is used which tweaks the pairing process based on the device type. The following is a summary of the steps:

- From a regular channel scan, discover the presence of a device.

- SDP sets up an L2CAP encapsulated ACL link as usual and exchanges information to discover device profiles.

- Devices exchange and discover I/O capabilities (have a keyboard, display, etc. or not). Some devices like a Bluetooth mouse and audio headsets do not have any capability to enter a key or display to see any code.

  - If no I/O, just connect once the user manually triggers a pairing.

  - If both the devices have a display and key entering capability, the user must enter or acknowledge (yes/no) a displayed key.

- If both devices support NFC, instead of manually entering the pairing key information can be learned out of band.

All these transactions can be tracked through Wireshark captures. This helps in detecting the failures in the pairing process. The following are some of the snapshots which show the steps mentioned earlier.

```
>  Frame 62: 257 bytes on wire (2056 bits), 257 bytes captured (2056 bits)
>  Bluetooth
v  Bluetooth HCI H1 Rcvd HCI Event
      [Direction: Rcvd (1)]
v  Bluetooth HCI Event – Extended Inquiry Result
      Event Code: Extended Inquiry Result (0x2f)
      Parameter Total Length: 255
      Number of responses: 1
      BD_ADDR: Plantron_a3:7b:19 (bc:f2:92:a3:7b:19)
      Page Scan Repetition Mode: R1 (0x01)
      Reserved: 0x00
      Class of Device: 0x240404 (Audio/Video:Wearable Headset Device – services: Rendering Audio)
      .010 1111 1011 0010 = Clock Offset: 0x2fb2
      RSSI: –60 dBm
      Extended Inquiry Response Data
      >  Device Name: PLT Focus
      >  Tx Power Level
      >  Manufacturer Specific
      >  16–bit Service Class UUIDs (incomplete)
      >  128–bit Service Class UUIDs
         Unused
```

Figure 7-11. *Regular channel scan: discover the presence of a device*

Time	Source	Destination	Protocol	Dest Port	source port	Length	Info
165 12970801_	Plantron_a_	localhost ()	L2CAP			20	Rcvd Connection Response – Pending (SCID: 0x0506)
166 13013750_	Plantron_a_	localhost ()	L2CAP			20	Rcvd Connection Response – Success (SCID: 0x0506, DCID: 0x0100)
167 13013750_	host	controller	HCI_CMD			7	Sent Write Link Supervision Timeout
168 13013750_	localhost _	Plantron_a3:7b:19 (PLT Focus)	L2CAP			20	Sent Configure Request (DCID: 0x0100)
169 13056700_	controller	host	HCI_EVT			8	Rcvd Command Complete (Write Link Supervision Timeout)
170 13099650_	Plantron_a_	localhost ()	L2CAP			20	Rcvd Configure Request (DCID: 0x0506)
171 13099650_	localhost _	Plantron_a3:7b:19 (PLT Focus)	L2CAP			22	Sent Configure Response – Success (SCID: 0x0100)
172 13185549_	controller	host	HCI_EVT			7	Rcvd Number of Completed Packets
173 13228499_	controller	host	HCI_EVT			7	Rcvd Number of Completed Packets
174 13357348_	Plantron_a_	localhost ()	L2CAP			22	Rcvd Configure Response – Success (SCID: 0x0506)
175 13357348_	localhost _	Plantron_a3:7b:19 (PLT Focus)	SDP			21	Sent Service Search Request : L2CAP
176 13443247_	controller	host	HCI_EVT			7	Rcvd Number of Completed Packets
177 13615046_	Plantron_a_	localhost ()	SDP			46	Rcvd Service Search Response
178 13615046_	localhost _	Plantron_a3:7b:19 (PLT Focus)	SDP			27	Sent Service Attribute Request : 0x00010001 – Attribute Range (0x0000 – 0xffff)
179 13743095_	controller	host	HCI_EVT			7	Rcvd Number of Completed Packets
180 13872744_	Plantron_a_	localhost ()	SDP			56	Rcvd Service Attribute Response (fragment)
181 13915694_	localhost _	Plantron_a3:7b:19 (PLT Focus)	SDP			29	Sent Service Attribute Request : 0x00010001 – Attribute Range (0x0000 – 0xffff)
182 14001593_	controller	host	HCI_EVT			7	Rcvd Number of Completed Packets
183 14087492_	Plantron_a_	localhost ()	SDP			56	Rcvd Service Attribute Response (fragment)
184 14130442_	localhost _	Plantron_a3:7b:19 (PLT Focus)	SDP			29	Sent Service Attribute Request : 0x00010001 – Attribute Range (0x0000 – 0xffff)

```
>  Frame 180: 56 bytes on wire (448 bits), 56 bytes captured (448 bits)
>  Bluetooth
v  Bluetooth HCI H1 Rcvd ACL Data
      [Direction: Rcvd (1)]
>  Bluetooth HCI ACL Packet
v  Bluetooth L2CAP Protocol
      Length: 48
      CID: Dynamically Allocated Channel (0x0506)
      [Connect in frame: 163]
      [Disconnect in frame: 251]
      [PSM: SDP (0x0001)]
v  Bluetooth SDP Protocol
      PDU: Service Attribute Response (0x05)
      Transaction Id: 0x0002
      Parameter Length: 43
      Attribute List Byte Count: 38
      Data Fragment
      >  Continuation State: yes (00 36)
```

Figure 7-12. *Discover services: SDP sets up an L2CAP encapsulated ACL link*

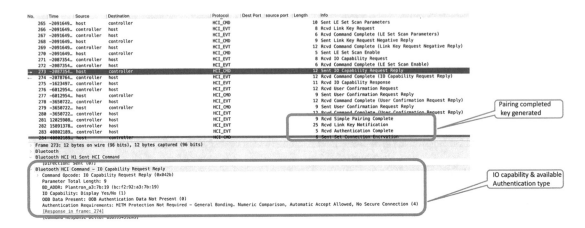

Figure 7-13. *Discover I/O capabilities and pair*

Paired Device Discovery and Data Transfer

When the devices are already paired and come in range, a set of procedures must be completed before data is transferred:

- Devices do a link scan, signal strength measurement, etc.

- Initiate a role discovery and agree on the master. Exchange the link encryption keys generated during pairing (both sides must have the same key). The key is not encrypted and can be seen as clear text.

Source	Destination	Protocol	Length	Info
host	controller	HCI_CMD	6	Sent Role Discovery
controller	host	HCI_EVT	7	Rcvd Link Supervision Timeout Changed
controller	host	HCI_EVT	10	Rcvd Command Complete (Role Discovery)
host	controller	HCI_CMD	11	Sent Switch Role
controller	host	HCI_EVT	7	Rcvd Command Status (Switch Role)
controller	host	HCI_EVT	9	Rcvd Link Key Request
host	controller	HCI_CMD	26	Sent Link Key Request Reply
controller	host	HCI_EVT	13	Rcvd Command Complete (Link Key Request Reply)

Figure 7-14. *Link scan role discovery and key exchange*

- SDP initiates an ACL link over L2CAP for peer service profile and capability discovery.

Source	Destination	Protocol	Length	Info
Plantron_a3:7b:19 ()	localhost ()	L2CAP	17	Rcvd Connection Request (SDP, SCID: 0x0080)
localhost ()	Plantron_a3:7b:19 ()	L2CAP	21	Sent Connection Response – Pending (SCID: 0x0080)
localhost ()	Plantron_a3:7b:19 ()	L2CAP	21	Sent Connection Response – Success (SCID: 0x0080, DCID: 0x0040)
localhost ()	Plantron_a3:7b:19 ()	L2CAP	21	Sent Configure Request (DCID: 0x0080)

Figure 7-15. *SDP ACL connection initiation*

Source	Destination	Protocol	Length	Info
Plantron_a3:7b:19 ()	localhost ()	SDP	22	Rcvd Service Search Request : Headset Audio Gateway
localhost ()	Plantron_a3:7b:19 ()	SDP	19	Sent Service Search Response
Plantron_a3:7b:19 ()	localhost ()	SDP	22	Rcvd Service Search Request : Handsfree Audio Gateway
localhost ()	Plantron_a3:7b:19 ()	SDP	23	Sent Service Search Response
Plantron_a3:7b:19 ()	localhost ()	SDP	22	Rcvd Service Search Request : Phonebook Access Server
localhost ()	Plantron_a3:7b:19 ()	SDP	19	Sent Service Search Response
Plantron_a3:7b:19 ()	localhost ()	SDP	22	Rcvd Service Search Request : Audio Source
localhost ()	Plantron_a3:7b:19 ()	SDP	23	Sent Service Search Response
Plantron_a3:7b:19 ()	localhost ()	SDP	22	Rcvd Service Search Request : A/V Remote Control Target
localhost ()	Plantron_a3:7b:19 ()	SDP	23	Sent Service Search Response
Plantron_a3:7b:19 ()	localhost ()	SDP	22	Rcvd Service Search Request : A/V Remote Control Controller
localhost ()	Plantron_a3:7b:19 ()	SDP	23	Sent Service Search Response
Plantron_a3:7b:19 ()	localhost ()	SDP	36	Rcvd Service Search Request : Unknown
localhost ()	Plantron_a3:7b:19 ()	SDP	19	Sent Service Search Response
Plantron_a3:7b:19 ()	localhost ()	SDP	27	Rcvd Service Search Attribute Request : Handsfree Audio Gateway: [Protocol Descriptor List 0x0004]
localhost ()	Plantron_a3:7b:19 ()	SDP	38	Sent Service Search Attribute Response
Plantron_a3:7b:19 ()	localhost ()	SDP	30	Rcvd Service Search Attribute Request : A/V Remote Control Target: [Bluetooth Profile Descriptor List 0x0009] [(AVRCP) Supported Features 0x031…
localhost ()	Plantron_a3:7b:19 ()	SDP	40	Sent Service Search Attribute Response
Plantron_a3:7b:19 ()	localhost ()	SDP	30	Rcvd Service Search Attribute Request : A/V Remote Control Target: [Bluetooth Profile Descriptor List 0x0009] [(AVRCP) Supported Features 0x031…
localhost ()	Plantron_a3:7b:19 ()	SDP	40	Sent Service Search Attribute Response

Figure 7-16. *SDP service profile discovery*

- Based on the profile discovery required, upper layer protocols initiate additional connections for the exchange of configuration parameters.

- In our example, the Bluetooth headset is connected to a laptop. So we can see RFCOMM for the configuration setup and AVCTP and AVDTP protocol connections for audio control and data.

Source	Destination	Protocol	Length	Info
Plantron_a3:7b:19 ()	localhost ()	HFP	21	Rcvd AT+CLCC
localhost ()	Plantron_a3:7b:19 ()	HFP	20	Sent OK
controller	host	HCI_EVT	8	Rcvd Number of Completed Packets
Plantron_a3:7b:19 ()	localhost ()	RFCOMM	14	Rcvd UIH Channel=1 UID
Plantron_a3:7b:19 ()	localhost ()	HFP	34	Rcvd AT+BIA=0,1,1,1,0,0,0
localhost ()	Plantron_a3:7b:19 ()	HFP	20	Sent OK
Plantron_a3:7b:19 ()	localhost ()	RFCOMM	14	Rcvd UIH Channel=1 UID
controller	host	HCI_EVT	8	Rcvd Number of Completed Packets
Plantron_a3:7b:19 ()	localhost ()	L2CAP	17	Rcvd Connection Request (AVDTP, SCID: 0x0141)
localhost ()	Plantron_a3:7b:19 ()	L2CAP	21	Sent Connection Response – Pending (SCID: 0x0141)
localhost ()	Plantron_a3:7b:19 ()	L2CAP	21	Sent Connection Response – Success (SCID: 0x0141, DCID: 0x0043)
localhost ()	Plantron_a3:7b:19 ()	L2CAP	17	Sent Configure Request (DCID: 0x0141)
controller	host	HCI_EVT	8	Rcvd Number of Completed Packets
controller	host	HCI_EVT	8	Rcvd Number of Completed Packets
Plantron_a3:7b:19 ()	localhost ()	L2CAP	25	Rcvd Configure Request (DCID: 0x0043)
localhost ()	Plantron_a3:7b:19 ()	L2CAP	19	Sent Configure Response – Success (SCID: 0x0141)
controller	host	HCI_EVT	8	Rcvd Number of Completed Packets
Plantron_a3:7b:19 ()	localhost ()	L2CAP	27	Rcvd Configure Response – Success (SCID: 0x0043)
controller	host	HCI_EVT	8	Rcvd Number of Completed Packets
Plantron_a3:7b:19 ()	localhost ()	L2CAP	17	Rcvd Connection Request (AVCTP-Control, SCID: 0x0182)
localhost ()	Plantron_a3:7b:19 ()	L2CAP	21	Sent Connection Response – Pending (SCID: 0x0182)
localhost ()	Plantron_a3:7b:19 ()	L2CAP	21	Sent Connection Response – Success (SCID: 0x0182, DCID: 0x0044)
localhost ()	Plantron_a3:7b:19 ()	L2CAP	28	Sent Configure Request (DCID: 0x0182)

Figure 7-17. *Upper layer connection setup*

- After the upper layer connections are set up, actual data transfer can be seen. Here in our case, AVDTP is used to transport audio using aptX codec.

Source	Destination	Protocol	Length	Info
localhost ()	Plantron_a3:7b:19 ()	AVDTP	12	Sent Command – Start – ACP SEID [2 – Audio Sink]
controller	host	HCI_EVT	8	Rcvd Number of Completed Packets
Plantron_a3:7b:19 ()	localhost ()	AVDTP	11	Rcvd ResponseAccept – Start
localhost ()	Plantron_a3:7b:19 ()	aptX	681	Sent aptX
controller	host	HCI_EVT	8	Rcvd Number of Completed Packets
localhost ()	Plantron_a3:7b:19 ()	aptX	681	Sent aptX
localhost ()	Plantron_a3:7b:19 ()	aptX	681	Sent aptX

Figure 7-18. *Data transfer*

Summary

This chapter is all about how Wireshark helps with Bluetooth packet capture and analysis. In this chapter, we learned about

- Bluetooth standard evolution from versions 1 to 5.3

- Overall architecture and protocol stacks of Bluetooth Classic (BR/EDR) and Bluetooth Low Energy (LE)

- How to use Wireshark to filter out each protocol type in the protocol stack

- Wireshark Bluetooth packet capture and tools used on Linux, Windows, and macOS

- How to use Wireshark to understand the complete communication flow starting from device discovery, pairing, service discovery, and data transfer

References for This Chapter

Bluetooth specification: www.bluetooth.com/ specifications/specs/

Bluetooth IEEE standard: https://standards.ieee.org/ ieee/802.15.1/1180/

Bluetooth Test Platform: https://docs.microsoft.com/en-us/ windows-hardware/drivers/bluetooth/testing-btp-tools-btv s?source=recommendations

CHAPTER 8

Network Analysis and Forensics

Wireshark has been one of the important tools for network analysis and troubleshooting. Wireshark gives complete visibility of how a packet is treated at various stages of its propagation from one application endpoint to the other over the network. This visibility powers a network operator to understand what an application is doing, if it's behaving as expected or there is an unexpected malicious attempt to disrupt the network, application, and IT resources.

The Internet has helped people come closer and isolated networks get interconnected. However, it is also the common entry point for security attacks. The threat origin is not limited to the Internet, most of them are traced to internal sources. With clouds spanning both local and the Internet, the threat landscape has expanded manyfold. The overall cybercrime cost for year 2021 is estimated as $6 trillion and expected to double in the next four years.

In previous chapters, you learned about the use of Wireshark for a specific protocol or network type. In this chapter, we take a more generalized deep dive and security-focused approach. You will learn about how to use Wireshark for

- Network security attack identification, postmortems, and prevention

- Discovering malware and covert communications

- Tips and tricks for Wireshark forensics

- DDoS and malware step-by-step analysis with real attack pcap files

Network Attack Classification

Cyber-attacks have evolved with time, and there are hundreds of new variants of these getting discovered each day. Every attack type tries to exploit some vulnerability

© Nagendra Kumar Nainar and Ashish Panda 2023
N. K. Nainar and A. Panda, *Wireshark for Network Forensics*, https://doi.org/10.1007/978-1-4842-9001-9_8

on the end hosts, networks, networking protocols, and even firewalls and security appliances too.

Every attack type can be completely different or may be minor or major variants of any known vulnerability exploit. However, the popular ones can be broadly categorized into a few buckets. The following section will discuss the same in more detail. We will discuss in detail how their signature can be detected through Wireshark.

Packet Poisoning and Spoofing Attacks

It's practically possible for an attacker to follow a packet stream of communication between two devices and impersonate one of the participants. This becomes easy in broadcast media like Ethernet where all devices in the same VLAN have reachability with each other. ARP spoofing and poisoning are common forms of this type of attack:

- With the ARP spoofing type of attacks, the attacker sends ARP replies of the same IP with a different MAC.

- In ARP poisoning, the attacker sends ARP replies with different IPs for the same MAC.

ARP spoofing aims at impersonating another machine, thereby redirecting data meant for the victim machine toward itself. ARP poisoning on the other hand is normally aimed at corrupting the ARP table of a victim machine. Both ARP poisoning and spoofing have a common motive and operate through malicious ARP or gratuitous ARP replies.

Often, both of these terms are used interchangeably. The following figures will demonstrate the subtle difference between these techniques.

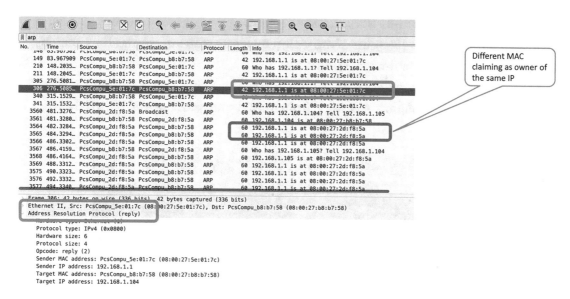

Figure 8-1. ARP spoofing

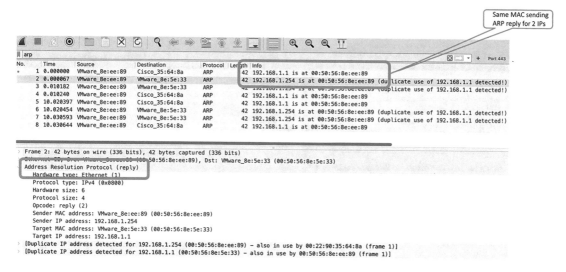

Figure 8-2. ARP poisoning

DHCP Spoofing

Like ARP spoofing, in this type of attack the attacker machine waits for DHCP requests and sends DHCP offers and ACK with its own address as the default gateway or DNS server. This directs all traffic from the victim machine to the attacker and creates the perfect scenario for a man-in-the-middle attack. The attacker machine may also act as a proxy for all communications of the victim machine with any destination, thereby stealing sensitive information, passwords, etc.

DHCP spoofing can be traced through Wireshark by using a display filter as "***dhcp***" and checking if DHCP offers are coming from a valid source or not and if the DHCP options are correct.

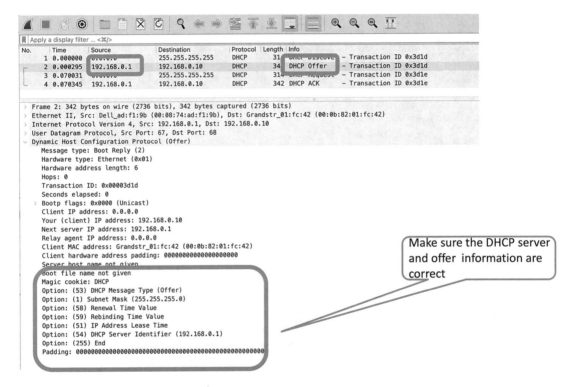

Figure 8-3. *DHCP verification*

DNS Spoofing and Poisoning

Consider the previous scenario of ARP or DHCP spoofing causing traffic to be diverted to the attacker machine. Also, it can act as a DNS server if the DHCP offer is compromised by specifying the attacker's IP as the DNS server IP.

Like ARP poisoning, the DNS server cache entry can be poisoned with adding incorrect entries by an attacker DNS client.

With both DNS spoofing and poisoning, the stage is set by the attacker to respond to DNS queries with incorrect mappings pointing to one of the attacker machines, which can further exploit the victim device.

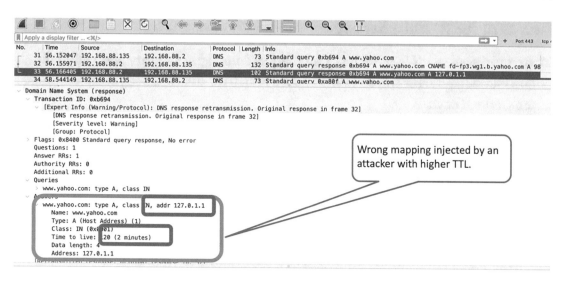

Figure 8-4. *DNS spoofing*

Prevention of Spoofing Attacks

Apart from ARP, DHCP, and DNS discussed earlier, practically any networking protocol (e.g., OSPF, BGP, STP) can be spoofed or poisoned unless protected. Most of the protocols these days have authentication built in for every packet. Some also have antireplay and encryption protection built into the protocol. Both must be used wherever available. DNSSEC (authentication and integrity protection) and DNS over TLS (encryption) are recommended over traditional DNS.

For ARP and DHCP spoofing, layer 2 switches have port security, and dynamic ARP inspection (DAI) features are available and recommended for secure operation.

Network Scan and Discovery Attacks

These types of attacks are not meant to cause any real damage but are used as a reconnaissance method before a real attack. With these attacks, the attacker gains an understanding of the network topology, endpoint IP/IPv6 addresses, open ports, what kind of operating system is being used, what kind of security infrastructure is in place, etc. This is a very vital and sensitive information as it can be further used to exploit the known vulnerabilities on those network and infrastructure devices. The following subsections discuss in more detail some of the common attacks.

ARP and ICMP Ping Sweeps

This type of scan sends ICMP echo or ARP request messages for every host within the defined subnet. Attackers prefer doing an ARP scan if the attacker is in the same subnet as the scanned device.

With Wireshark, you can clearly identify this type of sweep attack as a burst of ARP or ICMP packets from one IP going to multiple IPs.

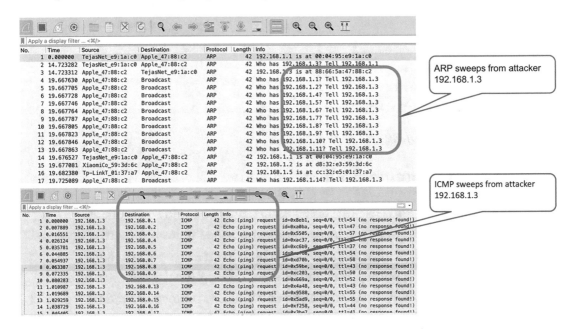

Figure 8-5. Sweep attacks – ARP and ICMP

UDP Port Scan

With UDP port scan, the attacker sends a burst of UDP packets to the target victim, sequentially increasing the destination port value from 1 to max 65535.

If there is no service running on the UDP port, the victim replies with an ICMP unreachable message saying the port is not reachable. However, some hosts do not do. Sometimes, if the port is open and the application behind this port consumes the packet and if the packet payload is not the expected format, the attacker may not get a response. Based on this logic, the attacker gets an understanding of open and closed ports on a device.

With Wireshark, you can see these attacks as a flood of packets going to a single IP with different UDP port values.

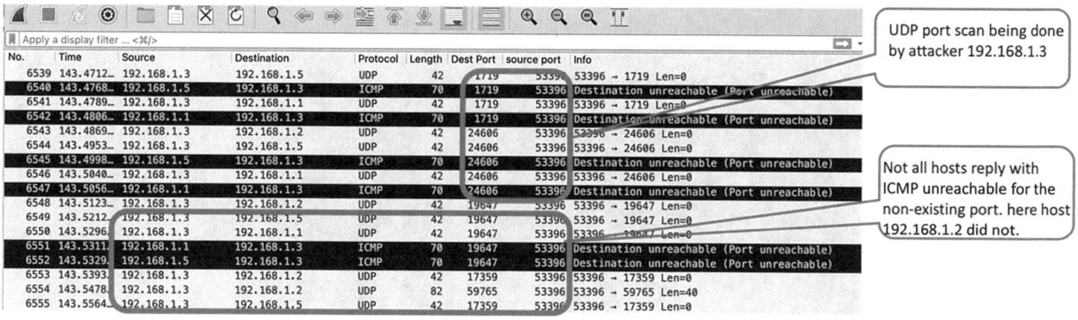

Figure 8-6. *UDP port scan*

TCP Port Scan

For an attacker, TCP scan is easier than UDP as all hosts send an RST message for a port if the port is not open. Figure 8-7 shows the simple form of TCP scan known as TCP SYN scan. The attacker sends a TCP packet with a SYN flag set to the victim port.

- If the port is closed, a TCP packet with RST is returned.

- If the port is open, a TCP packet with SYN ACK is returned.

  - The attacker then quickly sends RST and moves on to scan the next port.

Like SYN scan, the attacker can utilize other TCP flags (ACK, FIN, PSH, URG) when sending the packet by setting any of these flags. By interpreting the response type, it can be determined whether a port is open, closed, or filtered by any access list or firewall.

This type of scan also can be easily identified by a set of SYN and RST response flood exchanges between the attacker and the victim.

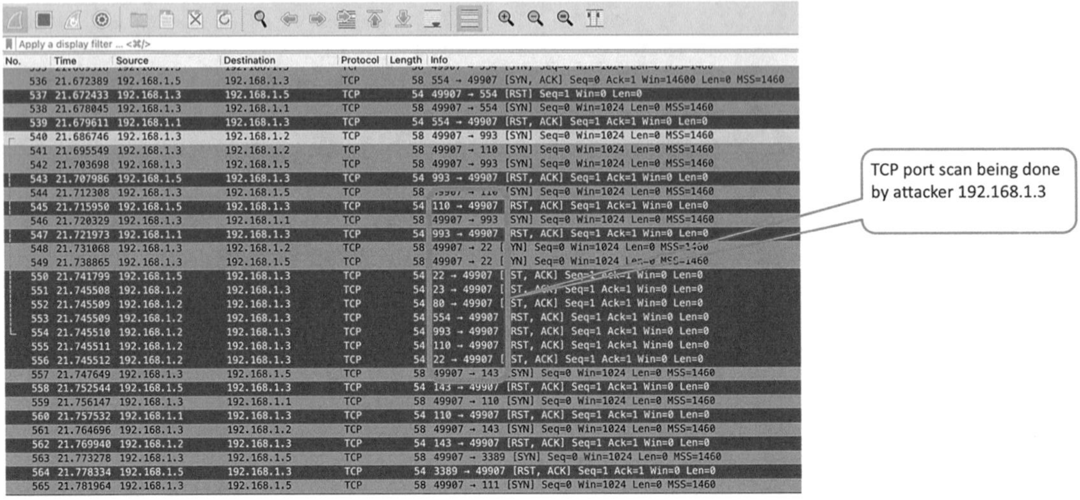

Figure 8-7. TCP port scan

OS Fingerprinting

There may be minor differences between operating systems in the way they respond to a TCP/IP connection attempt. For example, one OS may have a different initial sequence number than the other. Similarly, the IP Identifier field, TCP options support, and TCP initial window size may be different too.

An attacker may use this to its advantage and try to identify the victim's operating system version.

Figure 8-8 shows what the Wireshark capture looks like for a fingerprinting attempt through **nmap**. The attacker first initiates a TCP port scan, then an ICMP scan for IP Identifier signature, and then TCP window and initial sequence number signature fingerprinting:

Nmap scan report for scanme.nmap.org (45.33.32.156)
Host is up (0.26s latency).
Not shown: 995 closed tcp ports (reset)

PORT	STATE	SERVICE
22/tcp	open	ssh
53/tcp	filtered	domain
80/tcp	open	http
9929/tcp	open	nping-echo
31337/tcp	open	Elite

Aggressive OS guesses: Linux 2.6.32 (95%), Linux 2.6.32 or 3.10 (94%), Linux 2.6.39 (94%), Linux 3.10 - 3.12 (94%), Linux 3.4 (94%), Linux 3.5 (94%), Linux 4.2 (94%), Linux 4.4 (94%), Synology DiskStation Manager 5.1 (94%), WatchGuard Fireware 11.8 (94%)

No exact OS matches for host (test conditions non-ideal).

Uptime guess: 49.243 days (since Fri Jul 29 08:14:04 2022)

Network Distance: 12 hops

TCP Sequence Prediction: Difficulty=262 (Good luck!)

IP ID Sequence Generation: All zeros

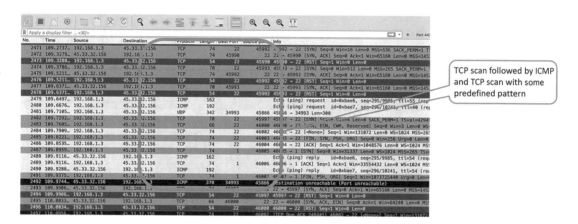

Figure 8-8. *OS fingerprinting*

Preventing Port Scan Attacks

The use of a good firewall and intrusion detection/prevention systems will help with this. Honeypots can be useful too. After the scan is detected, it can be redirected to a honeypot instead of forwarded to the victim.

Brute-Force Attacks

Brute-force attacks are used to gain access to any device by guessing the username or password. Although guessing the username or password can take a long time to crack, there are a lot of techniques like rainbow table, dictionary of known credentials, hybrid brute force, etc. which can make it quicker.

All of these techniques generate a flood of traffic like port scans and can be easily detected through Wireshark analysis. Also, at the end device side, multiple failed attempts should raise a red flag.

In Figure 8-9, we have demonstrated a telnet brute-force connection attempt. We can see a flood of TCP connection attempts from sequential source ports. Further, the TCP data can be inspected by clicking one of the packets and navigating through the Wireshark menu *Analyze ➤ Follow ➤ TCP stream*.

Preventing Brute-Force Attacks

This type of attack can easily be prevented by delaying failed attempts, using a strong password policy, multifactor authentication, and monitoring devices for failed attempts.

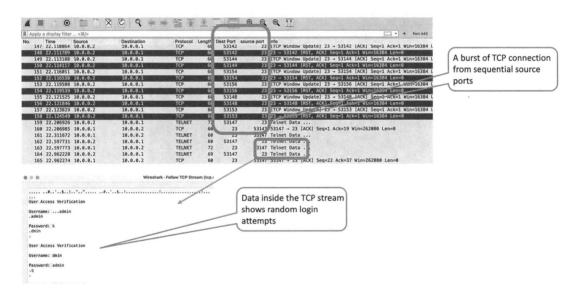

Figure 8-9. *Brute-force attack detection*

DoS (Denial-of-Service) Attacks

Denial-of-service attacks aim to disrupt a network or service by generating authorized data or connections in such volume that it overwhelms the capacity.

For example, if a server can handle 100,000 connections at a time, and if an attacker generates connections that exceed this number, the server is overloaded and cannot handle legitimate connections. Similarly, if a service provider has a 10 Gbps Internet link and an attacker generates data that clogs the network capacity, then the legitimate data and users are affected.

Most of the time, the attack doesn't come from a single source. Either the attacker has a huge globally distributed infrastructure or infects multiple devices with malware and controls them to generate a coordinated attack against the victim network or service endpoint. Such distributed DoS attacks are termed **DDoS** attacks. DDoS attacks can cripple a network and server very quickly due to the distributed, synchronized nature that generates a huge load on the infrastructure.

Figure 8-10 shows two examples from real data set where packets were flooded with random source IPs and IP protocol values. The second Wireshark snapshot shows a flood of UDP packets with random ports and source IPs.

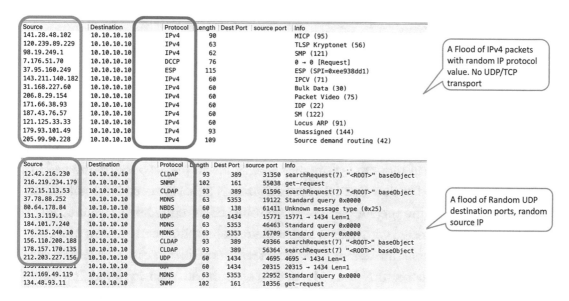

Figure 8-10. *DDoS examples, random UDP and IP protocols*

Figure 8-11 shows two examples from real DDoS attacks. The first example shows TCP packets with SYN ACK flags and are coming from the same source and destination ports.

In the second one, DNS amplification attack symptoms are seen where DNS replies from random sources are directed toward the victim.

Source	Destination	Protocol	Length	Dest Port	source port	Info
136.243.174.154	10.10.10.10	TCP	74	9069	55680	5680 → 9069 [SYN] Seq=0 Win=42340 Len=0 MSS=1460 SACK_PERM=
75.136.225.254	10.10.10.10	TCP	60	21	21	1 → 21 [SYN, ACK] Seq=0 Ack=1 Win=65535 Len=0 MSS=1460
42.51.60.58	10.10.10.10	TCP	60	2376	57635	7635 → 2376 [SYN] Seq=0 Win=1024 Len=0
75.136.225.254	10.10.10.10	TCP	60	21	21	TCP Retransmission] 21 → 21 [SYN, ACK] Seq=0 Ack=1 Win=6553
75.136.225.254	10.10.10.10	TCP	60	21	21	TCP Retransmission] 21 → 21 [SYN, ACK] Seq=0 Ack=1 Win=6553
136.243.174.154	10.10.10.10	TCP	74	9069	55684	5684 → 9069 [SYN] Seq=0 Win=42340 Len=0 MSS=1460 SACK_PERM=
93.114.150.139	10.10.10.10	TCP	60	21	21	1 → 21 [SYN, ACK] Seq=0 Ack=1 Win=64240 Len=0 MSS=1412
75.136.225.254	10.10.10.10	TCP	60	21	21	TCP Retransmission] 21 → 21 [SYN, ACK] Seq=0 Ack=1 Win=6553
163.158.248.5	10.10.10.10	TCP	74	9070	54496	4496 → 9070 [SYN] Seq=0 Win=64240 Len=0 MSS=1460 SACK_PERM=
75.136.225.254	10.10.10.10	TCP	60	21	21	TCP Retransmission] 21 → 21 [SYN, ACK] Seq=0 Ack=1 Win=6553
40.77.226.250	10.10.10.10	TCP	66	43796	443	43 → 43796 [SYN, ACK] Seq=0 Ack=1 Win=65535 Len=0 MSS=1420
136.243.174.154	10.10.10.10	TCP	74	9069	55688	5688 → 9069 [SYN] Seq=0 Win=42340 Len=0 MSS=1460 SACK_PERM=
75.136.225.254	10.10.10.10	TCP	60	21	21	TCP Retransmission] 21 → 21 [SYN, ACK] Seq=0 Ack=1 Win=6553
93.114.150.139	10.10.10.10	TCP	60	21	21	TCP Retransmission] 21 → 21 [SYN, ACK] Seq=0 Ack=1 Win=6424
75.136.225.254	10.10.10.10	TCP	60	21	21	TCP Retransmission] 21 → 21 [SYN, ACK] Seq=0 Ack=1 Win=6553
91.121.144.97	10.10.10.10	TCP	60	3199	45335	5335 → 3199 [SYN] Seq=0 Win=1024 Len=0
75.136.225.254	10.10.10.10	TCP	60	21	21	TCP Retransmission] 21 → 21 [SYN, ACK] Seq=0 Ack=1 Win=6553

TCP SYN ACK packets with same source & destination port from random sources

Source	Destination	Protocol	Length	Dest Port	source port	Info
45.179.193.111	10.10.10.10	DNS	1490	22	53	Standard query response 0x3b76 RRSIG pizzaseo.com RRSIG
185.49.192.170	10.10.10.10	DNS	1052	22	53	Standard query response 0x3b76 RRSIG pizzaseo.com RRSIG
24.199.33.46	10.10.10.10	DNS	72	22	53	Standard query response 0x6fd9 Server failure RRSIG pizz
24.199.33.46	10.10.10.10	DNS	72	22	53	Standard query response 0x3b76 Server failure RRSIG pizz
36.92.44.202	10.10.10.10	DNS	1004	22	53	Standard query response 0x6fd9 RRSIG pizzaseo.com RRSIG
36.92.44.202	10.10.10.10	DNS	1004	22	53	Standard query response 0x6fd9 RRSIG pizzaseo.com RRSIG
36.92.44.202	10.10.10.10	DNS	1004	22	53	Standard query response 0x6fd9 RRSIG pizzaseo.com RRSIG
36.92.44.202	10.10.10.10	DNS	1514	22	53	Standard query response 0x3b76 RRSIG pizzaseo.com RRSIG
36.92.44.202	10.10.10.10	DNS	1004	22	53	Standard query response 0x3b76 RRSIG pizzaseo.com RRSIG
36.92.44.202	10.10.10.10	DNS	1004	22	53	Standard query response 0x3b76 RRSIG pizzaseo.com RRSIG
36.92.44.202	10.10.10.10	DNS	1514	22	53	Standard query response 0x3b76 RRSIG pizzaseo.com RRSIG
36.92.44.202	10.10.10.10	DNS	1514	22	53	Standard query response 0x3b76 RRSIG pizzaseo.com RRSIG
185.49.192.170	10.10.10.10	DNS	1052	22	53	Standard query response 0x3b76 RRSIG pizzaseo.com RRSIG
80.83.233.167	10.10.10.10	DNS	1004	22	53	Standard query response 0xfddf RRSIG pizzaseo.com RRSIG
80.83.233.167	10.10.10.10	DNS	1514	22	53	Standard query response 0xfddf RRSIG pizzaseo.com RRSIG

DNS reply from SSH port 22 from random IP sources

Figure 8-11. *DDoS example: TCP SYN ACK with the same port, DNS replies amplification with an SSH port*

Preventing DDoS Attacks

Normally, it's not possible to completely block the ports or links that bring in offending connections and data as they are legitimate traffic. For example, web traffic directed to a web server and upload or download data on an Internet link. However, if the pattern of the attack is unusual, the specific sources can be blocked or redirected to a honeypot.

A good network design with proper segmentation and redundant systems and servers should help lower the damage and help recover quicker in case of attacks seen.

Network and infrastructure should be beefed up with web security, good firewall, and intrusion detection and prevention policies. Endpoint security, antivirus, and antimalware tools should be deployed to protect the edge devices.

Malware Attacks

This type of attack constitutes a significant portion of the overall cyber-attacks recorded. Malware stands for malicious software. Malware has a broad category of software that infects and exploits networks, servers, and end hosts in various ways.

Virus, worms, and trojan horses: They enter a computing device through physical, Internet, emails, file attachments, and all possible digital transfer means. They infect the system, can encrypt or delete all data, and replicate and propagate to other computers by exploiting existing vulnerabilities. Sometimes, they can act like ransomware too.

Spyware, adware, keyloggers, and phishing: These types of malware aim at collecting sensitive information from the victim and don't cause much damage. They can replicate and propagate like viruses and worms through all possible means.

Botnet and crypto miners: These types of malware use the computing resources of the victim system to cause DDoS-type attacks or earn money through crypto mining.

Ransomware: This type of malware after infecting the victim device or network demands ransom to not cause damage to the system.

Every malware has its own way of communicating over the network and replicating. By monitoring the same Wireshark can detect malware communication signatures through packet capture. However, some of them can be extremely stealthy and may not communicate at all. Those are difficult to analyze through Wireshark.

Figure 8-12 shows an example of Turkish redirect malware from a real data set. This caused all file downloads redirected to another infected destination. We have a step-by-step guide for the analysis approach for malware attacks discussed in the section "Wireshark Malware Analysis."

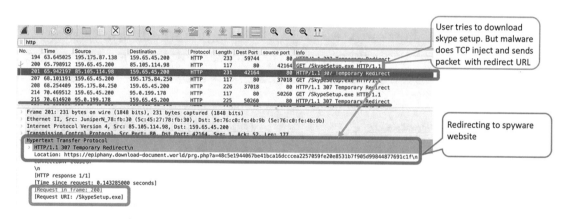

Figure 8-12. *Turkish malware redirect*

Prevention of Malware Attacks

Following a proper network and security hygiene will go a long way in preventing malware attacks.

Network and infrastructure should be beefed up with web security, good firewall, and intrusion detection and prevention policies. Multifactor authentication, endpoint security, and antivirus and antimalware tools should be deployed to protect the edge devices.

All devices should have updated software, and any known vulnerabilities should be patched at the earliest. Email, web, and cloud security protection mechanisms must be deployed.

Most malware attacks rely on social engineering and phishing techniques which trick the end user into clicking malicious links and opening malicious attachments. User education is important to prevent malware attacks through all such means.

Wireshark Tweaks for Forensics

Autoresolving Geolocation

It is very important to know the attacker's source IP geolocation. Wireshark supports the integration of the **Country**, **AS** number, and **City** database provided by MaxMind. The details can be downloaded free of cost from MaxMind as a .mmdb file format at the following location after creating an account:

www.maxmind.com/en/accounts/767404/geoip/downloads

The geolocation feature can be enabled by navigating the Wireshark preference menu. After it's activated, Wireshark needs to be restarted. Post activation, the location, AS, and country details can be seen from the *statistics* ➤ *endpoints* ➤ *ipv4* menu.

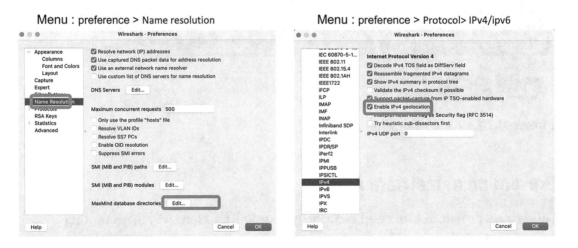

Figure 8-13. *Enabling geolocation*

Changing the Column Display

Including the TCP/UDP port, the location, country, and window size help in the quick identification of the traffic flow and the distribution. It can be added or changed from the menu *Preferences ➤ column*.

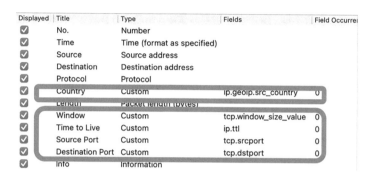

Figure 8-14. *Wireshark display custom column*

Frequently Used Wireshark Tricks in Forensics

Find Exact Packets One at a Time

Though the display filter has good features, if regular expression matching or packet hex matching is required, this method is useful.

This process finds one packet at a time and moves to the next one once the Find button is clicked again.

Hex: Find a packet with a hex pattern matching the specific hex value.

Regular expression: It matches the string in the dissected text shown in the packets.

String: The string matches the text in the info field.

Trigger this menu with *Edit ➤ find packet*. Alternatively, one can use shortcut keys [Ctrl+F] on Windows or [Command+F] in macOS.

Contains Operator

This is a useful search operator in the display filter. We can have flexible searches like the following:

frame contains GET: Looks for the value GET inside the complete frame

http contains facebook: Looks for the text value facebook in the HTTP fields

data-text-lines contains "javascript": Finds all web pages containing a certain string

Following a TCP Stream

This helps stitch payload fields in the TCP and decode. This gives visibility into what the application is doing and is very useful while analyzing HTTP streams.

This option can be triggered with the menu option *Analyze* ➤ *Follow* ➤ *TCP stream*.

Wireshark Forensic Analysis Approach

Wireshark packet inspection can help identify the type of attack. In this section, the analysis approach for two important types of attacks is discussed in detail.

The basic approach here is to find out the **IOCs** (Indicators of Compromise) and logically determine whether the packet communication behavior is legitimate or malicious. IOCs can be an IP, domain name, user agent, hostname, geolocations, communication pattern, etc.

Wireshark DDoS Analysis

The DDoS attacks are normally geographically distributed. The steps may change based on the attack but broadly remain the same for most of the analysis. The IOCs and analysis steps can be as follows:

- When did the issue start?

- What are the targets?

- What is the IP source of the attack?

- What are the geographical locations and is traffic expected from them?

- Is the traffic pattern similar to the baseline?

- What are the protocols involved?

- Are the TCP/IP fields and communication pattern normal?

  - TCP/UDP port matching

  - HTTP string and substring matching

  - Check for embedded URLs in the TCP stream

  - Check the authenticity of the websites in use

- Is the packet flow expected or indicate a DDoS attack?

The analysis in this section considers a packet capture from a real-world DDoS attack. The sample is taken from the StopDDoS GitHub repository:

`https://github.com/StopDDoS/packet-captures`

At first look, it looks like a SYN flood. We will follow our steps to conclude if it's legitimate or not.

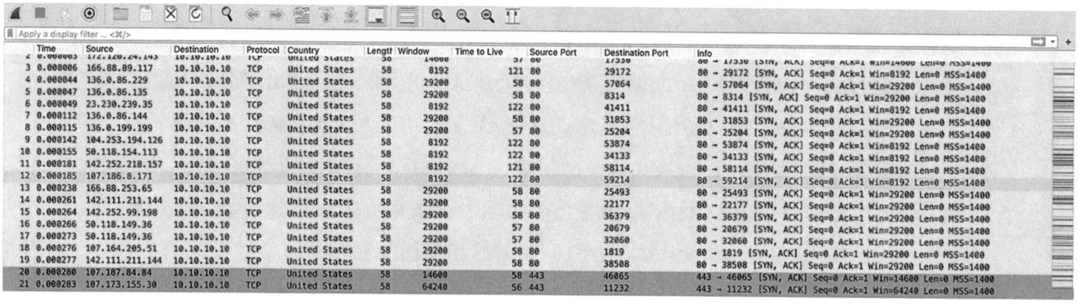

Figure 8-15. *DDoS capture file display*

The following are the answers to our IOCs:

- When did the issue start?

As seen in the first frame, Jun 5, 2021, 09:28:45.551136000 IST.

- What are the targets?

All packets are directed to 10.10.10.10.

- What is the IP source of the attack?

The sources are distributed. The endpoint graph **statistics ➤ endpoints** and conversation graph **statistics ➤ conversations** show the details.

Address A		Address B	Packets	Bytes	Packets A → B	Bytes A → B	Packets B → A	Bytes B → A	Rel Start	Duration	Bits/s A → B	Bits/s B → A
8.12.164.27	▲	10.10.10.10	1	58	1	58	0	0	0.121788	0.0000	—	
8.12.164.100		10.10.10.10	1	58	1	58	0	0	0.100161	0.0000	—	
8.14.147.4		10.10.10.10	1	58	1	58	0	0	0.032061	0.0000	—	
8.17.250.110		10.10.10.10	1	58	1	58	0	0	0.129280	0.0000	—	
23.27.5.50		10.10.10.10	1	58	1	58	0	0	0.068146	0.0000	—	
23.27.6.47		10.10.10.10	1	58	1	58	0	0	0.015931	0.0000	—	
23.27.7.25		10.10.10.10	1	58	1	58	0	0	0.117946	0.0000	—	
23.27.7.53		10.10.10.10	1	58	1	58	0	0	0.095669	0.0000	—	
23.27.7.190		10.10.10.10	1	58	1	58	0	0	0.116451	0.0000	—	
23.27.11.17		10.10.10.10	1	58	1	58	0	0	0.004348	0.0000	—	

Figure 8-16. *Source of the attack*

- What are the geographical locations and is traffic expected from them?

  The endpoint graph **statistics ➤ endpoints** shows the geographic locations and AS numbers of sources in a tabular format. Also, it can be visually inspected by choosing the map option. It can be seen that most of the packets are concentrated at the United States; one of the origins shows 5000+ sessions, which doesn't look normal. Also, the conversation is not limited to a single IP. IP addresses seem to be increasing in sequence, which is also unusual. Mostly, it appears as a distributed botnet attack, or the IP addresses are possibly spoofed and manually generated by some DDoS attack tools.

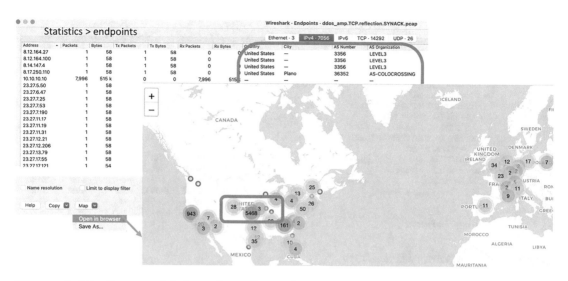

Figure 8-17. *Geographic location of attack*

- Is the traffic pattern similar to the baseline?

  Traffic TCP sessions look unusual, but the rate of traffic is very
  nominal (9 Kbps). The traffic rate can be verified from the I/O graph.
  All the sources in the 7000+ sessions are sending only a single SYN
  packet. They don't attempt to establish the session also.

- What are the protocols involved?

- The *statistics ➤ protocol hierarchy* chart lists all the protocols seen
  in the capture file and is very useful to see all the applications and
  protocols involved on a single page. Based on the output, it can be
  seen it's predominantly TCP traffic (96%), but no applications are
  involved on top of TCP. This also looks unusual.

Wireshark · Protocol Hierarchy Statistics · ddos_amp.TCP.reflection.SYNACK.pcap

Protocol	Percent Packets	Packets	Percent Bytes	Bytes	Bits/s	End Packets	End Bytes	End Bits/s
Frame	100.0	8000	100.0	515475	28 M	0	0	0
Ethernet	100.0	8000	21.7	112000	6103 k	0	0	0
Internet Protocol Version 4	100.0	7996	31.0	159920	8714 k	0	0	0
User Datagram Protocol	2.0	163	0.3	1304	71 k	0	0	0
Simple Network Management Protocol	0.2	14	3.8	19803	1079 k	14	19803	1079 k
Real-Time Transport Protocol	0.9	70	2.2	11098	604 k	64	10288	560 k
RFC 2833 RTP Event	0.1	6	0.1	642	34 k	6	642	34 k
Real-time Transport Control Protocol	0.1	4	0.0	172	9372	2	36	1961
Malformed Packet	0.0	2	0.0	0	0	2	0	0
OpenVPN Protocol	0.9	75	3.0	15474	843 k	75	15474	843 k
Transmission Control Protocol	96.0	7679	35.1	180732	9848 k	7675	180124	9815 k
SSH Protocol	0.1	4	0.1	528	28 k	4	528	28 k
Internet Control Message Protocol	1.9	153	2.9	14696	800 k	139	6912	376 k
Data	0.2	14	1.4	7280	396 k	14	7280	396 k
Data	0.0	1	0.3	1432	78 k	1	1432	78 k
Address Resolution Protocol	0.1	4	0.0	184	10 k	4	184	10 k

Figure 8-18. *Protocol hierarchy*

- **Are the TCP/IP fields and communication pattern normal?**

    - IP TTL field analysis

        - Seems in similar range but not exactly the same. Indicating the attack source is not the same device but geographically not too far

    - TCP/UDP port, sequence number, window, and other fields

        All the packets are SYN ACK packets coming from source port 80 to a random destination port. A group of sources have the same TCP window size. It looks like the end sources are tricked to send the packet to the victim. This looks like a TCP reflection attack.

    - HTTP string and substring matching: Not applicable

    - Check for embedded URLs in the TCP stream: Not applicable

    - Check the authenticity of the websites in use: Not applicable

- Is the packet flow expected or indicate a DDoS attack?

    The flow is not expected based on all the preceding observations. The sources are distributed across the United States mostly, and it looks like sources are tricked to send SYN ACK toward the victim in response to SYN from the attacker as the attacker has possibly spoofed the source IP in the SYN packet as the victim's IP. The sources are generating SYN ACK toward the victim based on the source field in the SYN packet.

Conclusion: It can be concluded as a distributed denial-of-service attack involving a TCP reflection mechanism.

Wireshark Malware Analysis

In this analysis, we have used a pcap file of a true malware download that happened when a user clicked a tiny URL link. The PCAP file is taken from the *malware-traffic-analysis.net* portal.

Caution   Be careful while handling this pcap file. Use a controlled and restricted environment to analyze.

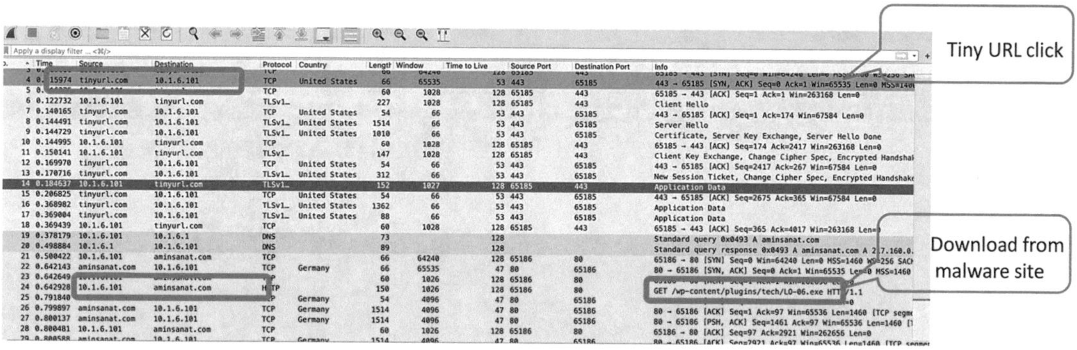

Figure 8-19. Malware download

A slightly similar approach is done here compared to the DDoS analysis but is more focused on verifying the content provider and content authenticity. The following are the IOCs (Indicators of Compromise) and steps to follow:

- When did the issue start?

   Ans: As per the first URL click, Jan 7, 2021, 01:52:24.437356000 IST

- What are the targets?

  Ans: The download was triggered from the IP 10.1.6.101.

- What are the websites/download IPs involved? Check the authenticity of the websites in use.

  Ans: The IPs are autoname resolved by Wireshark (GeoIP integration). The websites involved are tinyurl.com and aminsanat.com.

  When a query is done for both on virustotal.com, the download website **aminsanat.com is tagged as malicious**.

- What are the protocols involved?

  Ans: The chart seen with *Statistics ➤ Protocol hierarchy* shows the majority of data is for HTTP. We can create a filter for the same.

Wireshark · Protocol Hierarchy Statistics · 2021-01-06-Remcos-RAT-infection.pcap

Protocol	Percent Packets	Packets	Percent Bytes	Bytes	Bits/s	End Packets	End Bytes	End Bits/s
∨ Frame	100.0	1681	100.0	868301	4563	0	0	0
∨ Ethernet	100.0	1681	2.7	23534	123	0	0	0
∨ Internet Protocol Version 4	100.0	1681	3.9	33620	176	0	0	0
∨ User Datagram Protocol	0.4	6	0.0	48	0	0	0	0
Domain Name System	0.4	6	0.0	316	1	6	316	1
∨ Transmission Control Protocol	99.6	1675	93.2	809223	4252	1072	758812	3987
Transport Layer Security	0.5	9		5768	30	8	3553	18
> Hypertext Transfer Protocol	0.1	2	85.1	738628	3881	1	96	0
Data	35.3	593	3.8			93	32643	171

Apply as Filter ▶
Prepare as Filter ▶   Selected
Find   Not Selected
Colorize   ...and Selected
                    ...or Selected
Copy as CSV   ...and not Selected
Copy as YAML   ...or not Selected

Figure 8-20. *Protocol hierarchy*

- If HTTP is involved, filter GET and POST requests: http.request

  - HTTP string and substring matching

  - Check for embedded URLs in the TCP stream

  - Check the authenticity of the websites in use

  Ans: Found one GET request which contains a file download URI. The last packet shows the successful download of a file named LO-06.exe.

  On *virustotal.com*, **aminsanat.com is tagged as malicious**.

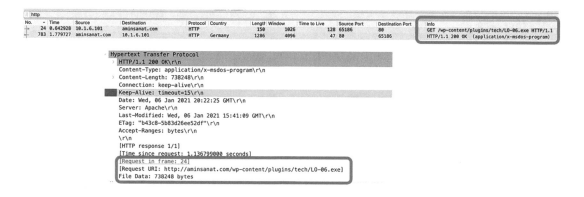

- Are the TCP/IP fields and communication pattern normal?

  Ans: The TCP/IP flow looks normal. It's a single flow which stops after the download is over.

- Verify authenticity of downloads or content transferred.

Caution   Be careful with the malware content analysis. Only work within a controlled and restricted environment. Don't open the content. We can verify the hash of the file without opening the same. And then compare the hash with a known database.

Ans: The file transferred through HTTP can be extracted through Wireshark by navigating through the menu **File ➤ export objects ➤ HTTP**.

Click the file shown and click save. At this point, your antivirus may delete the file.

- Check the file hash (md5/sha1)

Ans: Without opening the file, use any hash generation tool to verify the hash. Then search and validate the hash value on virustotal.com, which shows this as a malicious content

- Is the packet flow expected or indicate any malicious activity?

Ans: Based on the website reputation and also the content verification, it is concluded as a malicious activity.

243

Summary

With the evolution of networks and the Internet, security threats are evolving too. Attacks by cybercriminals are getting more result oriented. Cyber war is real. While real war is being fought on the battlefield, cyber war is being used as a virtual aid for the same. Latest statistics show the overall cybercrime costs stand at $6 trillion and are projected to touch $10 trillion in the next three years.

Cyber security trends show that ransomware, crypto mining, supply chain attacks, deepfake, video conferencing attacks, and IoT attacks are hot. Cyber security and analysis need to keep pace with all the emerging threats.

Wireshark has been one of the important tools in forensic analysis and will continue to be one in future too. This chapter helps you gain a deep understanding of the same. In this chapter, you learned about

- All categories of network and security attacks and how to prevent them

- How Wireshark can be used to analyze each of these attacks

- Tips and tricks and filters for Wireshark forensic analysis

- Step-by-step troubleshooting and analysis approach to DDoS and malware attacks through Wireshark

References for This Chapter

DDoS analysis pcap files: `https://github.com/StopDDoS/packet-captures`

Malware analysis pcap files: `https://malware-traffic-analysis.net/`

Wireshark geolocation database: maxmind.com

Cyber security trend statistics: forbes.com

CHAPTER 9

Understanding and Implementing Wireshark Dissectors

Imagine sending a message to a friend. Easy, just write a letter and mail it to them. Alright, now imagine not one but a city's population wanting to send a message to their friends along the borders. And not just one time message but messages every minute or even every second. In this case, it wouldn't be plausible for each one of those senders to write their own letter and expect a service to deliver it to the right person, first because the number of senders needed to individually transmit each packet to their respective recipient, and second is the amount of unnecessary movement done even if two senders live right next to each other. The first fix would be to decrease the size of the envelopes being used by cutting up the letter and delivering them sequentially. Postal men can then collect more of these smaller messages of multiple people living nearby so that the distance traveled decreases.

When the receiver gets each message through their mailbox, they might organize and put it into a folder. Consequently, their child might investigate the letters and read them in any order they like.

This entire system of postal delivery mimics the communications done through the combination of Wireshark and the Internet.

N. K. Nainar and A. Panda, *Wireshark for Network Forensics*, https://doi.org/10.1007/978-1-4842-9001-9_9

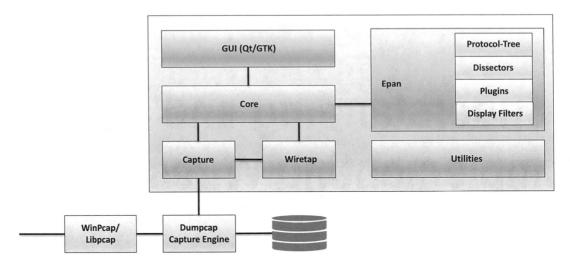

Figure 9-1. *Wireshark architecture*

In this depiction, each action done at a particular step of the process corresponds to the process in which data over the Internet travels and enters the view of a Wireshark user. Here is a detailed walk-through:

- The network interface card is what enables the computer to connect to the Internet. This hardware can directly be monitored during a capture.

- Npcap is a newer version of WinPcap, a packet sniffer that utilizes the libpcap library and pcap API. Many applications like Wireshark and tcpdump incorporate this tool to capture the packets.

- Dumpcap, the default capture engine for Wireshark, allows multiple interfaces to be captured using npcap and serves as a buffer between the application used and the network.

- The information captured can either be saved to a hard disk and read by the libwiretap library or sent straight to the core build of Wireshark. Libwiretap also supports individual dissectors to access its network data.

- Once captured, data can be sent through the EPAN (Enhanced Packet Analyzer), Wireshark's own packet analyzing engine, which primarily consists of four parts:

  - **Protocol tree**: A tree structure of packets that break down key statistics

Protocol	Percent Packets	Packets	Percent Bytes	Bytes	Bits/s	End Packets	End Bytes	End Bits/s	PDUs
▾ Frame	100.0	1413	100.0	717001	39 k	0	0	0	1413
▾ Linux cooked-mode capture	100.0	1413	3.2	22608	1,242	0	0	0	1413
▾ Internet Protocol Version 4	100.0	1413	3.9	28260	1,553	0	0	0	1413
▾ User Datagram Protocol	6.4	91	0.1	728	40	0	0	0	91
Domain Name System	6.4	90	0.9	6378	350	90	6378	350	90
Data	0.1	1	0.0	31	1	1	31	1	1
▾ Transmission Control Protocol	93.3	1319	91.9	658589	36 k	960	338701	18 k	1319
Transport Layer Security	9.0	127	15.4	110215	6,059	127	83785	4,606	134
▾ Hypertext Transfer Protocol	5.0	70	40.9	293086	16 k	39	15325	842	70
Online Certificate Status Protocol	0.6	8	1.0	7031	386	8	8629	474	8
Media Type	0.1	1	0.0	282	15	1	282	15	1
Line-based text data	0.8	12	63.9	458331	25 k	12	226139	12 k	12
JPEG File Interchange Format	0.4	6	9.1	65439	3,597	6	67006	3,683	6
eXtensible Markup Language	0.2	3	49.7	356175	19 k	3	33811	1,858	3
Compuserve GIF	0.1	1	0.0	43	2	1	43	2	1
Git Smart Protocol	11.5	162	31.4	225057	12 k	162	33299	1,830	3142
▾ Internet Control Message Protocol	0.2	3	0.1	407	22	0	0	0	3
Domain Name System	0.2	3	0.0	299	16	3	299	16	3

Wireshark · Protocol Hierarchy Statistics · git_smart.pcapng

No display filter.

Help — Copy ▾ — Close

Figure 9-2. *Image of a protocol hierarchy statistic*

- **Dissectors:** Breaking down each of the protocols contained into an appropriate format for a graphical view

- **Dissector plugins:** Externally implemented dissectors that act as separate modules

- **Display filters:** The display filter functionality for viewing only certain packets

- Finally, there is the nice GUI interface Wireshark provides where dissected packets can be seen in real time. Plugins are unique features of Wireshark that can be used for added functionality within the environment. They can be added through *Wireshark ➤ About Wireshark ➤ Folders ➤ Personal Lua Plugins* or *Personal Plugins*.

Note   The dissector source files normally reside within the */epan/dissector* folder. More details about locating other plugins are explained in the later part of this chapter.

As an analogy, we compared it with the postal service as depicted in Figure 9-3.

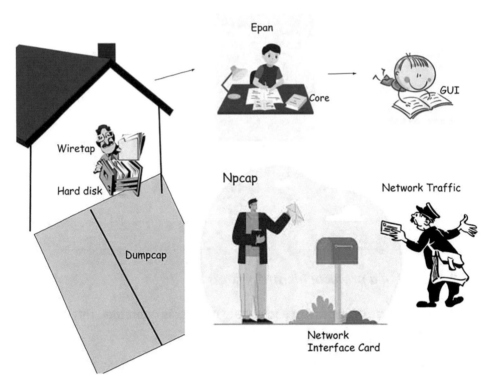

Figure 9-3. *Visual analogy of Wireshark with the postal system*

Zooming into the message, the envelope needs to contain a few essential features to successfully deliver. First and foremost, their destination IP needs to be written so that the postal service knows where to send the letter. The letter might also contain a "from" address and a name to indicate where it is coming from. Lastly, as we touched on in the previous example, this letter might not be sent at one time regarding each of these messages has to be sent every second, thus a sequence number must be attached to alert the receiver of the progress of that send.

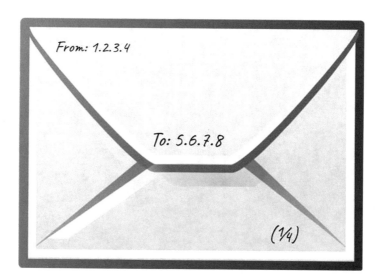

Figure 9-4. *Envelope design for postal communication*

The information contained on this envelope is easily decipherable by any person, even the sneaky receiver's kid, but only deals with a fraction of the security and transmission issues that occur in modern networking.

First off, even in this scenario, we as the sender are assuming that the postal service is completely trustworthy and that they will deliver the messages on time. Switching gears to real network interfacing, we hope that the information we send is only viewable by the intended receiver, but there is a possibility that a request or piece of information is intercepted by a third party or that one of the connections to the destination was not working. Therefore, so many protocols were created to administer these mishaps and prevent them from ever causing an inconvenience to the end user. One of the most common of them was specifically named asymmetric encryption, which essentially secured any data being sent within two users. This protocol, along with many other specifics that were needed to transport information successfully, really made understanding where a packet came from and how it came here difficult from an analyzer perspective. Now this is what it might look like:

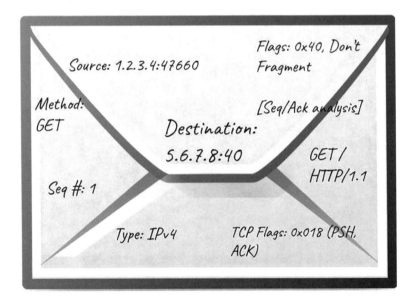

Figure 9-5. *Envelope design for a modern network packet*

All this information wouldn't be necessary to a browser or viewer who wants to just get that information, but information gets messy when shown only decrypted. This is where Wireshark's EPAN stack helps the breakdown of these large and almost continuous streams of data arrange into headings and subheadings that can be shown as a packet tree. There are different dissectors created and implemented as part of EPAN that help decode different such protocols, fields, and subfields along with expert info highlighting the basic observability from the decoded packet data.

While installing Wireshark is sufficient to have all the created dissectors to decode the packet capture, there are scenarios where a new dissector is required to decode the proprietary packet type or a new protocol which is still under development or standardization. In the next section, we will discuss about creating our own dissectors to handle such scenarios.

Protocol Dissectors

As briefly explained in Chapter 1, Wireshark uses built-in dissectors to decode each block of the received data into the packet view. Dissectors are tree-like structure where each dissector will decode portion of the binary data and hand the remaining payload to the other dissectors based on the decoded information.

High-level dissectors can register its focus to handle a specific type of protocol using a stack of lower-level protocol dissectors, enabling multiple operations to be inserted in between. As this dissector goes on to analyze more data, it provides the following set of outputs:

- Sets the protocol column of the packet list pane

- Sets the info column of the packet list pane

- Creates and includes values for tree and subtree entries of the packet detail pane

- Calls other subsequent subdissectors to decode the payload

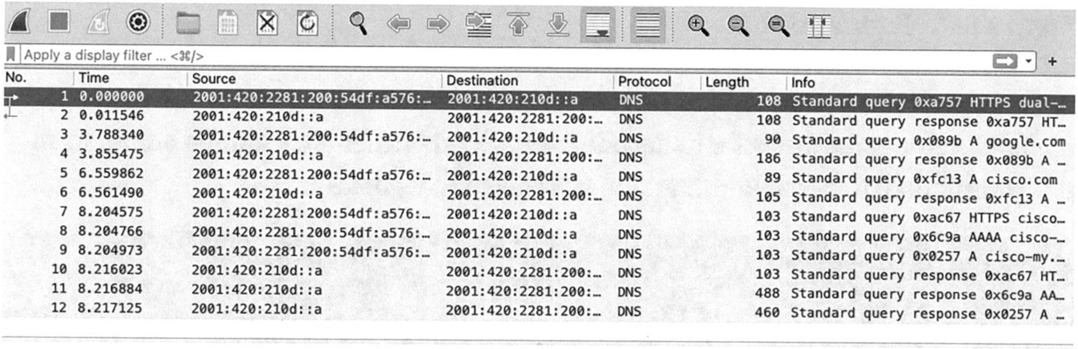

Figure 9-6. *Packet headers on the list and detail pane*

The preceding capture shows a real utilization of the dissection process that leverages the dissector to classify this packet as a DNS packet. The relevant expert info is included in the Info field of the display pane. We will focus on all the protocol headers except the frame header, which rarely gets accessed in a custom dissector.

Each packet dissector starts with a frame dissector that decodes the frame-specific details such as the timestamp of the captured packet, frame length, protocol type, etc. This is a metadata added after the capture and is not a data carried in the packet itself. An example frame dissector field is shown in Figure 9-7.

```
∨ Frame 1: 108 bytes on wire (864 bits), 108 bytes captured (864 bits)
    Encapsulation type: Ethernet (1)
    Arrival Time: May 17, 2022 08:46:46.051164000 EDT
    [Time shift for this packet: 0.000000000 seconds]
    Epoch Time: 1652791606.051164000 seconds
    [Time delta from previous captured frame: 0.000000000 seconds]
    [Time delta from previous displayed frame: 0.000000000 seconds]
    [Time since reference or first frame: 0.000000000 seconds]
    Frame Number: 1
    Frame Length: 108 bytes (864 bits)
    Capture Length: 108 bytes (864 bits)
    [Frame is marked: False]
    [Frame is ignored: False]
    [Protocols in frame: eth:ethertype:ipv6:udp:dns]
    [Coloring Rule Name: UDP]
    [Coloring Rule String: udp]
```

Figure 9-7. *Frame dissector*

The frame dissector classifies this captured frame as Ethernet and hands it over to the Ethernet-specific dissector to decode the payload further. An example output from the Wireshark GUI for the Ethernet frame is shown in Figure 9-8.

```
› Frame 2: 83 bytes on wire (664 bits), 83 bytes captured (664 bits) on interface lo, id…
∨ Ethernet II, Src: 00:00:00_00:00:00 (00:00:00:00:00:00), Dst: 00:00:00_00:00:00 (00:00…
  › Destination: 00:00:00_00:00:00 (00:00:00:00:00:00) 6 bytes
  › Source: 00:00:00_00:00:00 (00:00:00:00:00:00) 6 bytes
    Type: IPv4 (0x0800) 2 bytes
› Internet Protocol Version 4, Src: 127.0.0.1, Dst: 127.0.0.1
› Transmission Control Protocol, Src Port: 80, Dst Port: 47660, Seq: 1, Ack: 318, Len: 17

                            46-1500 bytes

0000   00 00 00 00 00 00 00 00   00 00 00 00 08 00 45 00    ········  ······E·
0010   00 45 a6 07 40 00 40 06   96 a9 7f 00 00 01 7f 00    ·E··@·@·  ········
0020   00 01 00 50 ba 2c d4 ba   e9 5f f1 2d 45 e0 80 18    ···P·,··  ·_·-E···
0030   01 5e fe 39 00 00 01 01   08 0a cb 1d a6 0d cb 1d    ·^·9····  ········
0040   a6 0c 48 54 54 50 2f 31   2e 30 20 32 30 30 20 4f    ··HTTP/1  .0 200 O
0050   4b 0d 0a                                             K··
```

Figure 9-8. *Ethernet tree with other subtrees*

The subsections shown under the Ethernet header are attributes that have been decoded initially from the hexadecimal display section. If we were able to see the Ethernet traffic transmitting to the device, there would be an additional 8 bytes and 4 bytes before and after this dump. Those values, both the preamble and frame check sequence (FCS), respectively, are only accessed during the hardware process and not passed onto the software side. The Ethernet dissector classified the payload based on the "Ether Type" field as an IPv4 packet, and the remaining packet payload is handed over to the respective dissector to decode it further.

This approach continues till any dissector is able to classify the subsequent data type, and the relevant dissector is available to decode it further.

Post and Chain Dissectors

These two dissectors are very similar in that the former is called after all dissectors have been called already, while the latter runs after individual packets have been decoded. Both can benefit being able to access accumulated fields.

Creating Your Own Wireshark Dissectors

There are the three different methods of creating dissector plugins. We will briefly look into each of the options to better understand the methods.

Wireshark Generic Dissector (WSGD)

This method has the lowest barrier to entry with the protocol definitions being typed in text files as text definitions, which are compiled to produce dissectors. It was created by Olivier Aveline as a side project, but then added on as a plugin for Wireshark available for both Windows and Linux. Although the accessibility of this technique is accessible, text interpretation is the slowest at dissecting packets, and it has limited access to the general libwireshark libraries. A basic example of creating a dissector using WSGD is shown in Figure 9-9.

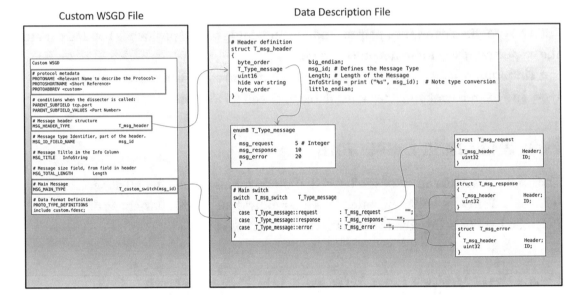

Figure 9-9.

The WSGD plugin leverages two types of files to create the dissector as follows:

- Custom WSGD file

- Data Descriptor file

The Custom WSGD file describes the metadata about the protocol for which the dissector is created. The metadata includes the name to refer to the protocol in the Wireshark interface, the message fields, and the message length (if fixed). This file will also have the reference to the second file known as the Data Descriptor file.

The Data Descriptor file defines the data format for the message payload. This file defines different message types and the associated field.

Note   Make sure to copy the appropriate version of the WSGD plugin into the Wireshark application.

Lua Dissectors

Lua is a scripting language that can be held simply in a text file but still formatted according to its syntax. It can be executed by its own Lua interpreter at runtime, and it has access to some libwireshark infrastructure, but not all. Lua, being a simple scripting language, helps the users to create their own dissectors in a much easier manner. The disadvantage of using a Lua-based dissector is that it still performs a bit slower than C dissectors during the deployment due to the need to interpret the scripting language. A basic example of creating a dissector using Lua is shown in Figure 9-10.

```
-- Protocol Declaration [Ex: objectName = Proto(name, Description)]

new_proto = Proto("TestProto",  "Test Protocol")          Declaring the Protocol with a
                                                              name and Description
-- Define Message Type Values
local msg_types = {
    [05] = "msg_request"       Setting different message types
    [10] = "msg_response"
    [20] = "msg_error"
}
                                                   Defining the protocol fields

message_length = ProtoField.int32("testproto.message_length", "messageLength", base.DEC)
message_id     = ProtoField.int32("testproto.msgid"      , "msgID"     , base.DEC)
opcode         = ProtoField.int32("testproto.opcode"     , "opCode"        , base.DEC)

new_proto.fields = {message_length, message_id, opcode}

function new_proto.dissector(buffer, pinfo, tree)
  length = buffer:len()
  if length == 0 then return end

-- Defines the name in the "Protocol" Column in the wireshark interface
                                         Define the name for
  pinfo.cols.protocol = new_proto.name   Protocol field in the GUI
-- Creates a subtree and capture the payload

  local subtree = tree:add(new_proto, buffer(), "Test Protocol Data")  Subtree creation
end

-- Associate the protocol to the respective transport layer port   Associating with transport
local tcp_trans_port = DissectorTable.get("tcp.port")                 layer ports
tcp_trans_port:add(65123, new_proto)
```

Figure 9-10. *Example of Lua Dissector*

The name and the description for the new protocol are defined using the **Proto** object. The protocol field table is created using the **<name>.fields** option. Optionally, this field can also be left empty if not required for the protocol. The dissector further defines the **function** which is called every time for the packet. The **Pinfo** object, which is one of the parameters of the **function**, defines the name for the protocol field Column in the Wireshark GUI interface. Optionally, subtrees are created as required, and finally the transport layer port numbers or ranges are associated to the protocol.

Lua is enabled by default and can be enabled as a non-root user. The dissector file is saved with .lua extension and moved to the plugin folder that varies depending on the operating system. From the Help option, open "About Wireshark" ➤ Folder to see the location where the personal Lua plugins can be loaded. An example is shown in Figure 9-11.

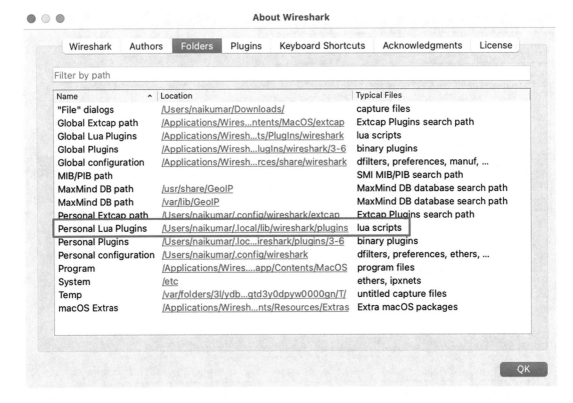

Figure 9-11. Personal Lua Plugins

By copying the file to the respective location and restarting the Wireshark application, the new dissector can be used to decode the packet.

Note   Unlike other scripting and programming languages, Lua uses double hyphen (--) to exclude the line from execution.

C Dissectors

C is a general-purpose programming language used by Wireshark in its prebuilt dissectors. It is faster in deployment time compared to Lua or WSGD and does not need any interpreter to build. All the libwireshark infrastructure is available, with preexisting dissectors and the developer guide serving as an example. It does however require a full development environment, an understanding of the libwireshark API, and lots of experience with the language structure to pursue.

The dissector created using C can be included as part of the main Wireshark program libwireshark or can be developed as a plugin. A basic example of a C-based dissector is shown in Figure 9-12.

Figure 9-12. *Example of C based Dissector*

The steps to create the dissector using the C language are as follows:

- The relevant global functions that will be called by the dissector to handle the packet payload are included in the start of the file. Then the variables for header fields, subtrees, and expert info are defined using hf_variables and ett_variables.

- Further, the function to register the new protocol, header fields, and subtree types is defined using the proto_register_name function.

- The relevant details to include the expert info fields for different handlers are defined by using expert_add_info and expert_add_info_format.

- Once the expert info details are included, the protocol, fields, subtree, and expert info arrays are registered using proto_register_protocol, proto_register_field_array, proto_register_subtree_array, expert_proto, and expert_register_field_array functions.

- The dissector handles are created using the dissector_name function by defining the packet data buffer and the display tree.

Such created dissector is compiled and validated to ensure that the dissector works as expected and doesn't crash for different unexpected or corner case scenarios. A detailed dissector for the NSH protocol is in the following link that can be used as a reference while creating a new dissector:

`https://gitlab.com/wireshark/wireshark/-/blob/master/epan/dissectors/packet-nsh.c`

Note   If the intention is to distribute the dissector to the external community, then the dissector plugin must be developed with GPL compliance.

Creating Your Own Packet

When any of the preceding methods are used to create a custom or a new dissector, it is necessary to validate the dissector using a packet. While one simple option is to capture the respective packet, it may not be readily available for capture if the protocol in itself is still under development. In this section, we will discuss about creating our own packet to open with Wireshark and validate the newly created dissectors.

While there are different options available to create packets, the simplest and easiest one is to create one using a TXT file. An example is shown in Figure 9-13.

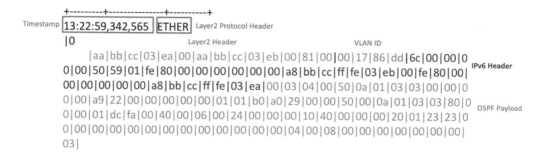

Figure 9-13. *Hex based Packet Format*

Instead of creating it from scratch, one option is to open an existing pcap file and choose a basic packet with minimal details. Now, choose *File ➤ Export Specified Packets* to get the pop-up window shown in Figure 9-14.

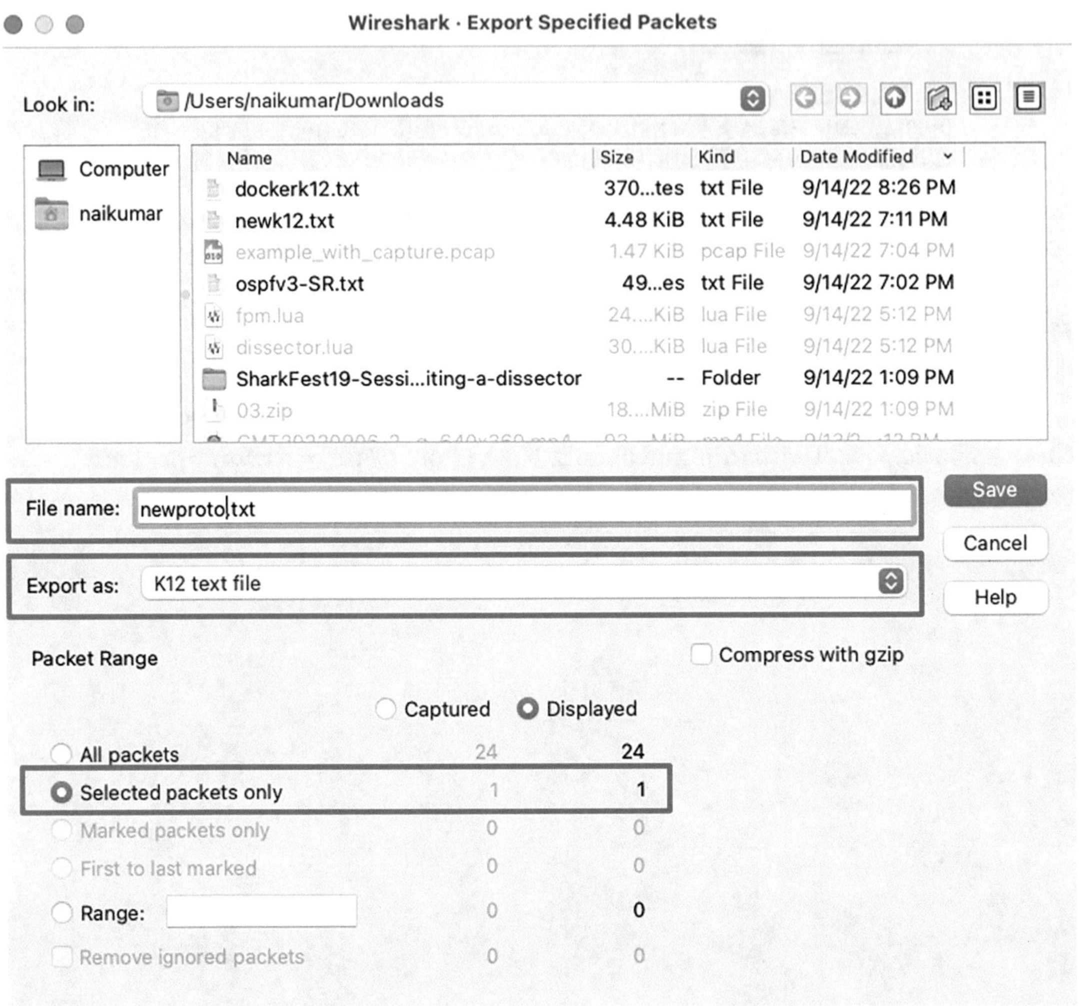

Figure 9-14. *Exporting packet as TXT file*

By setting the ***Export as*** field to **K12 text file**, we can save the packet as an editable text file as shown in Figure 9-14. The text file will have all the data fields in hexadecimal format. The respective fields can be edited, updated, or extended to validate the new dissector created. Once the respective fields are updated, the new packet can be opened with Wireshark using the ***Open Capture File*** option as shown in Figure 9-15.

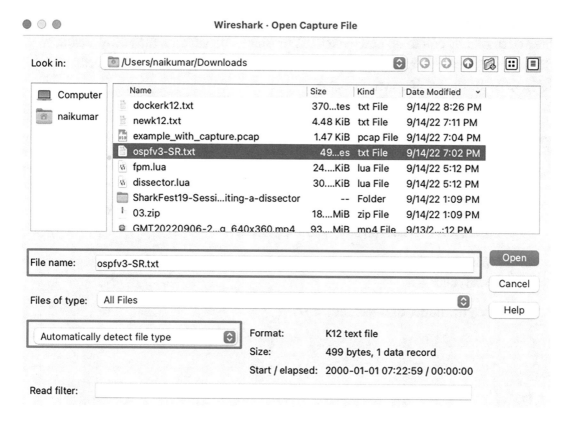

Figure 9-15. *Opening text packet file*

By using this option, we can create our own packets not only to validate the dissectors but also to play around by setting different invalid fields and see how the dissector reacts without crashing. For example, the dissector may be defined to expect value a or b for a specific field. By setting the value to c manually in the packet, the dissector can be validated to see how it reacts to such unexpected value in the field.

Summary

In this chapter, we spruced up the knowledge of the readers about Wireshark architecture and how the same can be leveraged for developing our own dissectors.

We further discussed about different ways of creating a new dissector. Each such method is explained with a very basic example for a better understanding. Further references are included along with an example.

Finally, we discussed about manual options to capture or convert a packet in a text file and manually edit to upload it back to Wireshark and validate the newly created dissectors. This chapter helps the reader to understand the basics and use further references to create their own dissector.

References for This Chapter

WSGD Introduction: `http://wsgd.free.fr/index.html`

Dissector Template: `https://github.com/boundary/wireshark/blob/master/doc/packet-PROTOABBREV.c`

Wireshark Developer's Guide: `www.wireshark.org/docs/wsdg_html_chunked/`

Lua Introduction: `www.lua.org/`

Index

A

Advanced Encryption Standard (AES), 74, 117, 149, 163
Amazon Prime, 145
Amazon Web Services (AWS), 179–187, 193
Amplitude, 109
Application security
  business applications, 66
  HTML file, 66
  HTTP, 66, 67
  HTTPS, 67, 68
  IPSec, 67, 68
  protocols, 67, 68
ARP poisoning, 223
  and spoofing, 222
ARP request messages, 226
ARP spoofing, 222, 223
Authentication Key Management (AKM), 126, 127
AWS environment, 181–182

B

Basic Service Set (BSS), 114–116
Berkeley Packet Filter (BPF), 56–60
Bluetooth, 203, 210
  classic *vs.* LE, 205
  communication model, 204
  concepts, 203
  controller, 207, 208
  HCI, 209

host and peer device, 203, 207
instructions, 204
LELL, 209
protocols, 212
protocol stack, 207
radios, 205, 206, 208
versions, 205
Bluetooth headset, 219
Bluetooth host, 215
Bluetooth packets, 212–215
Bluetooth protocol stack, 207
Brute-force attacks, 229, 230
Brute-force connection, 230
Business-critical application, 174

C

Capital expenditure (CAPEX), 174
Capture filters, 55, 56
  advanced filters, 61–63
  BPF, 56
    CLI, 57
    GUI, 57
    instructions, 59
    IPv4 TCP packet, 59, 60
    syntax, 58
  deep packet filters, 61–63
  vs. display filters, 56
  libcap-based capture applications, 56
  libpcap filter syntax, 56
  primitive expressions, 55
  tcpdump man page, 55
  telnet traffic, 55

Capture modes and configurations
    monitor mode, 46
    promiscuous mode, 45, 46

C dissectors, 257–258

Cloud computing, 173, 201

Cloud Native Computing Foundation
    (CNCF), 195, 200

Cloud service providers (CSP), 179, 187

CloudShark
    API
        capture files, 23
        Curl, 24, 25
        options, 24
        permissions, 24
    capture.sh script, 26
    GitHub repository, 26
    HTTP/FTP, 22
    log in, 22
    uploading, 25
    user credential, 22
    web page, 21
    vs. Wireshark, 22, 23

Command line interface (CLI),
    1, 24, 36, 196

Computer quantum, 173

Containers, 144, 180–181, 193–196

Counter Mode Cipher Block Chaining
    Message Authentication Code
    Protocol (CCMP), 117

Cyber-attacks, 65, 221

Cyber war, 244

D

Data Descriptor file, 254

DDoS capture file, 237

Denial-of-service attacks, 230, 231

Destination connection ID (DCID),
    88, 90, 91

DHCP spoofing, 223–225

Digital transformation, 66, 173

Display filters/graphs, 10, 11, 19, 247

DNS amplification attack symptoms, 231

DNS over HTTPS (DoH), 68, 103, 104

DNS over TLS (DoT), 102, 225

DNS spoofing, 225
    and poisoning, 224

Docker, 181, 193–195, 201

Domain Name System (DNS), 68
    hierarchy, 101
    internet resource, 99
    IP address, 100
    IPv4 address, 100
    IPv6 address, 100
    machinery, 99, 100
    packets, 102
    Query message, 100, 101
    resource records, 100
    response message, 102
    RFC1034, 99
    Secure DNS
        GET/POST methods, 103, 104
        HTTPS connection, 103
        SSL key, 104
        TLS connection, 103
        Wireshark capture, 104

Dynamic ARP inspection (DAI), 225

E

Elastic Compute Cloud (EC2), 179–182

Electromagnetic radiation, 107–109

Electromagnetic spectrum, 107, 108

Embedded multimedia objects, 151

Encapsulated Remote SPAN (ERSPAN), 32, 33, 35

End-user devices, 117, 121

Ethernet, 1, 8, 46, 61, 110, 111, 117, 161, 222, 252, 253

Evolution, computer quantum, 173

Extended Service Set (ESS), 115, 116, 130

F

Federal Communications Commission (FCC), 109, 113

Flow graphs, 20, 21

Forensics

    DDoS attacks, 236

    IOCs and analysis, 236

    packet hex matching, 235

    search operator, 236

    TCP and decode, 236

    TCP/IP fields, 240

    TCP/UDP port, 235

Forward error correction (FEC), 208

Frame check sequence (FCS), 252

Frequency, 108, 109, 112–114, 212

Full virtualization, 175, 176

Fully Qualified Domain Name (FQDN), 100

G

Galois/Counter Mode (GCM), 74

Geolocation, 234, 236

GNU General Public License (GPL), 2

Google Cloud Platform (GCP), 181, 187–189, 193

Graphical user interface (GUI), 1, 120

Groupwise Temporal Key (GTK), 136

H

Hardware-assisted full virtualization, 175, 176

HCI packet filter, 209

Honeypots, 229

Host Layer Operation, L2CAP, 209, 210

Host-to-controller communication, 216

HTTP multimedia file export, 151

HTTP stream, 151, 236

Hypertext Transfer Protocol (HTTP), 66–70, 73, 78, 79, 82–85

Hypertext Transfer Protocol Secure (HTTPS), 67

    alert messages, 72

    capturing/filtering, 72, 73

    client, 71, 72

    CLIENT HELLO message

        key exchange extensions, 74, 75

        Wireshark capture, 74

    CLOSE NOTIFY message, 72

    decryption

        SSL key, 79–82

        TLS packet, 81, 82

        Wireshark frame option, 79

        Wireshark preference option, 80, 81

    filters, 69

        HTTP2 statistics, Wireshark, 83–85

        port, 82

        TCP handshake, 82

        TCP transport, 82

        TLS message types, 82

    GET messages, 70

    peers, 72

    port 80, 69

    prefix, 70

    private key, 70

Hypertext Transfer Protocol
    Secure (HTTPS) (*cont.*)
    public key, 70
    request traffic, 70
    secured connection, 72
    server, 71
    SERVER HELLO message
        certificates, 76
        Cipher Suite, 76
        encryption, 76, 77
        frames, 77
        TLS, 75, 76
    sessions, 70, 71
    SSL key
        macOS-based machine, 77, 78
        Windows-based machine, 78
    Wireshark capture, 69
    workflow, 70, 71
Hypervisors
    definition, 177
    revolutionary introduction, 175
    type 1 hypervisor, 178
    type 2 hypervisor, 178
    types, 177

I, J

IEEE 802.11 frame format, 122
    BSSID, 123
    captures, 123
    definition, 122
    duration, 122
    flags, 122
    Frame Control Field, 122
    Frame/Sub Types, 122
    MAC address, 123
    radio-specific details, 124
    radiotap header, 124

    radiotap metadata, 124
    types, 122
Input/output (I/O) graphs, 14, 165
Institute of Electrical and Electronics
    Engineers (IEEE), 110, 111
International Telecommunication Union
    (ITU), 109
Internet, 86, 99, 143, 182, 189, 221,
    232, 246
Internet-based businesses, 66, 173

K

Kubernetes, 181, 195, 196, 201

L

L2CAP packet filter, 210
Libsrtp, 160, 161
Link Management Protocol (LMP),
    208, 209
Linux kernel, 56, 212
Local area network (LAN)
    challenges, 110
    connection, 110
    definition, 110
    IEEE 802.3, 110
Lua dissectors, 254–256

M

macOS, 3–4, 118, 119, 214, 235
Malicious hackers, 65, 67, 68
Malware attacks, 232–234
    devices, 234
    network and infrastructure, 233
    prevention, 233
Mesh Basic Service Set (MBSS), 114, 116
Message Integrity Check (MIC), 116, 135

Modern network packet, 250
MP4, 144, 146
Multimedia applications, 143, 171
Multimedia streaming, 144
    streaming format, 146
    streaming implementations and
        providers, 145
    streaming transport, 145

N

Nested virtualization, 175, 176, 178
Netflix, 143, 145
Network analysis
    ARP poisoning, 222
    packet stream, 222
    protocol, 221
    spoofing and poisoning, 222
    visibility powers, 221
Networking protocol, 222, 225
Network interface cards (NICs), 117, 246
Network Virtualization using GRE
        (NVGRE), 110

O

OS fingerprinting, 228, 229
OS-native traffic capture tools
    BSD, 36–38
    Linux, 36–38
    macOS, 36–38
    UNIX, 36–38
    Windows, 39–41

P

Packet dissector, 251
Packets
    capture point, 35

hub, 34
    packet characteristics, 60
    packet encapsulations, 61
    port mirroring, 30, 31, 34
    remote port mirroring
        capabilities, 32
        ERSPAN header, 32, 33
        methods, 31
        mirror destination device, 32
        mirrored traffic, 33
        Router-1 mirrors, 32
        Switch-1 mirrors, 32
    TAP, 34
    types, 30
Packet stream
    protocols, 19
    TCP conversation, 19
    YAML, 19, 20
Paired device discovery
    data, 218
    link scan role, 218
Pairing, 216–218
Pairwise Master Key (PMK), 133
Pairwise Transient Key (PTK), 134
Paravirtualization, 175, 176
Port mirroring
    capture packets, 30, 31
    mirrored source ports, 30
    network devices, 30
Postal communication, 249
Premaster keylog file, 154

Q

QoS markings, 164, 165
Quick UDP Internet Connection (QUIC)
    capturing/filtering, 89
    comparision, 86, 87

Quick UDP Internet Connection
  (QUIC) (*cont.*)
  connection identifiers, 87
  filters, 98
  handshake message, 88, 96
  header, 90–92
  initial message
    TLS Client Hello, 92–94
    TLS Server Hello, 94–96
  protected payload, 97, 98
  reliability components, 87
  RFC9000, 86
  session layer protocol, 86
  streams, 87
  TCP, 85, 88
  TLS, 86
  TLS traffic, 98
  UDP, 86
  workflow, 87, 88

R

Radiocommunication Sector, 109
Radio Frequency Communication, 212
Radio technologies, 111
Radio waves/spectrum, 107
  amplitude, 109
  frequency, 108, 109
  frequency bands, 109
  license, 109
  radiation, 108
  radio wave spectrum, 109
  range of spectrum, 109
  speed of light, 108
  wavelength, 108, 109
  wireless spectrum, 108
Real-Time Messaging Protocol
  (RTMP), 145

Real-time multimedia
  decrypting secure RTP (*see* Secure RTP
    decryption)
  decrypting signaling, 153–157
  media transport
    RTCP, 148, 149
    RTP Protocol, 148
    SRTP and SRTCP, 149
    WebRTC, 149, 150
  multimedia transport, 148
  secure SIP, 153
  signaling
    H.323, 148
    SDP, 146, 147
    SIP, 146
    SIP over TLS (SIPS), 147
  telephony and video analysis, 163 (*see*
    Telephony)
Real-Time Streaming Protocol
  (RTSP), 145
Real-Time Transport Control Protocol
  (RTCP), 148, 149
Real-Time Transport Protocol (RTP), 145,
  146, 148, 149, 152
Reconnaissance method, 225
Regular channel scan, 216, 217
Remote packet capture
  android devices, 49, 50
  extcap
    androiddump, 49, 50, 52
    interfaces, 47
    sshdump, 47, 48
    utilities, 47
  PCAP remote
    Android app, 52, 53
    sshdump, 54
    Wireshark, 53
Robust Security Network (RSN), 126

RSA keys dialogue, 154, 155
RSA keys list dialogue, 155, 156
RTP player voice graph, 171
RTP streams, 168, 169

S

SDP service, 219
Secure RTP decryption
    decryption, SRTP, 158
    filter SRTP-only packets, 159, 160
    libsrtp, 160, 161
    libsrtp and text2pcap, 162
    SDP packet, 158
    SRTP encryption key extraction
        from SDP, 159
    in text format, 161
    Text2pcap utility, 161
Secure Simple Pairing (SSP), 216
Secure Socket Layer (SSL), 67
Security compliance team, 65
Service Discovery Protocol (SDP), 211
Service Set Identifier (SSID), 115
Session Description Protocol (SDP), 146
Session Initiation Protocol (SIP), 146
Signal-to-noise ratio (SNR), 124
Signature fingerprinting, 228
Simultaneous Authentication of
        Equals (SAE), 117
Source connection ID (SCID), 88, 91
SourceVM, 182, 183, 186, 187
SRTP payload, 158
Streaming, 143
Streaming RTP video captures, 152
Sweep attacks, 226
Switched Port Analyzer (SPAN),
        30–32, 35, 45
SYN and RST response, 227

T

TCP packet, 7, 56, 227, 231
TCP port scan, 228
TCP stream graphs
    packets, 15
    round trip time, 17
    throughput/goodput, 16
    time sequence
        Stevens, 15
        tcptrace, 15, 16
    window scaling, 18
Telephony, 165
    Control Protocol, 211
    QoS and network issues, 164, 165
    RTP RTP streams, 168–170
    SIP flows, 167
    VoIP analysis, 165
        call flow and I/O graph, 166–168
        RTP payload, replaying, 170
        RTP statistics, packet loss, delay
            and jitter analysis, 169
        RTP stream analysis, 165, 166,
            168, 169
    VoIP calls, 166
    VoIP, Wireshark optimization, 164
Temporal Key Integrity Protocol (TKIP), 116
Test Access Point (TAP), 34
TLS packet protocol preference, 157
Traffic capture
    in AWS environment (see VPC traffic
        mirroring)
    in Docker environment, 193, 194
    in GCP environment, 187–192
    in Kubernetes environment, 195–200
Transistor-based processors, 173
Transport Layer Security (TLS), 67, 70,
        102, 147

Trivial File Transport Protocol (TFTP), 86
Turkish malware, 233
Turkish redirect malware, 233

U

UDP load balancer, 188–192
UDP port scan, 226, 227

V

Virtual Extensible LAN (VxLAN), 110
Virtualization, 173
    classification, 175, 176
    concept, 174
    containers, 180, 181
    evolution, 174, 175
    full virtualization, 176
    hardware-assisted full
        virtualization, 176
    nested virtualization, 176
    paravirtualization, 176
    virtual machine (VM), 178, 179
Virtualization stack, 177
Virtual machine (VM), 178, 179
Virtual private cloud (VPC), 182
    traffic mirroring (see VPC traffic
        mirroring)
Voice communication, 110
VoIP packets, 165
VPC network, 192
VPC traffic mirroring
    AWS VPC example setup, 182
    configuration option, 183
    EC2 instances, 182
    filter configuration, 185
    final configuration, 186
    mirror filter, 184, 185
    mirror session, 186, 187
    mirror target, 184
    SourceVM, 182

W, X

Wavelength, 108
Web multimedia content, 144
Wi-Fi Protected Access (WPA), 116
Windows operating system, 213
Wired Equivalent Privacy (WEP), 116
Wireless capture
    AirPort Utility, 119, 120
    Diagnostic Tool, 120, 121
    Native Wireshark Tool, 118, 119
Wireless LAN (WLAN)
    AP, 110
    BSS, 114, 115
    channels
        frequency, 114
        2.4 GHz band, 111–113
        5 GHz band, 113
        multiple adjacent, 113
        non-overlapping, 112
        overlapping, 112
        U-NII-1 frequency band, 113
    encryption protocols, 116, 117
    ESS, 115, 116
    MBSS, 116
    spectrum bands, 111
    types, 114
Wireless network discovery
    beacons, 125
    802.11 beacon frame, 125, 126
    endpoint station, 125
    filtering mechanisms, 127
    home network, 125
    RSN parameter, 126
    802.11 SSID broadcast, 125
    SSID parameter, 126

Wireless technology, 107
Wireshark, 220, 221, 226, 228, 235, 258, 260
   applications, 29
   community support, 2
   data representation, 12, 13
   Ethereal, 2
   features, 2
   launch page, 6
   Linux, 4
      packets, 5
      Red Hat and Alike, 4
   live capture, 7
   macOS, 3, 4
   with multimedia communication, 150
   packet capture, 8
      bottom panel, 8
      capture filters, 9
      display filters, 10, 11
      dissectors, 8
      layers, 8
      Pcap *vs.* Pcapn, 11, 12
   packets, 29, 30
   source code, 2
   Traffic Capture
      CLI, 41, 42
      GUI, 43
      multiple interfaces, 44
      stopping capture, 44
   Ubuntu/Debian derivatives, 5
   uses, 1
   website, 3
   Windows, 5
Wireshark analysis, 215
Wireshark application, 256
Wireshark architecture, 261
Wireshark captures, 217
Wireshark dissectors
   analogy, 248

   architecture, 246
   communications, 245
   installing, 250
   messages, 245
   outputs, 251
   packets, 253
   protocol, 247, 250
   user, 246
Wireshark generic dissector (WSGD),
      253, 254
Wireshark malware analysis, 233
   DDoS analysis, 241
   protocol, 242
   TCP/IP flow, 243
   URL link, 241
Wireshark packet inspection, 236
WiresharkTarget, 182
WLAN data exchange
   802.11 data frame
      decryption, 137, 138, 140
      encryption, 136, 137
      WPA-PSK key, 138, 139
WLAN endpoint onboarding
   registration process, 128
      association phase, 132, 133
      authentication phase, 131
      probing phase, 128–130
      802.1X exchange phase, 133–136
   wireless channels, 127
WLAN statistics, Wireshark, 140, 141
World Wide Web (WWW), 66

Y

YouTube, 145, 146

Z

Zooming, 248

Printed in the United States
by Baker & Taylor Publisher Services